Mom Heart Moments

DAILY DEVOTIONS FOR
LIFEGIVING MOTHERHOOD

MOM HEART
MOMENTS

SALLY CLARKSON

TYNDALE
MOMENTUM®

A Tyndale nonfiction imprint

Visit Tyndale online at tyndale.com.

Visit Tyndale Momentum online at tyndalemomentum.com.

Tyndale, Tyndale's quill logo, *Tyndale Momentum*, and the Tyndale Momentum logo are registered trademarks of Tyndale House Ministries. Tyndale Momentum is a nonfiction imprint of Tyndale House Publishers, Carol Stream, Illinois.

Mom Heart Moments: Daily Devotions for Lifegiving Motherhood

Designed by Sarah Susan Richardson

For information about special discounts for bulk purchases, please contact Tyndale House Publishers at csresponse@tyndale.com, or call 1-855-277-9400.

ISBN 978-1-4964-8322-5

Printed in China

30	29	28	27	26	25	24
7	6	5	4	3	2	1

INTRODUCTION

---✦---

MOTHERHOOD IS PROFOUNDLY IMPORTANT.

Today I sat on a crumpled bed with a soft, pink blanket, a half-drunk bottle of milk next to me as I watched my small, fragile grandbaby, one-year-old Lilian, finally begin to breathe the deep breath of a little one deeply in need of rest.

With the terrible respiratory infection our whole family had shared with her, she had cried for twenty minutes as she gasped and wheezed to clear her congested lungs. Now, as she slept with little rattles emerging from her open mouth, she looked like a soft, squishy little angel to me—so very precious and dear to my heart.

As I sat in the growing darkness, I actually thought of you who will read this book. I know that every day, your life is challenging, demanding, and perhaps isolated as you fulfill this important role. But you are my hero. You are shaping the history of the next generation by choosing to be a lifegiving mother.

As I look back on the years of mothering my own four children to adulthood, I am more convinced than ever that God created us to be lovers, teachers, spiritual directors, friends, and so much more to our children.

When we become God's agents in passing on lifegiving messages to our children, we are serving Him and His Kingdom purposes in meaningful ways. We sacrifice our lives so that they can go into the world spiritually strong, emotionally healthy, and with a virtuous character intact.

I wanted to write some messages from my heart to yours that might, for just a moment every day, encourage you in your task, grant you a bit of wisdom, remind you that your life today will reap rewards for all eternity, and show you truths from His Word.

You are not alone. God sees you and is with you. I am praying for you and count you as a woman of great worth because you are giving of your life to bring His life to your precious children. May He give wind to your sails and guide you through your journey with generous grace and His unfailing love.

Sally Clarkson
Fall 2019

JANUARY 1

Watch over your heart with all diligence,
for from it flow the springs of life.

PROVERBS 4:23

A WOMAN CANNOT PASS ON what she herself does not have. If we want to pass on health and beauty and goodness to our children, we must discipline ourselves to pour into our minds and souls truth from Scripture, seek out wise people, and read great books, as well as protect our souls from all that is base.

And so, as I ponder what I want to become more of this year, I must take seriously the cultivating of my own soul, so when others come to draw from me, they are drawing from Him, because I have invested time in Him, His Word, His wisdom, His truth, and His ways. I am working on my own personal goals, so I may determine how I will use my time this year to ensure that I am growing in all the elements that are beautiful, true, wise, good, and lovely.

Here's my advice: seek out a time to get away alone to consider how you would like to grow this year. Evaluate the habits you practice and how they influence your soul, your heart, and consequently, your worship of God. Make a plan of how you will grow in wisdom, beauty, and truth this year. What will you read? When will you have a quiet time? What do you need to stop doing?

Make a plan for all the ways you will pour beauty, goodness, wisdom, and truth into your children this year. What books and stories will you read to them? When will you have devotions with them? How do you need to change in order to reflect love and graciousness to them, so they will form their relationship habits on gentleness and generous love?

What do you need to change in order to focus more on investing, rather than just passing time with emptiness?

Take this opportunity to put time away for evaluation
and planning on your calendar!

JANUARY 2

Love is patient, love is kind . . .
does not take into account a wrong suffered.

1 CORINTHIANS 13:4-5

TIME AND AGE HAVE CONVINCED me of my own propensity to be selfish and immature. Consequently, my gratitude has grown immensely, since I know that I don't have to perform for the Lord. He is mindful of my imperfections, yet He still calls me His own special child. The number of times He has had to bear with me, love me, and give me grace has made me so much more apt to bear with, love, and forgive my sweet but human children, husband, and friends.

I know they will make mistakes and be selfish and sinful—just like me!—but I also know that I can only please God and have peace in my own heart when I choose to love them back. And in practicing loving them, my own heart swells with more love, good thoughts, and generosity.

This is how it works in my own life. I will have a critical thought toward Clay or the kids or a friend. If I foster that thought, it nurtures self-righteousness, resentment, and anger. When I choose to look at the relationship with eyes of love instead, I can get perspective: this is a person dear to me. They have a personality that comes with many flaws, just as mine does. They do not live to hurt my feelings!

I need to remember that love covers a multitude of sins. I remember how much I need grace in all of my own fragile times. I also remind myself that I will please my precious, patient Lord Jesus if I obediently act in love.

So, I cover the person with grace, say words of patience and kindness, and then I am amazed that my feelings of love follow and the relationship improves, rather than being broken. Good feelings often accompany acts of obedience.

These words in 1 Corinthians describe God, who tells us that
He actually is love! Too often, these words do not describe me.
Do patience and kindness come easily to you?

JANUARY 3

Where there is no vision, the people perish:
but he that keepeth the law, happy is he.

PROVERBS 29:18, KJV

"THE MOTHER IS THE FOUNTAIN-HEAD of the Home. The home is the fountain-head of society and of the Church of Christ. And no influences in the universe contribute so much toward guiding immortal souls Heavenward as the Home and the Mother. If I were asked to name any one principle that seems to have an almost universal application, it would be this one: show me the mother and I will show you the man! Next to the sovereign grace of God, the influence of a mother's teachings and example is the most effective in moulding character and shaping destiny."*

These words, written over a hundred years ago, are still very powerful today. Perhaps they are even more powerful now, in a culture where an understanding of the importance of mothers to the overall well-being of soul of the next generation has been lost. How affirming it is to see that truth of past generations still applies to us today.

Often, I find that in the absence of a clear enough vision for their children and homes, mothers replace conviction and vision with lots of activities and distractions for their children. As a result of all this rushing around to endless lessons and buying the newest curriculum and technology for their children, moms feel like they are accomplishing something. However, a focus on home life is the key to civilizing our children, and thereby our nation.

From the beginning of time, God created the home to be a place sufficient to nurture genius, excellence, graciousness, and grand civility. But the key factor is nothing that can be purchased or owned. The accomplishment of this grand life is found only in the soul of a mother personally mentoring her children through the power of the Holy Spirit.

Do you have a vision for your family?
Write down your dreams and goals in order to have
a true focus for the time you spend together.

---

* Gene Fedele, ed., Golden Thoughts of Mother, Home, and Heaven (Gainesville, FL: Bridge-Logos, 2003), 221.

You shall teach [these commandments] diligently to your sons and shall talk of them when you sit in your house and when you walk by the way and when you lie down and when you rise up.

DEUTERONOMY 6:7

IT IS IN A PERSONAL RELATIONSHIP with a real person whose soul is alive that the deepest imprints of life are given. The secrets and deep emotions shared during the good-night hours, in which the soul of a child is tender and open; the comfort of warm, homemade food prepared and eaten in the early evening as ideas are discussed, prayers are said, and devotions are read; the advice given in the midst of washing dishes together after a meal; the heroic and riveting stories read aloud and enjoyed together that establish common patterns of morality, values, and dreams in the comfort of the blazing hearth; the mugs of steaming hot chocolate savored while squishing against each other on a couch—these are the heavenly moments when we can share God's Word with our children. His Word is food to the soul and nourishment to the mind and conscience of a child fully awake to all that is important in life.

There is no computer, television, software, or textbook that can pass on such passion, love, and motivation.

When the invisible strings of a mother's heart are tied to the hearts of her children through loving sacrifice and nurture, the stability and foundations of a nation become secure and stable. A mother, living well in her God-ordained role, is of great beauty and inestimable value to the future of any generation. Her impact is irreplaceable and necessary to the spiritual formation of children who will be the adults of the next generation. Fun, comfort, humor, graciousness, spiritual passion, compassion for the lost, hospitality, chores, meals, training, lifegiving words, hours and hours of listening and playing and praying and reading—all are parts of the mosaic of soul development.

Are the words of God on your heart? They must be there before they can be given to your children. Take a moment to work on memorizing today's important verse.

JANUARY 5

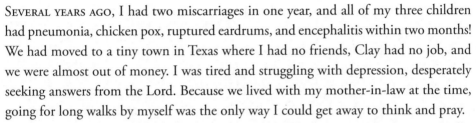

Without faith it is impossible to please Him, for he who comes to God must believe that He is and that He is a rewarder of those who seek Him.

HEBREWS 11:6

SEVERAL YEARS AGO, I had two miscarriages in one year, and all of my three children had pneumonia, chicken pox, ruptured eardrums, and encephalitis within two months! We had moved to a tiny town in Texas where I had no friends, Clay had no job, and we were almost out of money. I was tired and struggling with depression, desperately seeking answers from the Lord. Because we lived with my mother-in-law at the time, going for long walks by myself was the only way I could get away to think and pray.

One day, as I was walking and pondering, it was as if the Lord said to me, "Sally, if I took everything away from you that you hold dear, would you still believe in Me?" It was as though God was shining a spotlight onto the deepest part of my soul. And I found at the very bottom of it that I would rather hold on to my faith in God and believe in His love and goodness for the rest of my life than choose a life of existentialism and despair. I also knew this choice would require constant vigilance—that I would have to guard my heart and feed it with the truth of God's Word and His constancy in my life.

Faith was planting a flag in my heart that day. Faith was my assurance of things hoped for but not seen. Faith meant choosing to hope in Him every day, acting on that faith and hope, and understanding that without this commitment of my will to choosing to believe and hope, I couldn't be pleasing to God or sense His wisdom and hand upon my life.

I would look back on that day as a day that would determine the course of my walk with God.

Have you made a decision to plant a flag of faith in your own life? What challenges that faith?

Let us draw near with a true heart in full assurance of faith.

HEBREWS 10:22

MAKING A DECISION TO STAND FOR and in faith means many things. It means I choose to believe the best and act in light of what Scripture says about God—that He is loving, righteous, good, kind, wise, and so on. I believe in light even when I find myself in darkness. I believe love is redemptive and is a perfect bond of unity, even when I am confronted with unloving, immature people.

It means choosing to believe that God listens to my prayers and that the prayer of a righteous person avails much—trusting that in His time, I will see eternal results, even if it isn't on my time schedule.

If I put God on trial every time something difficult happened to me, I would only be unstable and insecure in life—wondering and fearing when the next trial or danger would come my way. But if I build my life on the foundation of believing in Him— sowing faithfulness and goodness—I will reap the blessing of freedom and peace.

I determined long ago to never allow my mind to wander to an active place of doubt. In the way that I made a promise to stay married to Clay and choose to love him unconditionally for all of our years, with divorce never being an option, my promise to God meant the same thing. As I look back over the years, my commitment has determined my behavior and has always pointed me to the source of direct instructions— always to God and His Word, always to faith, and always to obedience.

Do you believe that God hears you? That He will answer in time? How can you strengthen your soul in order to continue choosing rightly in the midst of daily challenges?

JANUARY 7

*He has made everything beautiful in its time. Also, he has
put eternity into man's heart, yet so that he cannot find out
what God has done from the beginning to the end.*

ECCLESIASTES 3:11, ESV

WOMEN LONG FOR IDEALS, beauty, and goodness in the depths of their souls as a consequence of God's elegant design. Intuitively, we all sense there is a better way, a better place. A sense of justice tells us in our hearts that life should be fair, because we were created for a perfect world filled with the virtues of God's character. These shadows of a long-lost reality lead us to hope for heaven, that place where we will not be disappointed.

Our deep longings become a platform for our hope in God. Jesus' disciples depended on this hope, authentic to them because they had experienced Jesus face to face and knew their hope was founded on reality. Their sure hope of heaven gave them joy in this world.

Many years ago during a time of testing, I renewed a promise to God that I would trust Him. In light of my commitment, I would act in faith, believing that what I had learned from Scripture was true. Redoubling my efforts to give God the chance to speak to me as often as possible, I disciplined my life to have quiet times almost every day. Sometimes the quiet times would be full and fruitful; sometimes they were extremely short and empty; sometimes I was dull and dead inside. But over many years I learned to turn over my worries and fears, one by one, to God and leave them there with Him.

*One of the most important parts of my day is the time I set aside for prayer,
reading, and pondering God's Word. Have you found a special time to
set aside specifically to quiet your heart before the Lord? If not, may I
encourage you to do so? It's the best investment you will ever make.*

How great a love the Father has bestowed on us, that we would be called children of God; and such we are.

ONE EVENING I FOUND MYSELF knocking at my daughter Joy's door. She was singing loudly, and I joined in as I stepped into her bright, happy room. We sang at the top of our voices until we started giggling too hard to continue. I kissed her good night and tapped next at the door of my other daughter, Sarah, opening it to find her, as always, a veritable princess reclining in bed, shaking her head at Joy and me and our loudness. Suddenly, my heart was filled with thanksgiving. As I was delighting in my own sweet children, feeling I could be myself, resting and rejoicing in our mutual, close relationship, with the strings of their hearts tightly tied to mine, I was at rest.

You see, I prefer Joy and Sarah, my own children. I have given them my time, my body, and my sleepless nights; cooked thousands of meals; sought to make celebrations special in buying them gifts; crafted a life, putting them to bed with a blessing on countless nights; and forgiven them for their attitudes and messes. I still prefer my children over all the other people in the world—because they are mine—my very own beloved children.

And so God has bestowed such a great and endless and personal love upon me— I am preferred and forgiven and cherished and served and thought about by Him, because I am His very own child. I can, in my own limited, sinful way, enjoy and celebrate my children's lives and moments and be intimate friends sharing hearts, laughter, weariness, and needs. God, as my Father, has bestowed His perfect love on me, even knowing me to my depths, and yet willing to keep giving, celebrating life, listening, helping, comforting—because I am His very special, chosen, related-to-Him child.

The Father has given His all for you! Imagine how much He loves and prefers you today!

JANUARY 9

Our Father who is in heaven, hallowed be Your name.
Your kingdom come. Your will be done, on earth as it is in
heaven. Give us this day our daily bread. and forgive us our
debts, as we also have forgiven our debtors. and do not lead
us into temptation, but deliver us from evil. For Yours is
the kingdom and the power and the glory forever. Amen.

MATTHEW 6:9-13

GOD LISTENS TO US WITH ALL OF our concerns right where we live—what a wonder! This is just part of why I love coming to Him in the spirit of His prayer shared here in Matthew 6.

His will encompasses all of history and everything that must happen to accomplish His purposes. So in the spirit of humility, we come to Him with our prayers to seek His will and His grace, knowing that somehow, mysteriously, He allows those prayers to influence what takes place in the heavenlies in response to our issues here on earth. He does listen; He does respond; and He is our High Priest who prays alongside us, helping us to do His will.

Our world offers us plenty of opportunity to worry, to become anxious, to despair over where our nation is headed or whether the next generation will serve God. Economic concerns trouble many, and relationships always present their own difficulties. When we ask Him to work in our nations, let us ask Him to bring righteousness, knowing that righteousness exalts a nation. We need to be careful to live our own lives righteously! When crisis brings us to fear or catastrophes happen or national needs arise, these issues always put us in the place we should have been all along—on our knees before Him.

Are you tempted to be a worrier about big issues facing your
nation and the world? How might remembering God is bigger
than all of it help you leave your concerns in His hands?

Lord, teach us to pray.

LUKE 11:1

FOR MANY YEARS, Clay has used a popular acronym to guide our family in prayer. We call it the ACTS of Prayer.

A—Adore Him. Coming before Him puts us in the right frame of mind—acknowledging His greatness and power as we come into His presence with our requests. A good place to start is Psalm 145, especially verses 8-21. We take time to praise Him for some of the attributes mentioned there.

C—Confess our sin. We come to Him to humble ourselves, asking His forgiveness for our own sins as well as for those of the church of Christ and our nation. First John 1:9 says, "If we confess our sins, He is faithful and righteous to forgive us our sins and to cleanse us from all unrighteousness." Daniel confessing the sins of his whole nation is our model (Daniel 9:1-19).

T—Thanksgiving. This is where we remember what He has done personally to lead us, provide for us, and answer our prayers. We humbly recognize His great care. Psalm 95:1-3 gives us the pattern.

S—Supplication. We ask God to hear our requests and to answer what is on our hearts, according to His will. "Ask, and it shall be given you; seek, and ye shall find; knock, and it shall be opened unto you" (Matthew 7:7, KJV).

Times of crisis help us to understand that we are not in control of our lives and force us to cry out to Him. He wants us to seek Him and to ask for His will to be done in all circumstances—but times like these make it even more important and help us put the concerns of life in proper perspective. May all of us who believe around the world humbly seek His power and grace for our nations, and for His strength and glory to be more clearly seen.

When we spend time in prayer, He fills us with His own love and peace.

Have you taken time to teach your children how to pray?
Share this acronym with them and use it to pray together!

JANUARY 11

Does not wisdom call, and understanding lift up her voice? On top of the heights beside the way, where the paths meet, she takes her stand; beside the gates, at the opening to the city, at the entrance of the doors, she cries out: "To you, O men, I call, and my voice is to the sons of men. O naive ones, understand prudence; and, O fools, understand wisdom. Listen, for I will speak noble things; and the opening of my lips will reveal right things."

PROVERBS 8:1-6

IT'S ALWAYS A JOY WHEN all my children find their way back to the nest, and this time was no exception. We have had rousing discussions this weekend in our home with family and friends who have different opinions about so many issues—from "How should we try to reach a postmodern culture?" to "What is really important to the Lord?" and on to "What is the appropriate balance between ideals and grace, passion, and redemption?" It has been good for me to enter the world of a younger generation, to see how they think, and to ask what my part is in offering truth in a way that can be understood. All of the input I receive from differing points of view prepares me to be a better thinker and more insightful into the souls and ways of people, and it ultimately makes me a better steward of His messages.

Yet I see from today's Scripture that there is a need for a voice of wisdom, to echo the voice of the Holy Spirit that calls to my children. Sometimes it's my voice box He uses! If I have taken time to fill my own soul with wisdom, I find I have great confidence to speak to my children and help shape their opinions about these important issues.

Do you see yourself as an echo of God's wisdom in your children's lives? Remember that taking time to listen to their ideas and opinions opens their hearts and helps them listen to your own.

JANUARY 12

You have need of endurance, so that when you have done
the will of God, you may receive what was promised.

HEBREWS 10:36

THIS IS THE VISION I SEE: if mothers rise to be gatekeepers, make their homes places of excellence, cultivate reverence for and worship of God as well as love for each other, spend personal time teaching and discipling their children, serve them through this training and nurture, and give up their own time to accomplish all of this, there will be hope.

When mothers abandon this important responsibility, there is a greater tendency for children to become the kind of adults who are self-centered and self-serving, and who overlook unrighteousness without any pang of conscience, because that conscience has never been developed. They become the kind of adults who can passively let others take responsibility for our government and country, who accept and validate those who would promise the moon even though the moon isn't available in reality.

For effective parenting to occur, there must be hundreds—thousands—of dinners made, laundry loads run, backs scratched, and cookies baked. There must be water-color projects and messes, hikes and games of hide-and-seek, wonderful lifegiving books and concerts and the theater. Time spent ministering to our children is time well spent, because that investment grants us the door to their hearts. When their hearts are soft to us because we have ministered to their needs, their minds will also be softened to hear our values, our convictions, and our guidance.

Moms, the way you invest your life today will indeed have a great impact on history. The cultivating and raising of great souls is of the utmost importance. Your life is making a difference. Spend time in the Word, read those books that call you to excellence, pray with friends of like mind—and don't give up!

Our culture doesn't put much value on endurance. Yet life requires
it! Determine that you will endure to the end regardless of situations.
Just making that decision goes a long way toward accomplishing your ideals!

JANUARY 13

Thus says the LORD, "Stand by the ways and see and ask for the ancient paths, where the good way is, and walk in it; and you will find rest for your souls."

JEREMIAH 6:16

As a young woman, I looked ahead to the adventure of having my own precious brood of children and idealized all the love, fun, and joy we would share as a family.

My life as a mom has created countless moments of joy, love shared, deep fulfillment, and wonderful memories. Yet I also have had times of dark depression, loneliness, and feelings that I couldn't keep going. I have often felt inadequate to know just how to discipline and train my children. Choices about their lives have often been a mystery amid so much parenting advice. On and on my questions go.

I felt so many times that I needed a guide, a map, the right resources to make the journey, and help along the way. I needed a companion to walk the road with me and to strengthen and encourage me when I felt so alone and forlorn. With so many people in my life who had such differing values and who had offered such a variety of advice, I didn't know where to turn for real tried-and-true wisdom.

Finally, I found a path that was sure and provided me with the steadiness and encouragement I needed. As I learned how to walk closely with the Lord, how to pray, and how to apply Scripture in very practical ways in my life, I began to have the resources for completing this journey well. I can now see how faithful my dear heavenly Father has been in my life, even though I was too young and limited to always understand the routes along which He was taking me.

What do the "ancient paths" and "the good way" in Jeremiah 6:16 refer to? How can you refocus yourself and your children on the ways of the ancient path?

There is an appointed time for everything.
and there is a time for every event under heaven.

ECCLESIASTES 3:1

SOME TIME AGO WHEN MY FAMILY was going through a difficult, troubled time, I had some discussion with the Lord and decided what I needed was to make some resolutions specifically for that season. A resolution is a determined commitment, an act of my will to decide in advance how I will behave and obey the Lord.

I resolved to reject any fearful thoughts by choosing to worship God and focus on His wonderful faithfulness and trustworthy character.

I resolved to be a strong pillar of faith for Clay in the midst of all he had to hold together. To not whine, complain, or falter unnecessarily in the midst of his hard work and commitment to figure out how to keep supporting our family. He needed me to "smile at the future," like the woman in Proverbs 31.

I resolved to make this time a blessed season of great memories—warm soups, candlelight, inspiring stories of heroes in other times, cards of encouragement to friends who needed them, phone calls and phone prayers with my boys who needed support and encouragement in the midst of their financial difficulties, Bible studies and life-giving words sent to all whom the Lord would bring to mind—simple efforts spent in eternal areas that would minister to the hearts of my precious family and friends.

I resolved to think of new ways that Sarah and Joy and I might serve others during those days. As we plan to be God's hands and voice and words, it gives us a way to be about God's business and to perceive the strategic role Christians can play in the lives of others.

Are you facing a particularly difficult season right now?
What resolutions can you make in advance that would help you
be prepared to make good decisions regarding your emotions,
actions, and intentions when the pressing times come?

JANUARY 15

You whom I have taken from the ends of the earth, and called from its remotest parts and said to you, "You are My servant, I have chosen you and not rejected you. Do not fear, for I am with you; do not anxiously look about you, for I am your God. I will strengthen you, surely I will help you, surely I will uphold you with My righteous right hand."

ISAIAH 41:9-10

RECENTLY, I recalled one of the first times I felt panic about the difficult circumstances of my life. There had been lots of tension in Poland between the Polish workers and the Russians who controlled the country, and I was a young missionary living there— illegally. People had begun to riot and rebel, and Russian tanks began to roll into Warsaw, where we lived. Many of the streets were lined with soldiers, and the threat of war was in the paper and on the news every day. I remembered thinking, *What am I doing over here in a time of war? I am not sure if I am ready to die in this conflict just now.* We had been ministering in Hungary and touched the bullet holes in apartment buildings of people we had worked with, where a similar revolt had caused the loss of hundreds of lives.

When I came across this passage in Isaiah, I camped on it. I resolved that I would stand on it emotionally and spiritually.

The Lord was faithful, and we came through the conflict with Him holding our hands.

Since then, many other times and seasons have come where fear threatened to take away my peace. Yet I have a pattern of remembrance now, of the ways He has been faithful through all the seasons and hard times.

Do you find yourself worried over many things?
Make a list. Then write at the top today's Scripture
from Isaiah . . . and throw the list away.

Be hospitable to one another without complaint.

I PETER 4:9

My wonderful friend Phyllis is such a joy to me. She is seventy-two, and yet her desire for bringing life and beauty and love to women so burns in her heart that she is always alive, energetic, and engaged whenever I see her. She has made her home a haven, so that just to be inside her rooms is a pleasure. There are soothing colors on her walls, and there are pictures, small relics, and treasures throughout her home that speak of the many places she has lived and traveled, her love of the Lord, and the great value she places on family. And always there is a candle lit, soft music playing, and a pot of fresh tea ready in case someone comes by for a few minutes of fellowship. There is a lovely little bedroom in her basement, just ready for someone who needs to get away—two single beds waiting for the next guests.

A woman is at her best when she is spreading life and light from the richness of her soul. I believe moms are true heroes who will be the bearers of light when shadows threaten to overtake. They weave peace and love in homes where burdens are weighing on the shoulders of husbands. They sing songs of faith in the midst of life's calamities. They can model a childlike faith and rest in God when they live in the Sabbath rest of His provision, even when physical provision is scant. I believe that moms can be the determining factor in our country during difficult times, to bring courage to families and nations as we wait on God and follow His ways.

If you have an introverted personality, it may be difficult for you to even think about purposefully inviting someone into your home! But making the effort is worth it. Ask the Lord if there's someone you could invite over for an encouraging visit.

JANUARY 17

*Whoever does not receive the kingdom of God
like a child will not enter it at all.*

MARK 10:15

LAST NIGHT, my two girls and I were on my bed talking of dreams and adventures we hope to experience together as a family. There are many dreams I have held all of my life that have not yet come true, but I still dream them. And of course, I know that some of my daughters' dreams will lead them far from me. But how precious this night was, when hearts were opened and deepest desires shared and we all snuggled together as I fought to stay awake.

Women have always been intended, through the family structure, to pass on righteousness and a loving relationship with God to every generation. Yet my girls find themselves in a broken world where few have the same values they do. Every day, I pray that my children yet unmarried will have the opportunity to meet godly, righteous spouses who also have a dream of passing on godly values to the next generation.

There is a temptation to become cynical and crusty as we make our way through life. Yet, in studying verses about God's will this year, I was impressed again to pursue childlike faith—to keep believing my God can do anything, to believe in His goodness, to believe in prayer.

So, I continue sharing my own dreams with Him! I pray for miracles and for Him to do great things in and through the lives of my family. I want to live with anticipation like a child, to not measure my life by what I can provide for myself but by what He is able to do as I believe in Him and trust Him.

*Have you found yourself becoming cynical . . .
maybe a bit too "adult"? Ask the Lord to help you return
to the childlike faith and hope that pleases Him.*

JANUARY 18

Be anxious for nothing, but in everything by prayer and supplication with thanksgiving let your requests be made known to God. and the peace of God, which surpasses all comprehension, will guard your hearts and your minds in Christ Jesus.

PHILIPPIANS 4:6-7

THE LORD HAS BROUGHT me through many difficult, busy, trying seasons. When I've come into His presence and spent time in His Word, He has been there for me. I didn't always feel His presence, but I took His Word and promises at face value and rested in them anyway, and then practiced taking steps of faith—one day, one issue at a time. Now, I can look back and see that He has used each part of the journey to shape me—my character, my love, my humility, my compassion—and has taught me to rest in Him.

I must guard my heart and my mind so that I don't spend unnecessary energy and time on worrying, but rather give everything into His hands and picture Him taking and working it all out on my behalf as His daughter.

I need courage. Courage is the ability to face difficulty, danger, fear, or pain without being overcome by present circumstances, but instead acting with resolve, and with strength of mind and behavior. I have made a decision of my will to take courage—to practice being strong, to put one foot in front of the other, to believe in a good outcome from a Father who is good. Courage lies in believing and behaving as though God will indeed be faithful. These habits create a life of faithfulness and are the foundation of a life well built and well lived.

What are you anxious about today? Make a list, and then in prayer and supplication—with thanksgiving!—make those requests known to God. Enjoy His peace!

JANUARY 19

Be devoted to one another in brotherly love; give preference to one another in honor; not lagging behind in diligence, fervent in spirit, serving the Lord; rejoicing in hope, persevering in tribulation, devoted to prayer, contributing to the needs of the saints, practicing hospitality.

ROMANS 12:10-13

So many mamas find themselves incredibly lonely. Entertainment is sought to fill the cavernous holes and vacuums in the soul, where it replaces real relationships, love, and service and only serves to placate and dull the one imbibing it. Television replaces visiting and sharing friendship, discussing books, being creative, cooking, painting, sewing, writing letters, enjoying articles and books, reading aloud, playing games . . . and so we live an isolated existence. Media has defined and determined the moral values and character of this current generation, but it has not satisfied souls. Real, hand-to-hand, voice-to-voice friendship and intimacy is what we long for and hope for.

That is why we must figure out a way in the midst of our busyness to create community and fellowship. We need to connect heartstrings from one person to the other—and lend a helping hand to each other in the midst of our burdens and our joys.

While I relish the ability to share encouragement and teaching through today's digital means, we all need to know that there is someone nearby who is real, someone to touch, talk to, cry with—to truly know. I have learned that often, if this kind of fellowship is going to happen, I need to be the one who initiates it. God was an initiator—He came to give: He healed and blessed and taught and sacrificed. It is what we also were created to do. I travel so much that I cannot always do as much locally as I would like, but I have come to really appreciate the encouragement I receive when I open my home to sweet, like-minded women.

Might God be calling you to open your own home and create real community right where you are? Pray about it.

JANUARY 20

*. . . not forsaking our own assembling together, as is the
habit of some, but encouraging one another; and all
the more as you see the day drawing near.*

HEBREWS 10:25

LAST WEEK, I had a precious conversation with a young, idealistic mama who said, "I just went upstairs for three minutes to put up laundry and when I came down, my three-year-old had used a permanent marker to draw all over the naked body of my eighteen-month-old, and then she went on to color on my favorite blouse—as well as the carpet! I thought to myself, 'Is this what I want to do for the rest of my life? Take care of these children? Stay home by myself and do this day in and day out? Am I not more talented than this? Will I never have a bigger life?'"

I sympathized with her, even as I giggled at her story! How I know those feelings. So many mamas struggle with isolation as they spend much of their time at home. I want you to know today that you are not alone! God loves you so much and is so proud of the ways you are bringing life and beauty into your home. He knows your struggles. He sees you and your need to be loved and appreciated and filled up.

If I could, I would have you into my little living room right now for tea and chocolate. But since that's not possible, I am going to pray for you. You must be a conductor of your own symphony and make a plan to add to your life some beauty, some pleasant times with people, and some outings away from the messy home. Sometimes you need to avoid being sequestered with too many sinful children and a sinful mama in one small place!

*While the verse from Hebrews above is generally interpreted in
the light of church meetings, I think we can apply it to gathering
together informally too! Who do you know who would appreciate a
call, an invitation, or perhaps a handwritten note from you?*

JANUARY 21

He who is slow to anger is better than the mighty, and
he who rules his spirit, than he who captures a city.

PROVERBS 16:32

NOT TOO LONG AGO, a lovely mom brought her two children along to our meeting in a coffee shop. They were sweet children, but they alternated between climbing all over her and making her chase them around the café! Later, my children and I were discussing the meeting. It was humorous to hear how opinionated they were, as each reminded me how intentionally we taught them to be patient and to wait their turn—because they all remembered it the same way. We were (and are!) strong believers in a concept called self-government.

The idea behind self-government is that all of us have power and authority over our own lives. This power comes from within, and can help us master problems, surmount obstacles, and use our self-will to achieve great things. The person who has cultivated this kind of strong character is useful and productive in every area of life.

This quality helps a believer exercise faith, courage, and perseverance in the midst of trials. It is what helps a pianist to practice long hours, an athlete to exercise rigorously in order to become a champion, a missionary to master a language and remain faithful in a foreign country until there is a multiplying ministry, a wife to bear up with grace when married to an immature husband, a mother to continue over and over to practice patience with a sick or rebellious child. It is the unseen power of governing life by mature, faith-based choices as opposed to temporary, self-centered feelings.

At the time today's Scripture was written, a city without walls
had no protection, no vantage point to watch for enemies, and
no means of defense. And so we are when we have no self-control.
Is self-control an area in your own life that could use some
work? How can you strengthen your own "city walls"?

*I call heaven and earth to witness against you today, that I have
set before you life and death, the blessing and the curse. So choose
life in order that you may live, you and your descendants.*

DEUTERONOMY 30:19

IN LIFE, all choices have consequences. Children need to understand they will reap what they sow. I used to tell my children over and over again, "Daddy and I cannot make you into great people. You have the power to determine how strong you become by how you exercise your will. We can train you and teach you how to be good and how to be righteous, but you have to decide to obey, that you want to become a person of godly character. God made you such a wonderful child, so I hope you will decide to do your best to become all that you can be. It is in your hands. It is yours to decide how to respond."

When we appeal to our children's hearts for excellence and choices of good behavior, we are giving them the will and desire to be excellent for themselves. But if we attempt to train them behaviorally by always forcing them to do what we want them to do because they might get a spanking or some other kind of discipline, their motivation is to avoid spanking or harshness, not to please God or to please their parents by having a good heart and responding in obedience.

My desire as a mom is that my children would internalize the precepts we've taught them over the years. I want them to love God and obey Him because they earnestly love Him and desire to please Him. Building a foundation will carry them throughout all the decision-making processes they will face for the rest of their lives.

*Do you tend to try to motivate your children's choices through
behavioral training, or through reaching their hearts? How can
you change the way you instinctively respond to your children?
Spend time in prayer asking the Lord's help in this area.*

JANUARY 23

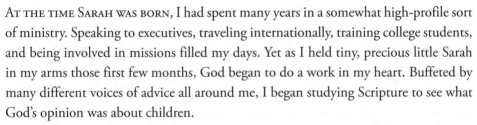

God blessed them; and God said to them, "Be fruitful and multiply,
and fill the earth, and subdue it; and rule over the fish of the sea and over
the birds of the sky and over every living thing that moves on the earth."

GENESIS 1:28

AT THE TIME SARAH WAS BORN, I had spent many years in a somewhat high-profile sort of ministry. Speaking to executives, traveling internationally, training college students, and being involved in missions filled my days. Yet as I held tiny, precious little Sarah in my arms those first few months, God began to do a work in my heart. Buffeted by many different voices of advice all around me, I began studying Scripture to see what God's opinion was about children.

I found the first blessing out of His mouth was, "Be fruitful and multiply" (Genesis 1:28). "The fruit of the womb is a reward," I was told in Psalm 127:3. Many other Scriptures convinced me of the high priority God places on the lives of children!

I have rarely met a mom who did not love and cherish her children. So many, however, feel lost in a sea of contemporary philosophies. Some have to work just to feed their families. Many are single and bear burdens alone. Many come from broken families and don't know how to love their children. Some feel they have never been given permission from our culture to stay home with their children. Others have simply never been taught the truth about their role in their precious children's lives.

Yet we know both from statistics and biblical wisdom that most children do not become righteous without the devoted teaching and intentional training of the parents. We know that if the next generation of adults—the children currently in our homes— is neglected, that generation will have no godly character, no purpose, and no direction and will contribute to the demise of our own culture.

Have you embraced God's view of children? In what
ways has common culture's negative attitude toward them
affected your own understanding and lifestyle?

*Do not be conformed to this world, but be transformed by
the renewing of your mind, so that you may prove what the will
of God is, that which is good and acceptable and perfect.*

ROMANS 12:2

WE WOULD NEVER THROW seeds out into the wind and expect them to grow into a beautiful garden. Similarly, we cannot throw our children out into the winds of culture and expect them to become people of great character and faith. This is especially true when media—the internet, television, movies, and magazines—and cultural values at large take commitment to marriage, purity, and godly character lightly. Both media and our culture scoff at those things and promote the adulation of celebrities such as actors, athletes, and musicians whose lifestyles are immoral and vain and who obviously reject those values.

When God places a child into our arms, we know it is one of the most significant treasures we will ever be given, because what we do to invest in that child's life will influence the course of history—not just that particular child's life but that of future generations.

My heart is to encourage you, mom, to do the hard thing—to take the time and pay whatever it costs to be that person in your children's lives, the one who gives them an appetite for God and the things of God. I want to see you do the work of making your home a place of real life, beauty, truth, and celebrated relationships, so that when you enter the gates of heaven, you can say to Jesus, "I did all that I could to whisper into the ears of my children the truths and secrets of the Kingdom of Heaven, and to pass on a love for You."

*Is your mind being transformed, so that it is different
from the world? How are you whispering the secrets of the
Kingdom of Heaven into the ears of your children?*

JANUARY 25

The fruit of the Spirit is love, joy, peace, patience, kindness, goodness, faithfulness, gentleness, self-control.

GALATIANS 5:22-23

WHEN MY CHILDREN WERE YOUNG, part of my duty as a mom was to train my children's wills to develop strength and self-control. They remember us saying all the time, "You have a choice to make. If you obey me, then you will be blessed. But if you choose to disobey me, then you are choosing disciplinary consequences that will be unpleasant." If a fussy little one continued whining after such a warning, we might remove the child from the area where the rest of us were, for a time. Thus, even our toddlers learned the self-control of calming down and communicating in a normal voice—gaining control of their little spirits. We wanted our children to find internal motivation to obey us and to learn that there were positive and negative consequences to their choices—just as it says in Scripture.

Of course, the key to this is being consistent and following through unless there are mitigating circumstances—a child is ill, exhausted, or overstimulated—which often happens because the parent led the child to be that way because of a demanding and overly busy schedule! Sometimes the only recourse a child has is to cry or complain if they have become physically or emotionally spent because of too much activity and demands on their young body.

Helping our children know beforehand what we expected of them in most situations gave them guidelines to follow and helped them obey. We see this modeled in Scripture, as God is also this kind of trainer—He was very specific in the law to teach His children how to live life well. And so we sought to let our children know, without fail, what the guidelines and expectations were that would define their lives.

Do you usually interact with your children in a spirit of compassion, or is your approach antagonistic? Ask the Lord to show you. And remember, tomorrow is a new day!

I will sing of lovingkindness and justice, to You,
O LORD, I will sing praises.

PSALM 101:1

ONE OF THE REASONS DAVID IS such a picture of a man after God's own heart is that he constantly wrote songs about God's goodness and faithfulness, desiring to thank and praise Him. While David was king, he led his people in giving God the glory due His name. He called them to sing, play instruments, worship, and dance, and he joined them with all his heart.

We must find ways to do the same in our own homes. Practical applications of thanksgiving give our children patterns that they will practice the rest of their lives.

Truth be told, most of my own prayers are petitions and requests. Yet I am learning that thanksgiving is an exercise of my character that eventually influences my heart. When I look at my life with thankful eyes, it lifts my heart to see how truly blessed I am and makes all the other issues of my life seem less important. Gratitude gives me power to believe Him for great things. It causes my soul to soar because it directs my gaze heavenward instead of toward the earth. It is impossible for my heart to be truly thankful, acknowledging God's sovereignty over all situations, and to be bitter at the same time.

Increasing thankfulness in my own life is something I am working on. I've determined to write down what I appreciate most about God each year. Choosing to be thankful and learning to be content will fill your soul with peace and kindness. It is a choice, a habit of practice, which will indeed create in you a more beautiful soul. Practicing what you want to be—what God wants you to be—just because it is right will always end up blessing you in the end.

Do you have a plan to build your thankfulness
toward God? How might you begin, today?

JANUARY 27

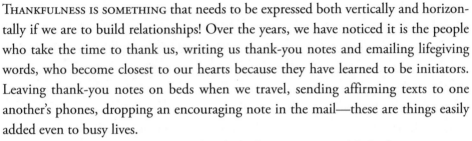

As you have received Christ Jesus the Lord, so walk in Him, having been firmly rooted and now being built up in Him and established in your faith, just as you were instructed, and overflowing with gratitude.

COLOSSIANS 2:6-7

THANKFULNESS IS SOMETHING that needs to be expressed both vertically and horizontally if we are to build relationships! Over the years, we have noticed it is the people who take the time to thank us, writing us thank-you notes and emailing lifegiving words, who become closest to our hearts because they have learned to be initiators. Leaving thank-you notes on beds when we travel, sending affirming texts to one another's phones, dropping an encouraging note in the mail—these are things easily added even to busy lives.

We all must tightly hold on to the ideal of community and fight for it, as it is in the community of loving believers where the reality of God is most felt. I have been so blessed to have a couple of friends who love me and reach out to me because they know I need to be cared for, just as they do.

My children didn't have lots of other people in their lives when they were younger, so I didn't have much competition! We loved and had fun with each other out of necessity, and the result is that we are friends and love and enjoy each other not because we have to, but because we truly enjoy each other and are interested in each other's lives. Even after so many years of fussing and tussling—they ended up in love.

Thanksgiving, joy, and strong relationships are interconnected! All of them can grow in our lives if we put some effort in.

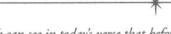

We can see in today's verse that before we overflow with gratitude,
we must be rooted and built up and established in faith!
Have you received Christ this way? He longs to have a relationship with you.

Do you think lightly of the riches of His kindness and tolerance and patience,
not knowing that the kindness of God leads you to repentance?

ROMANS 2:4

SOMETIMES WHEN PEOPLE FIND OUT Clay and I are grace-based in our approach to parenting, they assume we are lenient and undisciplined. However, we actually were very idealistic and had high expectations for our children. We instructed them through consistent training and a relational, discipleship-based life. Our philosophy also looked at each child as an individual, so we worked to figure out what appealed to and reached the heart of each one.

No matter what philosophy we have for discipline, we need to remember that our goal isn't primarily to make them obey, but to motivate them toward obedience from a sincere and loving heart. I always felt that if I expected my children to exercise self-control and to work hard, I had to be sure I was meeting their essential needs. They needed to be given a fairly routine life—plenty of sleep; an appropriate amount of stimulation; nutritional food; lifegiving, soul-filling words—so that their bodies could support my ideals and expectations for them as a mom.

Discipline is really about relational training in righteousness and taking time to instruct, train, praise, and correct. It lies in strengthening a child's moral character and will through all the moments of life, rather than referring to a list of rules and mandates about when and how and for how long to spank or punish. The Holy Spirit grants wisdom to each parent about how to apply biblical principles of training according to their own life puzzle and their unique children. While the final result will look different for each family and each child, philosophies that focus on reaching and training the heart have a more significant influence on the formation of the child's soul than those based on predetermined lists.

Have you ever taken time to think about the ways God relates to you
as a parent? How might this vision affect the way you relate to your children?

JANUARY 29

The Son is the radiance of God's glory and the exact representation
of his being, sustaining all things by his powerful word.

HEBREWS 1:3, NIV

PEOPLE HAVE OFTEN ASKED ME why I put so much emphasis on beauty—art, candles, beautiful music, a cup of tea, cinnamon rolls, great stories and books, and celebrating life—as I live, write, and teach. It seems there are so many "more important" things to focus on. I keep beauty primary because I wish to bring the reality of God and His life into my home in the most tangible way.

What did Jesus do? He gently touched human hands and feet, He told epic stories through prophets and in His sermons, He ate and celebrated among His own disciples. He comforted the sad, healed the brokenhearted, and inspired the vigorous young men sharing daily life with Him to continue living for a Kingdom that would never end. He modeled, through His every waking hour, the vast love, compassion, holiness, beauty, and servant leadership that expressed the very heart of God.

Jesus is not just a thought to be understood or a verse to be memorized, but a living, breathing, vibrant, loving, personal God who lives and moves among us right in our homes each day.

Young adults are confronted more than ever today with postmodern values. Almost every movie, television show, and book will inevitably turn to a focus on immorality, infidelity, and impurity. Our children are bombarded with it at every turn. There are fewer and fewer models that we can point to in order to say, "Follow this pattern of leadership, of sacrifice, of holiness." This is why our homes must become a true and vibrant picture of the living God, of the marvelous depth and beauty of Jesus.

If Jesus is the "exact representation" of the Father, what does that tell you
about God? What qualities do you see in Jesus that are most important to you?

JANUARY 30

You will make known to me the path of life; in Your presence is fullness of joy; in Your right hand there are pleasures forever.

PSALM 16:11

THESE PAST FEW YEARS, I have focused my spiritual study on Jesus Himself. Jesus is, according to Hebrews 1:3, "the exact representation of [God's] nature." In other words, when you see Jesus in Scripture, you see God Himself living in the flesh. To look at Jesus is to behold God the Father.

Jesus was a man who walked on water, was tossed about in the stormy sea on a smelly fishing boat, and hosted a picnic that satisfied the hunger of thousands of people. He didn't just talk about truth, He filled rumbling stomachs. Jesus touched the untouchables—a prostitute, lepers, the sick and dying—with tenderness and love. He held children on His knee and laughed with and loved them. Jesus was not afraid to rage at the religious leaders who led people in legalism and performance but were not compassionate—He was not afraid of them at all. He talked of birds, trees, lilies, mountains, and creation. Jesus, the very Son of God, washed 120 dirty toes the night before He died, and wiped them tenderly with a towel as a mother bathes the children she loves. He celebrated and drank wine at a wedding, cooked fish on the beach, and validated women for their service and tender love toward Him.

It is the life and reality of God that my children long for. For now, they experience this through my service, love, faith, and confident celebration of life. I can only give to them what I have found by loving Him on my own, by seeing Him with my own eyes, by understanding Him in my own quiet time, and then living from a soul fully engaged in Him.

Do you experience the truth of today's Scripture—of God's fullness of joy? Ask Him to open your heart to see it more clearly today.

JANUARY 31

A new commandment I give to you, that you love one another,
even as I have loved you, that you also love one another.

JOHN 13:34

WHEN I GRADUATED FROM COLLEGE, I worked on the staff of Campus Crusade for Christ (now Cru) for two years at the University of Texas, then moved to Eastern Europe to travel through Communist countries as a missionary. Because I had a committed heart, I was under the delusion that I was already mature! But since the Lord is a good parent and wanted me to grow into the likeness of Christ, He saw me as I was—young, immature, self-centered, and full of pride. The Lord knew I needed more practice and training to become more like Christ, to really grow in His kind of love.

So . . . He gave me a husband and children so I could find out what sacrificial love was really all about! It has not been easy to pull out the weeds of false expectations, to fight the storms of giving up my rights, to endure the drought of feelings that did not always match up to my ideals of what a loving wife and mother should feel in a happy home. Though still growing, I have learned so much about true love, self-sacrifice, commitment, and long-suffering. I have tested Him, misbehaved, thrown tantrums, and pulled away at times. Still He loves me; He died for me while I was yet a sinner, and His grace continues to extend to me now that I am His stumbling child.

Love must grow over years and years to become mature. It must be cultivated and watered and nurtured and protected and worked on again and again. Thank You, sweet Lord, for showing me the way and going before me to model real love.

How are you doing in the love department? Are there areas
where you know you're still striving against laying down your life?
Ask the Lord for help. He is ready to grant it!

FEBRUARY 1

Surely I have composed and quieted my soul; like a weaned child rests against his mother, my soul is like a weaned child within me.

PSALM 131:2

COME FEBRUARY, many of us have decided resolutions are for the birds. We've already failed to eat only whole grains, drink enough water, or exercise thirty minutes every day.

Many years ago, when I had hit my own wall during a particularly draining time, I looked at my life and thought, *How am I still doing this? No one knows how hard my life is. I'm still waiting on answers to prayer, hoping for people in my life to change, wishing my life would get a little easier. I have friends who are leaving their ideals behind because they're just worn out. Can I go on?*

As I sat on the bench that day, a sudden movement caught my eye. In the center of the square where I was reflecting, a young boy was dancing. His head was back, his arms were spread, and he was twirling in utter abandon. The look on his face was priceless—he was so full of joy! Unaware of anyone else, he danced among the falling leaves, perfectly happy. Then I heard the Lord speak to my heart and say, "That's what I want for you. I want you to be like a child. I don't want you to bear the burdens of your life. I want you to live a life of joy."

So the question becomes, what do we need to do so we won't lose our ideals—so we won't arrive gasping at the gates of heaven?

Godliness, wisdom, graciousness, joyfulness . . . these are qualities we want to have, and they don't happen by accident! They must be cultivated intentionally. We must develop habits that will help us build a foundation in our own lives to receive and experience and pass along His grace to others.

---

*Where might the Lord help you find room for more joy,
so His grace can flow to and through you?*

FEBRUARY 2

The Spirit of the Lord GOD is upon me, because the LORD has anointed me . . . to comfort all who mourn, to grant those who mourn in Zion, giving them a garland instead of ashes, the oil of gladness instead of mourning, the mantle of praise instead of a spirit of fainting.

ISAIAH 61:1-3

WE CANNOT PASS ON CIVILITY, beauty, intelligence, or excellence of mind and heart if we do not ourselves make these virtues a goal of our lives. As stewards of our souls, we must seek to cultivate a garden of beauty—it must be a regular habit, a discipline, to expose ourselves to great minds, the best musicians, fine artists, great theologians, and wonderful biographies, so that our souls will indeed reflect a museum of His great character and nobility—that of our great King.

There is so much ugliness in our world. The media is expert at creating new ways to celebrate and glorify evil, and it seems almost inescapable. Harsh realities are visually depicted for us on the news, in the papers, and online. If we don't intentionally pursue and reflect upon beauty, we will miss it as it is drowned out by the negative realities of life.

Creating an atmosphere of beauty, welcome, and hospitality takes work. I believe this is the work women in particular are called to do: to civilize, to make our domains beautiful, to invite others to see the life and glory of God.

Part of what God has done for us through Christ is to transform the way we experience all of life. He changes darkness to light and brings life to dead places!

Can you think of some specific areas of your own life where God has changed ugly things into beautiful ones? Write them down and thank Him!

FEBRUARY 3

God, after He spoke long ago to the fathers
in the prophets in many portions and in many ways,
in these last days has spoken to us in His Son.

HEBREWS 1:1-2

IN THE ABSENCE OF BIBLICAL CONVICTIONS, people will go the way of culture. If we don't regularly listen to the voice of God, we are doomed to obey the voices around us that may or may not have our best interest in mind—friends, culture, family, neighbors, television, magazines, Satan—the list goes on and on.

In Genesis, we find God walking in the Garden in the heat of the day to speak to Adam and Eve. He longs to have a conversation with them, to be with them and enjoy their company. He is not just a theological idea to be understood. He is a lover, a friend, a Father, a trainer, a Savior—and He wants to speak to us, too.

However, in the busyness of our lives, many just don't get this. Women read blogs to find out truth; they search for wisdom in the media; they write me and ask me to give them advice. I absolutely believe in seeking out the counsel of older women, but the fact remains that God wants to talk to us—to give us His insight about our situation, our puzzle. He, the Word Himself, has a word for us.

It seems that in our lives together, God has led Clay and me to make many out-of-the-box decisions. But they weren't arbitrary—we just kept looking at the Word and listening to His voice. He said, "Do not be conformed to this world, but be transformed by the renewing of your mind, so that you may prove what the will of God is, that which is good and acceptable and perfect" (Romans 12:2). In order to do God's will, you have to have your mind transformed to His will—which means not conforming to this world and all its voices.

Which voices are loudest in your own life?
How might you quiet those that aren't God's own?

FEBRUARY 4

The LORD came and stood and called as at other times, "Samuel! Samuel!" and Samuel said, "Speak, for Your servant is listening."

I SAMUEL 3:10

IN MY LIFE, I have found that most everyone will give me permission to give up on my ideals. They say, "You deserve a break—you need to find fulfillment!" and so on. Yet the more I walk with God, the more I realize I have just this one life to live a story that will show His excellence, His greatness, His love and mercy, His redemption and grace.

So many young women are listening to feminist voices, to popular culture, to contemporary thought. They do not know that certain choices, especially made after seeking the counsel of the wrong voices, will have great consequences in their lives. They unwittingly think that personal fulfillment comes from material things that will make them comfortable; work that will give them a sense of their own importance; experiences that will give them a surge of adventure and excitement; romance that will make them feel loved—but they do not really know or understand that in the long haul, no one and no thing can make them happy or fulfilled apart from the love and grace and forgiveness of God. So many decisions made for short-term gain have devastating consequences and leave ugly scars in the long run.

So we must seek wisdom where it is to truly be found—within God's Word.

No one loves you or has more grace for you than God! He is a God of love, second chances, forgiveness. All He wants is our hearts. He wants to inform our decisions, our ways, our attitudes, our convictions, and our values. He is waiting to talk to you . . . today!

Do you have an established quiet time? Set up an area where you can begin to develop a habit of meeting with God. Consider what you can do to make it more pleasant— a candle, cup of hot chocolate, lovely music to listen to?

Let us consider how to stimulate one another to love and good deeds.

HEBREWS 10:24

MANY YEARS AGO I heard a prominent speaker relate this wonderfully wise principle: "I will do anything to put myself in the company of people who make me want to love God more, to be more excellent, to set a standard of excellence in my life, to live up to my potential as a believer. I will also do whatever I can to avoid those who are drainers—those who steal my joy, who keep me from wanting to grow in my faith, who complain and criticize other people, or who tempt me to discouragement."

There are not many people whose lives really encourage me to press on, to walk in the presence of the Lord, to love others graciously and unconditionally, and to believe God with all my heart. Thankfully, though, there are a few people who do make me feel more filled up when I have spent time with them—ready to face life again, to finish well, to trust God. Those are the people I try to spend the most time with!

I have often shared that if you want to find the best kind of friend, find someone you can do ministry with—someone who loves God and wants to make a difference in the world. In the midst of working together, praying, and serving people, you will grow together in memory making, faith, and accountability. The strings of your hearts become knit together by the Holy Spirit as you invest together in Kingdom work.

Do you have friends who encourage you and push you forward?
Make a plan to get together with them soon. If not, begin to pray that
God will send you this type of friend—and make you one too!

FEBRUARY 6

For God so loved the world, that He gave His only begotten Son,
that whoever believes in Him shall not perish, but have eternal life.
JOHN 3:16

TAKING RESPONSIBILITY TO encourage and to speak lifegiving words is one of the best reflections of the reality of Christ in our lives. God always initiated—creating a Garden where Adam and Eve could thrive and be blessed; providing clothes after they had sinned; sending manna and quail for the Israelites in the desert; giving words of encouragement; miraculously multiplying fish and loaves when He noticed people's hunger; sharing promises of hope with His followers; and ultimately giving Himself as the final sacrifice.

When we pursue our children, our husband, our friends, and others in our lives who may be in need, we can protect them from despair, condemnation, and surrendering to less than God's best. We may even help them change their destiny by giving them the courage to hold fast their hope and wait long enough for God to show His grace in difficult circumstances.

This is why I pursue my children with the intention of giving them words of life. Calling my husband most days after lunch has become part of my daily routine, too, so I can let him know someone in the world is thinking of him and loves him and prays for him. Traveling across the globe to visit those I'm committed to, gathering women in my home, and hosting holidays all fall in this same category of purpose.

We don't initiate because we feel like it—we may be weary and discouraged ourselves. But we do it out of obedience, because He did, and His supernatural grace drives us to give of ourselves to others.

In today's verse, we see God's initiative! Because He
loved us, He gave His Son. Who does God bring to mind
that you might need to take initiative with today?

*Let us consider how to stimulate one another to love
and good deeds, . . . encouraging one another; and all
the more as you see the day drawing near.*

HEBREWS 10:24 25

THIS MORNING, in our small Bible study, a sweet mom came in, obviously overwhelmed by the busyness of her life. As several moms gathered, placing arms around her shoulders and asking about her day, she burst out sobbing and told us what an awful mother she was. She got bits of her story out between heaves, revealing that she hasn't gotten any sleep for some time, as she has a small baby and three other children under seven years old. No wonder she felt she was falling apart!

How happy I was that she came to our group today, because the Lord was just waiting to encourage her through the kindness and compassion of others. If she had not come, she would not have felt the fellowship of the Lord, His love, His encouragement, or His direction, because she would have remained alone.

We all feel inadequate at times, and just knowing we are not alone is so important. As believers, we have the Holy Spirit working in us, and He gives us the desire to minister to others. Some moms are great at bringing meals when someone is sick, some are practical, some are encouragers. But all of us who decide to initiate lifegiving care to those around us—including our children—influence them powerfully toward being faithful and having hope rather than giving up or surrendering to despair or moral failure. It is in praying for one another and loving one another that we will build community and true friendship.

---

*How can you be God's angel-messenger this week to
someone who is feeling invisible or alone?*

FEBRUARY 8

Whoever in the name of a disciple gives to one of
these little ones even a cup of cold water to drink,
truly I say to you, he shall not lose his reward.

MATTHEW 10:42

MANY YEARS AGO, when we had just moved to a new city and I was feeling quite alone, I wearily made my way to the local grocery store. When I reached the checkout stand, the very sweet cashier smiled and asked, "How are you today?" as I placed my items on the belt.

When I gave a weak smile and replied, "Fine," she squinted her eyes and wrinkled her nose as if she didn't quite believe me and said, "Really? You look like you just need to know someone cares."

I didn't know before that moment how close I was to tears! But just her simple kindness brought them spilling over. She gave me a hug, and when I got to the car, it struck me that though she was a checkout clerk, and not a pastor or ministry worker of any sort, she became an angel to me, by just letting me know that someone in the world cared!

All of us can be channels of the Holy Spirit's love, grace, and encouragement every day. It only takes a few minutes to be an angel-messenger of God's grace to someone—even to your own children! Just ask to be a vessel, and then initiate with those words that are in your heart, that baked bread, cup of tea, or phone call. I know that these small, loving acts of God's grace have blessed me so very much and have helped me to keep going. If all of us had a friend intentionally blessing us in some way each week, spurring us on to excellence and faith, we would all be such better warriors in this battle for our children's souls.

Is there something special you could do today to serve one of your children
in a way that would truly bless their heart and help them feel loved?

FEBRUARY 9

*Jesus said to him, "Have I been so long with you,
and yet you have not come to know Me, Philip?
He who has seen Me has seen the Father."*

JOHN 14:9

IF YOU WANT TO TRULY disciple your children, you have to model love yourself. You can't just say, "Jesus said we are supposed to love one another." If you want it to truly sink in, you have to do what Jesus did: spend focused time listening to the ones you love; give words of life and build them up; have fun, shared experiences with them; minister to them when they are sick or tired; appreciate their dreams; support and forgive them when they have failed. Then they do not just hear love as a word, but they experience love as a reality.

Similarly, if we want to change our own culture, we can't just tell people what is right and wrong; they must experience what is right by seeing it in our lives. We show people a realistic picture of marriage and family by inviting them into our home for meals, loving them actively and serving them as a family when they have needs, hosting them on holidays, and sharing Christ with them through our words and cups of cold water.

The role of motherhood is also extremely important in our days, just as it has always been! We must build our family culture in such a way that it builds anchor lines from our children's hearts to our hearts, giving them a reason to always think of home as the best place to be. Then, we invite others into our home so they, too, will catch the idea of having a strong family culture and seek to build one for themselves. The best way to do both? Model Jesus so those around us can see Him.

*Today's verse is such a powerful statement by Jesus.
We know perfection is impossible. But could you make
this statement yourself? Can those who watch your life see
God in it? What changes might you need to make?*

FEBRUARY 10

*Listen, my son, to your father's instruction and do not
forsake your mother's teaching. They are a garland to
grace your head and a chain to adorn your neck.*

PROVERBS 1:8-9, NIV

ONE AFTERNOON, I stood in the kitchen with one of my children while they brewed a cup of tea. As we stood there, this child suddenly said, "You know, a lot of our friends act like God makes them unhappy and sour."

"What do you mean?" I asked.

"Well, they always have a stern look on their faces, and say no a lot, and look like having fun is against the rules. But in our house, God is the one who made chili peppers for fajitas and Celtic music to dance to and stars to sleep out under on our porch. Our God is big and fun and good and interesting and loving and true. I like that kind of a God better than their kind." What a stunning and wise statement! I have observed again and again over the years how true this reflection is.

All children will balk at instruction and training; it's part of what strengthens their muscles! And yet maturity and growth comes for them, just as it does for us, as they learn to yield themselves to God's truths.

I've found that a yummy treat helps a young child stay quiet in their room each afternoon with less angst, calms a frazzled teen, and even softens the lines on my husband's worried brow. And offering one to myself does a lot of good too! Walking in a nearby park or taking a drive through the mountains resets our minds and reminds us even our most difficult situations are small beside God's majesty. All of us enjoy life more when we remember that our creative, beauty-loving God has given us much to enjoy.

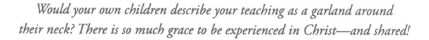

*Would your own children describe your teaching as a garland around
their neck? There is so much grace to be experienced in Christ—and shared!*

*Love your enemies, and do good, and lend, expecting nothing in
return; and your reward will be great, and you will be sons of the
Most High; for He Himself is kind to ungrateful and evil men.*

LUKE 6:35

IF WE ARE TO PLEASE CHRIST, there is no other option—we are commanded to love. Unconditional, grace-giving love must be our commitment, standard, and model every day if we want our children to know the Lord and commit their lives to Him. None of us is perfectly mature or strong in these areas; I have felt disqualified in this role as a mom many times when I became angry or irritated or said unkind words. But the ideal I get back to is to ask for forgiveness, give grace, and verbalize love. As we strive toward and practice God's ideals, our children will be given a foundation of emotional security.

The reverse is also true. If we harbor bitterness toward others, if we are regularly critical of people and do not forgive those who have offended us, we are leaving our children a wrong image of God, for we are their picture of His love and lovingkindness. Our words might say, "Love one another," but our actions may not. While many areas factor into rebellion, some children rebel because of hypocrisy in their home, where critical, pharisaical attitudes were the norm, rather than love—and it produced children who did not know God because the reality of His love was not the predominant character quality they witnessed.

Living together at home offers multiple opportunities on a daily basis for us to practice forgiveness! Perhaps we need to be reminded so often of our own need for God's forgiveness.

---

*Is there someone with whom you have had a disagreement,
harsh words, or a misunderstanding? God says that if He
has forgiven us, we need to forgive others—period!*

FEBRUARY 12

My heavenly Father will also do the same to you,
if each of you does not forgive his brother from your heart.

MATTHEW 18:35

JESUS ONCE TOLD THE STORY OF a wealthy man who forgave the debt of another to whom he had loaned money (Matthew 18:21-35). After being released from his great debt, this forgiven man ran into a man who owed him a small amount of money—but he showed him no mercy, demanding repayment at once. When the first man found out about his former debtor's lack of kindness to the other, he went looking for him and threw him in prison to be tortured until he had personally, completely repaid the original debt.

This story teaches much about our relationship with the Lord. Because He has forgiven us and humbled Himself to the point of death to bring about payment for our debt of sin, He says we owe everyone we meet the same grace, love, mercy, and forgiveness that we received. If we do not forgive others, then no matter how justified we feel in hanging onto our resentment and hurt, our hearts will be damaged, and we will feel far from God.

There is so much potential for broken relationships throughout life—hurt feelings, different values, varying philosophies, immaturity, insensitivity, harsh or careless words, and simple irritation offer just a few places where bitterness could take root.

We all have baggage of some sort from severed relationships in this broken world, and sometimes it's not at all our fault! But our hearts don't have to stay broken, and we don't have to react with bitterness, even in these circumstances. We can always choose to love, even when we are not loved by people—because God is absolutely, forever committed to loving us.

Are there relationships in your life that have been broken?
People you need to forgive? Ask God to bring them
to mind today, and lay a burden down.

Do nothing from selfishness or empty conceit, but with humility of mind regard one another as more important than yourselves.

PHILIPPIANS 2:3

IT WOULD BE IMPOSSIBLE TO count how many times I have found it necessary to humble myself in relationships. Sometimes I knew I was the one in the wrong. But many times, I chose to humble myself while still convinced the other person was guilty! The good news is, the more you practice humility, the easier it becomes. We are more like God when we love and "cover a multitude of sins" with our words and compassion than at any other time.

Does it hurt to be ignored or mistreated? Of course! But if we love Jesus, we are called to love and forgive not because the other person deserves it, but because Jesus tells us to love and forgive! We love out of our commitment to Him. Loyal, humble, long-suffering love—the kind that says, "I don't care what you have done; I will choose to forgive you"—is what makes us a picture of His reality to this world.

How important it is to train our children in love. The reason there is so much brokenness—so many divorces, so much child abuse, such prevalent feelings of abandonment in the hearts of children and adults—is because loving and serving one another takes a lot of work, sacrifice, and humility, and those are not natural to us. Only God's love and Jesus' example have the power to bring about change. We love because He first loved us. And love so often begins . . . with humility.

What if we choose to lay down our lives for our children, to humble ourselves and ask for and offer forgiveness, to model love, to set our own desires aside in favor of those in our families? We could change the world, starting in our own living rooms.

Take a moment to ask the Lord to show you your heart and its current position . . . and for help if it needs changing, as mine always does!

FEBRUARY 14

Behold, how good and how pleasant it is
for brothers to dwell together in unity!

PSALM 133:1

WHEN MY BOYS WERE YOUNGER and began to fuss, I read them the story of Cain and Abel and told them all boys are tempted to fight and be jealous, resulting in terrible consequences. Then I would read the passage in Psalms and admonish them: "That is the standard that pleases God—unity and peace. How could you have said that more graciously to your brother? You boys need to stay in this room until you have settled your differences. You cannot come out until you have made peace and have prayed together and can behave in a civilized way."

Often, the issues would be so petty. "He sat on my side of the cushion!" one would complain as I was reading out loud to them. Or, "Why do I have to clean up these dishes? I didn't even eat lunch here today!" There was a constant dripping of fussing and complaints over the years, always followed by correction, instruction, words of forgiveness, and prayer.

With the girls, too, much time was spent correcting disrespectful or condescending attitudes or looks—especially in the teen years. No one got away with an "attitude" toward me or Clay for too long. Heart correction was our focus.

This kind of training and instruction can be wearying. But we sought over and over again to love, correct, forgive, and give grace. We always said, "It is natural to fuss and disagree and hold grudges. It is supernatural to love and be humble and give grace. When we live in the power of the Holy Spirit, He calls us to love and give grace— period; no excuses—it is the standard of God's love and ways for us."

How's unity at your house? Ask the Lord to give you creative
ideas to encourage those in your family to love one another.

Two are better than one because they have a good return for their labor.
For if either of them falls, the one will lift up his companion. But woe
to the one who falls when there is not another to lift him up.

ECCLESIASTES 4:9-10

My WONDERFUL FRIEND Phyllis is a kindred spirit. She has a life full of responsibilities, and we don't get to see each other often because of our mutually busy schedules. But I set aside time to get together with her whenever possible because I know she will have been in the presence of the Lord, and I need the encouragement she has to offer! Whether we simply chitchat or share deep secrets, I will be exposed to a heart that has been planted in Scripture, watered with faith, and enlightened by the presence of the Lord.

Just being with her will fill my cup, point me in the right direction, and give me perspective. She has walked with the Lord for many years—one day, one devotional, one prayer at a time. Her wisdom is cumulative, from decades of experience in seeing God's faithfulness and learning how to live by faith. Every time we are together, I know she will share wise insight on how to look at life.

Over the years, I have purposefully sought to find friends who have the life of Christ bubbling up within them, in order to fill my own heart with wisdom from those who drive me to pursue God in His holiness. Positive peer pressure, you might say!

Excellent women are hard to come by. The ones I've known are dedicated to pursuing God no matter what, and their priorities show the investment they have made. Making it a habit to spend time with God on a regular basis, to walk obediently in service to Him, to study and follow Him, knowing His ways—these are just a few of their commitments that make them excellent friends.

What kind of friend are you? How are you shaping your
own soul to be one that others can draw from?

FEBRUARY 16

. . . strengthened with all power, according to his glorious might, for all endurance and patience with joy; giving thanks to the Father, who has qualified you to share in the inheritance of the saints in light.

COLOSSIANS 1:11-12, ESV

SOMETIMES PEOPLE BELIEVE THAT because their own pasts were difficult, it is impossible for them to create a lifegiving home for their families. I have known many excellent women over the years who had extremely difficult backgrounds. By following the Lord through studying and obeying His Word, they became beautiful reflections of Christ. It's a question of priority: Who will you spend the most time with? Who will you pay the most attention to? Whose voice will you tune your ear to hear? Whose words will be held nearest to your heart?

How can you become a lifegiving person, whether you had a lifegiving background or not? Determine that you will read the Word of God every day. Choose to believe in and trust Him each moment, in every circumstance. Pray for His guidance, and know that His presence goes with you. It is the engaged, loving heart that points others to Jesus, the wellspring of life. There is nothing else to replace it—no cleverness or self-strength or rules or formula that can replace the palpable life that comes from living day by day, holding on to God's hand.

Do you want your children to draw from the life that is bubbling over from your heart, mind, words, and attitudes? Then you must spend day after day with the Word of Life who will give you the true source of wisdom and love you long for. Even as a house is built one brick at a time and yet has the potential of becoming a mansion, so a wise woman builds her house—one brick at a time—into a home of spirituality that comes from spending regular time with Him.

Was the home you grew up in lifegiving? Because God has strengthened you, you are qualified to build your own lifegiving home! Begin by spending time with Him.

This I recall to my mind, therefore I have hope. The LORD's lovingkindnesses indeed never cease, for His compassions never fail. They are new every morning; great is Your faithfulness. . . . The LORD is good to those who wait for Him, to the person who seeks Him. It is good that he waits silently for the salvation of the LORD.

LAMENTATIONS 3:21-26

LIFE SOMETIMES SEEMS TO be an obstacle course. How I face each dip that must be straddled, each curve that must be managed, each barrier that must be jumped will indeed determine the outcome of my race. There is rarely a reprieve, and I always have to be on the alert so that my soul stays in the place of peace and hope.

I want to always go to the place where the truth is, where God's presence is, giving me guidance and hope. Struggling through difficulties is normal, and I still sometimes feel weariness, frustration, fear, and hopelessness right in the midst of feeling joy, deep appreciation, and love. But I continue persistently looking for His treasures of encouragement and truth.

Seeking God daily is my treasure. It must be when no one will talk to me or disturb my reverie. I light my candles, brew a cup of tea, and enter into the presence of the Lord. Usually I sit for a few minutes and take in the peace of being quiet and still. Sometimes I fail to calm my soul and instead stew and fret; sometimes I just sit and try to gather my wits and soul about me; sometimes I cry out; and other times, I dig for new truth and knowledge. He is the one Friend whom I go to every day. Without Him, there is no solution for me. Without His help and strength, I will find no path and no peace.

Are you talking to God in prayer as you would converse with a friend? Are you hoping in and waiting for the Lord, as today's verse suggests?

FEBRUARY 18

*When you pray, go into your inner room, close your door
and pray to your Father who is in secret, and your Father
who sees what is done in secret will reward you.*

MATTHEW 6:6

GOD HAS SEEN US THROUGH MANY, many difficult seasons as well as simpler, more pleasant ones in the past, so I can trust Him with the present and all that is to come. I've called on Him all these mornings, with secret prayers no one else could hear and hope for the future settled in my heart.

This life is a daily adventure. My own "inner room" helps see me through. It is a one-woman sanctuary, in the darkness of a presunrise room, where, through prayer and the living Word, miracles are taking place and the Father is whispering His love and assurance to my heart day by day, month by month, and year by year. It is a story of great blessing between a fragile child and a gentle, patient, strong Father who cares.

Most of us don't have space in our homes for a dedicated prayer room—but we can create a space for prayer, nonetheless! A corner of the couch, your favorite comfy chair, even a neighborhood sidewalk or park where you can run or walk and talk to God alone—plus maybe a basket or drawer where you can stash your Bible and journal and some encouraging books—that's all it takes. If your children wake before you're finished? No worries, just tell them you're having time with Jesus and need to be alone a bit longer—or have them get their own Bibles and join you.

*Developing a habit of praying in secret is essential to a life lived well.
Have you come to believe the truth here—that your Father sees
what is done in secret and that He will reward you? Pray that
He will help your unbelief and increase your faith.*

They are no longer two, but one flesh. What therefore
God has joined together, let no man separate.

MATTHEW 19:6

IT IS SO IMPORTANT TO UNDERSTAND that once a man and woman commit to getting married, that marriage becomes God's will in their lives. It becomes the place they will live out their faith and faithfulness, regardless of how foolish a match it was to begin with. It is to become a place for grace.

When a man and woman get married, they begin writing a brand-new story that has never been told before. It will be their heritage—the way they love each other, the way they live before God, the children they bring into the world, the homes they build, the impact they have on history, the stand they take for God and His Kingdom. The wedding day is potentially the beginning of a great epic. The tale that is written, of course, will not just be about the two—there are children, aunts, uncles, cousins, and more, both present and future, who will be affected by the quality and soundness and vision of a marriage and the choices the husband and wife make.

We have to choose not to give our children a legacy of compromise, disloyalty, and brokenness, and that choice will not be without cost. The way a husband and wife treat each other has a direct effect on how a child builds his or her internal sense of being. And the stability of the home affects a child's physical, emotional, intellectual, and spiritual health to an infinite degree.

While many promote a do-what-makes-you-happy ethic these days, the truth of God's Word is timeless. He intended marriage to be for life, and we honor Him when we honor the covenant we've made.

Today, pray for yourself and your family.
Ask God to help you honor your commitments.

FEBRUARY 20

an excellent wife, who can find? For her worth is far
above jewels. The heart of her husband trusts in her.

PROVERBS 31:10-11

To be a good wife draws upon all I can be in every area—my spirituality, intellect, wisdom, relational skills, creativity, artistry, perseverance, character, and beauty.

It seems that in this narcissistic time, all of life focuses on the "needs" of the person concerned. Is my husband gratifying me? Does his love fill me up? Could I have found someone better? But marriage is really about pleasing God—not my will but His be done. Most of us were not trained to be unselfish, so having to do so in marriage is a shock and surprise to our immature characters.

After the sparkle and ideals of marriage begin to wear off, a woman must settle in her heart that pleasing her husband and loving and respecting him is not about her own personal fulfillment, but about having a heart to please God in everything. It becomes a place of integrity before her children when they watch her loyal, gracious love given to a deserving or undeserving spouse. When I approach every attitude, every act of love and respect as a means of worshiping God by showing His reality in my marriage, then those acts have meaning—regardless of how my spouse behaves. There will also be conflict in every marriage, and sometimes our convictions will rub off on our husbands, but God will use us in their lives and them in ours. Learning how to stand on convictions and wise ways without nagging is an art to be learned. We are as iron sharpening iron when we live with the tension of friendship and love and are both so much better for the commitment to our ideals.

The first description we hear of an excellent wife is that the
heart of her husband trusts in her. Are you trustworthy?

A man has joy in an apt answer, and how delightful is a timely word!

PROVERBS 15:23

WORDS HAVE DEEP AND ABIDING POWER. They can give hope, redemption, and life; or they can bring guilt, anger, and death. We are to be stewards of our words, and if we are walking with God, we are to plant words as seeds in the hearts of our children, developing the fruit of life, beauty, hope, and confidence in them.

I have talked to a number of moms lately who struggle with anger and impatience and find themselves yelling a lot at their children. Of course, all of us have experienced this if we've been mamas for a while! We must remind ourselves that if we sow angry, condemning, guilt-producing words, we will produce children who feel hurt, condemned, guilty, criticized, and unloved. Studying Scripture in this area lately has really caused me to develop stronger convictions once again about the importance of guarding my lips and keeping them from pouring out anger—and of asking for forgiveness when I do! If we are to grow in righteousness, we need to use self-control in this area of angry words and learn to move more and more into His gracious, patient love as we mature.

Think of what would happen if our children grew up on lifegiving words: "I am so thankful for you!" "You are a blessing to me." "I appreciate you because . . ." "God has a special place for you in his Kingdom." "You encourage me." "I see that you are capable in _____ area." "You are a rock." "You are a joy." "You are faithful." "You are a lover." "I believe in you." "I believe in your dreams." There would be stored up in their hearts a deep confidence that they are loved, respected, appreciated, and called by God to accomplish great things for His Kingdom.

What word-seeds have you been planting in the hearts of your children lately? Ask the Lord to put a finger over your mouth and cause you to ponder before you speak.

FEBRUARY 22

The Lord GOD has given me the tongue of those who are taught,
that I may know how to sustain with a word him who is weary.
Morning by morning he awakens; he awakens my ear to hear
as those who are taught.

ISAIAH 50:4, ESV

IF SOMEONE WANTS TO REACH MY HEART, I need them to accept me for who I am. When I know they do that, I am much more likely to befriend them and draw close to them. However, if someone is critical of me and I always feel judged, I find myself avoiding that person.

Knowing I am best reached through the love and acceptance of others helps me understand my own children and their responses to my behavior and words. A legacy of good, kind, restoring, encouraging words will build souls and create memories of love, which sink into their very being. Conversely, words of complaint and condemnation drive our children, spouse, friends, and others far from us. We must choose and build the kind of legacy we want to have.

The same principle applies in friendship, ministry, marriage, and work. We can choose to be a blessing and sow seeds of faith in the lives of those God has brought into our lives, or we can sow death to our relationships.

I have been finding that the more I seek to sow words of life, to take initiative to really tell people how much I love and appreciate them, to give words of life, the more my own heart has grown in love and in peace and acceptance of them and of myself. In all areas of life, when I obey God, I eventually become blessed. How patient a Father He is! How wise are His ways in my life.

Do you sustain the weary with your words? Do you seek to be patient
with sleepy toddlers, an awkward and frustrated teen, a weary and
overloaded husband, a depressed and discouraged friend? Are your words
a fountain of hope and righteousness or death and discouragement?

FEBRUARY 23

Because of the LORD's great love we are not consumed,
for his compassions never fail. They are new
every morning; great is your faithfulness.

LAMENTATIONS 3:22-23, NIV

IT IS MORE THAN A COMFORT TO know that each day offers the promise of tomorrow—a new day, with no mistakes in it yet, as Anne Shirley would say.

The *yet*, perhaps, is the most important word in that phrase, because mistakes will surely be made. I will speak too sharply to someone, I'll gossip or criticize someone and then feel guilty, I will break a commitment I made to myself. Perhaps I'll forget to return a phone call, or to water a plant that then dies. The possibilities of ways to make mistakes big and small are endless. In the past, those sorts of things weighed heavy on my heart. Why couldn't I just get everything accomplished, as everyone else seemed to?

Sometimes it is assumed that anyone who speaks or writes or works to inspire other moms has "arrived" to some extent. There can be an illusion that at my house, everything is perfect, no one is ever cross, and there's no effort necessary to keep things running smoothly. This, I can assure you, is not the case!

My ability to idealize and aspire to great accomplishments often far exceeds my ability to achieve them. Yet my ideals and aspirations give me something to aim toward, a goal to define my daily path. I have learned so much the hard way—by making mistakes.

We will make mistakes, we will not always realize our ideals, and of course others will disappoint us even as we disappoint ourselves! But the wonderful truth, which I pray will go deep into my own heart and yours, is that the love of God is steadfast—it never changes, it remains strong, and it's forever loyal.

Aim high, sweet mama. And when mistakes come, know they
are covered by the One who holds everything in His hands,
and whose compassions are "new every morning"!

FEBRUARY 24

Fixing our eyes on Jesus [looking to Him, trusting in Him, depending on Him!], the author and perfecter of faith, who for the joy set before Him endured the cross, despising the shame, and has sat down at the right hand of the throne of God. For consider Him [ponder Him, understand His life, His sufferings] who has endured such hostility by sinners against Himself, so that you will not grow weary and lose heart.

HEBREWS 12:2-3

So OFTEN, I awaken at night after only a few hours of sleep, and the first feeling I experience is fear—concerns about the future, stress over a lack of finances, worry regarding my children, and so on. Yet I am learning so much, even now, about the importance of overcoming fear by faith.

As I study the stories of Scripture, it is obvious that when people looked at their obstacles in life—the storms, giants, and battles—they became fearful and useless and defeated. But when they looked at God Himself instead of their fears, they became strong. They conquered right in the midst of their battles, storms, and difficulties.

The only way I have found peace and assurance and confidence in life has been to let God hide me in the corners of His tent—to let Him fight my battles, to submit to His will, and to say, "You be my defender and provider, because I am your child." Fixing the eyes of my heart on Him, on His face, on His integrity of character and strength, is the only way I could live by faith and not by fear.

Resting in His presence and strength and power and goodness will put our hearts at rest. When we patiently face the storms, confiding, "This is too big for me to handle, but I am asking you to handle it for me," and then learn to wait—and sometimes wait and wait and wait!—we will see His purpose, ways, and, yes, salvation from our storms.

Where are your eyes? On Jesus? Or on the storm?

FEBRUARY 25

Let all who take refuge in You be glad,
let them ever sing for joy; and may You shelter them,
that those who love Your name may exult in You.

PSALM 5:11

JOY IS A SEED THAT MUST BE intentionally planted in the soil of life in the midst of our varying circumstances. It must be watered with faith, fertilized by obedience at every choice in life, and protected at every juncture. The weeds of selfishness and cynicism must be plucked when they first grow. Storms of bitterness must not be allowed to damage the fragile crop that has been planted.

In my lifetime, seeing so much sadness, brokenness, grief, and discouragement in the lives of people I loved, I realized that even believers could be overcome by the exhausting nature of living in a fallen world. It seemed to me that if joy was a fruit of His Spirit in my life, I needed to understand more how to live in that place in my heart, regardless of what storms were whirling around me. Jesus admonished His disciples that in this world they would have tribulation. He didn't cover it up or sugarcoat the truth.

Yet, the miraculous truth is that normal people like me can live a supernatural life and our actions can have eternal results in this world, bringing His light to manifest in very strategic, poignant ways. He is here with me and there with you. He is all-powerful to conquer kingdoms of darkness and to bring down strongholds. He lives to love, redeem, restore, and give hope and grace.

One interesting thing about today's verse is that it recognizes the fact that sometimes we need a place to take refuge! Thank God for sheltering you.

FEBRUARY 26

Dear friends, since God so loved us, we also ought to love one another. No one has ever seen God; but if we love one another, God lives in us and his love is made complete in us.

I JOHN 4:11-12, NIV

FOR SOME YEARS, I wondered if Joy and Joel could go for a day without chafing each other. Whatever personality issues lay between them, adding in a little sin nature and their age difference meant they often corrected each other's opinions or thoughts—there was always high friction. Some of my best memories recently have been seeing them come to the piano again and again, playing, singing, and harmonizing for literally hours, as they are both singer-songwriter types. Joel coached Joy as she practiced speeches and then spent hours judging at speech and debate tournaments. They even spent some time as flatmates while attending college in Scotland.

Amazingly enough, all of my children now seem to get along!

Moms often ask me, "When are they ever going to stop fussing? Will they ever be friends?" It does take longer than any of us would want, but training is the key to shaping each child's heart. Love must become a trained habit.

What we sow, we reap. And if we sow seeds of love, choosing to be kind, learning to be gentle, and showing respect, we will empower our children to have strong relationships. All of this must be taught, modeled, and then corrected again and again.

In short, training children to choose to love by showing kindness, gentleness, and respect will prepare them to go before both kings and paupers and to become leaders in their generation. This is one of the most important areas of training, so that our children can learn how to influence people with the messages of Christ. It starts with an attitude that says, "God has designed me to love people, to be humble like He was, and to show respect and kindness."

How are you training your children to love well today?

FEBRUARY 27

*This is the day which the LORD has made;
let us rejoice and be glad in it.*

PSALM 118:24

YEARS AGO, I began to reflect on what I saw and heard from many precious women all over the world whose lives had been shattered, whose hearts had been hurt, whose pathways had been quite wearisome and hard. I reflected, too, on what I saw in myself.

A few of these women seemed to have a secret delight, a light that came through their eyes and heart and demeanor—the way they valued others, the way they seemed to always picture themselves as givers of life, even in the midst of their own darkness. These few had joy even after many hard years. I wanted what they had, for this joy to be always surging through my own life.

Shouldn't one who knows Jesus, who is the God who spoke the world into being and created pink sunrises, babies' sweet chubby hands, rainbows amidst storm clouds, music that invites me to swing and sway, chili and chocolate, have the ability to find a life that is joyous beyond circumstances?

So I determined that joy would be a goal of mine, something I would seek, celebrate, live, and choose every day, desiring that I would hear the music of Him who was singing all the time. I determined to dance to the rhythm of His melody in and through my life. Jesus said, "In the world you have tribulation, but take courage; I have overcome the world" (John 16:33). The simple fact is, in the world we have tribulation. But we also have Jesus, and He has overcome the world. Therefore, we can have joy!

---

*Do you, too, want to be a woman of joy beyond your circumstances?
Where can you see the joy hidden in the darkness?*

FEBRUARY 28

He who is faithful in a very little thing is faithful also in much; and
he who is unrighteous in a very little thing is unrighteous also in much.

LUKE 16:10

CLAY AND I TALKED FOR HOURS and hours about our ideals for our children, even long before the first arrived. Our ultimate goal was to teach and model to our children what it looked like to walk with God. Not just to teach them morality, or to indoctrinate them spiritually, but to cultivate in them a heart for God and His Word, and to slowly give them independence so that they would be able to make good choices reflecting their own convictions.

We spoke often about "being faithful with much," and little by little, gave them opportunities to make their own decisions and practice being responsible with us, so that as we walked alongside them we could help them, pick them up, and teach them to learn from their mistakes. We often told them, "God has a work for you to do in your lifetime and in this world. Your personal integrity will be the platform from which you will give your messages. If you are faithful at home, we will help you to expand your borders."

Jesus sent his disciples into the world to bring His light and redemption and love. How can we as parents have a different goal? Having prayed for our own children and told them all their lives that they were to be Kingdom bearers in the world, we then had to support them, pray for them, and be accountable to them as God began to give them dreams and to open doors for them.

Most of all, we depended on the Lord, prayed a lot, and asked His Holy Spirit to work. He is always our confidence.

Do you try to shield your children from the possibility of making mistakes?
Can you see how this might be more harmful than good? Think of some
ways you can extend opportunities for responsibility to your children today.

MARCH 1

The wise woman builds her house,
but the foolish tears it down with her own hands.

PROVERBS 14:1

OUR ENTIRE FAMILY HAS BEEN captivated by the care and intentionality George Vanderbilt put into creating the Biltmore Estate, a place of great beauty and uniqueness that would serve as a refuge and resource for all who lived and visited and worked there. A great structure never just accidentally comes into being. It starts with careful planning and prep work—acquiring permits, hiring professionals, sourcing materials and fixtures, drawing up blueprints. Then comes the hard work of construction—board by board, brick by brick, paint for each room, adding all the beautiful details that make the home unique.

This great work of home building is a long-term construction project that takes what sometimes seems like endless years of care and hard work. In particular, the formation of the children of a family—nurturing excellent souls, filling minds with truth, inspiring hearts with the purposes of God, instilling a taste for God's goodness and beauty—requires planning and intentionality.

I also see motherhood as akin to being a home decorator. My job in my family involved setting the tone: celebrating life by bringing color, music, and beauty into every aspect of our home; gathering great, hopeful stories through books; cultivating wonderful memories with friends through parties and Bible studies, meals and traditions; lighting candles in the darkness and playing music to lift our souls. Purposefully inserting goodness and beauty into the moments of our days became a primary goal, so that our living would reflect the reality of what we believed about God.

What kind of "house" do you want to build in your life?
This can be anything from your actual home to your spiritual
heritage or even something personal to you. List at least three tools
you have for constructing your spiritual/emotional home.

MARCH 2

*Jesus said to them, "The Sabbath was made for man,
and not man for the Sabbath."*

MARK 2:27

MARCH IS THAT END-OF-WINTER time when the moms I know are a little bit weary of
the school year and feeling no inspiration ahead! That is exactly why I almost always
took a break from homeschooling in March. I made up my own holiday time for
just a few days, because my soul needed rest and refreshment. Life is a long journey,
and if we are to make it to the end with resilience, we have to plan for refreshment
along the way.

A friend once told Sarah that her love for beauty seemed a bit frivolous. However,
I have always taught my children that they are responsible to keep a light burning in
their souls—whatever it takes. Creating beauty and joyful moments in the midst of a
fallen, sad world is what gives light to others and nurtures that same light in our own
souls. By taking a break, I am not ignoring the pain or difficulties but admitting that
in order to keep going and giving of myself for many years to come, I have to take
responsibility for replenishing my soul and seeking to fill the spiritual, emotional, and
physical cup of my life with nourishment.

Going for long walks, reading a magazine or frivolous book, sleeping in, having
a tea party or lunch in the middle of the week with friends for no reason, creating a
scavenger hunt in the house for kids, taking a long bubble bath with divine music and
candlelight and not answering the phone or the door . . . Whatever sounds good and
within reason, I do because I know the principle of the Sabbath—God designed for
us to need rest because without it, we do not endure well or see Him clearly or have
the strength to believe in order to get perspective.

Do you need to schedule a Sabbath for yourself sometime soon?

MARCH 3

The LORD of hosts will prepare a lavish banquet for all peoples on this mountain; a banquet of aged wine, choice pieces with marrow, and refined, aged wine.

ISAIAH 25:6

IN ALL THE YEARS OF the Clarkson family, feasting together has been a lifegiving activity. And we've always called it feasting, whether it involves a full-blown banquet, a one-on-one treat of milk and cookies, or a bowl of fresh-popped popcorn enjoyed around the fire. The word *feasting* reminds us of God's bounty, the gift of our relationships, and the response of pleasure and thanksgiving that the act of sharing a meal requires of us.

When God created the world and pronounced it good, He lavishly provided an abundance of delights to please every possible palate. His artistic hand can be seen in all of the food He provided, not just to satisfy our basic need for calories, but also to gratify our senses with color, aroma, texture, and taste—orange carrots and red peppers, purple-black eggplant, rust-colored cinnamon, yellow and green squash, golden honey, sweet green and red and purple grapes, yellow and multicolored corn, brown rice and pale grains of wheat, pink sea salt, speckled trout, crunchy pecans and bumpy walnuts, rich maple syrup, mild hominy, spicy green and red chilies.

God created all these and more for our pleasure and our satisfaction. And He created us in such a way that we make emotional and spiritual connections in the process of enjoying them, especially when we share them around the table with people we love.

Adults and children are not just bodies to be fed, but also minds to be challenged, hearts that depend on emotional input to survive and to grow as healthy human beings, and spirits that long for connection with God and purpose in life. Feasting together is a powerful way to fulfill physical, emotional, and spiritual needs.

Do you see your table as a place to feast?
How might you change your perspective?

MARCH 4

He satisfies the thirsty and fills the hungry with good things.

PSALM 107:9, NIV

As Jesus celebrated His final Passover meal with His disciples, He gave the familiar food and rituals an eternal and spiritual significance beyond their temporary and physical natures, pointing His disciples to the future day when they would "eat and drink at [His] table" (Luke 22:30)—a real feast at a real table in the new Kingdom to come.

The Old Testament is filled with tables, foods, and feasts—stories of God's provision of food and drink and of God's people gathered together to enjoy it. We see stories of Abraham's hospitality to strangers and of the Israelites' first Passover meal together—both table gatherings with profound spiritual significance. And consider these tasty passages from the Pslams:

- "You prepare a table before me in the presence of my enemies; . . . my cup overflows" (Psalm 23:5).
- "He satisfies the thirsty and fills the hungry with good things" (Psalm 107:9, NIV).

You'll also find tables and food everywhere in the Gospels. Jesus often ate and reclined at tables with others. Many of His parables involved food, eating, and tables. Some of His miracles involved food and drink, and some of His most memorable teachings took place at tables.

But Jesus didn't simply use food as a tool in His ministry. He made it integral to His explanation of who He was and what He had come to do. When challenged to give a sign better than the manna in the wilderness, Jesus said, "I am the bread of life. Whoever comes to me will never be hungry again. Whoever believes in me will never be thirsty" (John 6:35, NLT). That statement took on added resonance at that final Passover table the night before He died. Bread and wine, the physical food and drink that give us physical life, represented His body and blood, the spiritual foods that give us eternal life.

---

*How could you use your family table time to remind
your family of Jesus' offering on the cross?*

I am the bread of life. Whoever comes to me will never be hungry again. Whoever believes in me will never be thirsty.

JOHN 6:35, NLT

IF MY TABLE COULD TALK, I know it would tell of innumerable moments. Toddlers munching on bits of food and Cheerios scattered over plastic place mats. Birthday breakfasts with cinnamon rolls, mugs of hot tea, and presents companioned by words of love and appreciation. Warm soup and stories shared on cold winter nights. Sunday afternoon teatimes with James Herriott's animal stories read dramatically. Countless lively discussions about morality and worldview as we filled up growing teenage bodies with satisfying food.

But souls grow by seasons as well. As we celebrate the passage of time by establishing and commemorating joyful traditions, honoring milestones (however small), cultivating a taste for greatness through the stories shared, books read, memories made, and faith lived out, we also make a path for growth and development.

Godly legacies are built, in other words, when we bring the life of Christ to the table through the grace of loving relationships and intimacy shared moment by moment. This is the essence of table discipleship. But doing it well requires both vision and commitment.

What is my vision for my lifegiving table? I picture that I am nourishing souls and spirits with both physical food and the everlasting food of the Word of God. I am providing grace and peace through gently accepting whoever joins us at the table. I am speaking hope forward by articulating my confidence in God's love, faithfulness, and kindness for each person.

I picture that I can be an instrument through which God brings life, beauty, and redemption to the limitations of my marriage and my family—because, in His Spirit, I am filled with the life that always brings light to the dark places and redemption to the broken places.

What is your vision for your own lifegiving table?

MARCH 6

*The heavens are telling of the glory of God; and their expanse
is declaring the work of His hands. Day to day pours forth
speech, and night to night reveals knowledge.*

PSALM 19:1-2

LIVING MOST OF MY LIFE within sight of some part of the Rocky Mountains has established a lifelong love of the high mountain terrain. Spring wildflowers begin with blues and purples, move to reds and whites as summer heats up, and finally end in fall with a flourish of yellows and golds. Stars sparkling in the night sky above our home at 7,300 feet altitude call us to linger long in the evenings, stretched out on blankets, cuddling in the cool night air, and listening quietly to God's voice speaking to us in the overwhelming velvet sky. Shimmering crystal snow blankets our pines and wild grasses in the winter, reminding us of the purity and holiness of our God and His transcendent loveliness.

Even as God's beauty calls out to us in what He has created, beauty in our homes lifts the spirits of all who live or visit there. There is great joy in creating something for the table that pleases the eyes, delights the creative juices, and satisfies our created longing for aesthetic pleasure.

Why does beauty matter? Because our Creator cared enough to fill His world with color, form, design, sound, and tastes that would reflect a part of His personality as well as His skill as an artist—and because He created us humans both to respond to that beauty with pleasure and to find joy in our own creations. When we strive to bring beauty into our lives and our homes, we reflect the nature of the One who made us. Beauty and creativity are the melodies that wrap around our souls and sing to us of His amazing, infinite life.

---

*How might you bring some of God's amazing outside
beauty inside your own home today?*

Do not be conformed to this world, but be transformed by the renewing of your mind, so that you may prove what the will of God is, that which is good and acceptable and perfect.

ROMANS 12:2

I HAVE PONDERED MANY TIMES what it means to be transformed, changed, reshaped as an antidote to being conformed to the world. To be transformed means to become something other, to be changed into something different. And the idea of being transformed in order not to be conformed to the world applies so clearly to family culture.

The more we can do to instill a sense of "This is who we are," "This is why we believe," and "This is what we stand for," the better chance we and our children will have of resisting the urge to conform to the world. A family culture that is distinct and grace giving has the power to both change and protect us.

It won't happen by accident, however. Establishing and shaping a family culture requires intentionality, thoughtful planning, commitment, and sacrifice. But the result can be truly transformative.

Austria has resisted being shaped by contemporary global culture because its own national culture is so strong and lively. So must we construct a strong, definitive, faithgiving, biblical family culture. Then those in our homes will be better able to resist the compromising draw of the world because they will have been shaped and changed by the place where they spend the majority of their days. If they grow up steeped in Scripture and truth, beautiful and lifegiving practices, and the sacrificial example of love at home, chances are they will carry these virtues with them. In the absence of such foundational shaping, they will by default go the way of the world.

Paul urges his readers to offer themselves as "a living and holy sacrifice" (Romans 12:1). How can that apply to parents trying to establish a family culture that is strong enough to resist the culture of the world around it? What kind of sacrifices do we have to make?

MARCH 8

Let your speech always be with grace, as though seasoned with salt,
so that you will know how you should respond to each person.

COLOSSIANS 4:6

I'M NOT THE FIRST PERSON to observe that conversation is becoming a lost art in this age of cell phones, instant messaging, and social media. Technology makes it so easy to communicate that we become accustomed to lazy forms of messaging. Instead of meeting a friend for tea, we send a text. Instead of dropping into an office to ask a question, we hide our request behind an email. Instead of working out a disagreement with a friend, we write an anonymous rant in a blog comment.

While digital communication, social media, and even snail mail are helpful in connecting us with others, especially those far away, they lack the personal, satisfying, impacting effect of a face-to-face conversation complete with questions, answers, smiles, laughter, tears, and even touch.

This is a great loss. One of the essential parts of being human is our capacity for connection. We are made in the image of a triune God, which is to say a relational God. To reflect His image is to live in communion with and response to our fellow image bearers. Texts and emails and even videoconferencing can bring us only so close to that kind of relationship. Sooner or later we need to have a direct connection.

Conversation is essential to discipleship. In fact, discipleship can be thought of as a long conversation about the things of Jesus over a lifetime. If we are to live into God's fullness for us and be skilled disciplers, we must pursue the art of conversation.

Learn to be the conductor of your table. Set the rhythm and the rules of your conversation. Make sure the quiet are heard, make sure the talkative are loved. Through your example, teach your children to be "quick to listen, slow to speak, and slow to get angry" (James 1:19, NLT). Let your table be the training grounds for graciousness and consideration.

Are your words full of grace and seasoned with salt?

MARCH 9

Taste and see that the LORD is good.
Oh, the joys of those who take refuge in him!

PSALM 34:8, NLT

THIS COMMAND IS NOT ONLY METAPHORICAL. I believe that God intended us to experience the full range of beauty in the world as a testament to His generous love for us. To neglect delight, feasting, and celebration is to neglect worshiping God in the way He intended us to. Our family's Sunday breakfasts also helped establish a positive attitude toward church.

Sometimes, in our weary and broken world, celebration almost seems wrong. When we look at our news feeds and TV screens, we see a profoundly fractured world. And even in our own homes and hearts, there are wounds, losses, and difficulties. Can celebration, feasting, and joy possibly be an appropriate response?

Yes!

Jesus was born into a world just as broken as our own, and the definitive first miracle of His ministry was to add His personal touch to a profoundly important celebration—a wedding feast.

Later, even when faced with crucifixion, Jesus gave His disciples reason to celebrate: "When everything is ready, I will come and get you, so that you will always be with me where I am" (John 14:3, NLT). The Gospels are focused toward a good ending—another wedding feast and a home to belong in. In celebration, we declare that God is not done with us yet. Ultimately, evil does not have the final word. We celebrate in thanksgiving for what God has done, and we celebrate in expectation of His final victory.

I have always loved that one of Jesus' last actions on earth was to make breakfast for His friends. "'Now come and have some breakfast!' Jesus said. None of the disciples dared to ask him, 'Who are you?' They knew it was the Lord. Then Jesus served them the bread and the fish" (John 21:12-13, NLT).

Why do you think Jesus served His disciples a meal on the
beach that morning? How could you—and your children—
literally taste and see that the Lord is good?

MARCH 10

One day some people said to Jesus, "John the Baptist's disciples fast and pray regularly, and so do the disciples of the Pharisees. Why are your disciples always eating and drinking?" Jesus responded, "Do wedding guests fast while celebrating with the groom? Of course not. But someday the groom will be taken away from them, and then they will fast."

LUKE 5:33-35, NLT

CHRISTIANS SOMETIMES FEEL a pressure to be "spiritual" all the time. But to separate the spiritual from the ordinary is to say that Jesus is not King over those everyday moments in life. We should learn from Jesus to embrace the mundane moments—even the silly, fun ones—and find God's fingerprints of grace within them. If we can do this, we will learn to see God in a fuller dimension.

Jesus didn't come just to save our souls; He came to redeem every part of our lives. When we give our whole lives to Him—food, drink, work, play, body, spirit, and family—we glorify God by living into the beauty He meant for us.

I like to picture what the feasts in the Bible must have been like. In the time when Jesus lived, meals were not nice, orderly things. I imagine dusty garments, loud arguments, pungent spices, and stinky feet. Jesus' ministry not only allowed for these meals; it took place in the context of them.

Not all holy moments are somber and serious. If Jesus discipled His apostles in the midst of food, drink, laughter, and mundane moments, I believe we should too. Instead of viewing them as spiritual "downtime," we should see them as the times when God is most likely to work.

Our laughter can glorify God as much as our thoughtful meditation.

Serving pizza to a houseful of teenagers can strike spiritual gold.

We must learn to cherish all the moments of our lives and to call them holy.

What did people accuse Jesus of in today's Scripture? How did this show their disdain for the joy and fellowship of eating and drinking together? What does Jesus' response tell you?

Why worry about your clothing? Look at the lilies of the field and how they grow. They don't work or make their clothing, yet Solomon in all his glory was not dressed as beautifully as they are. and if God cares so wonderfully for wildflowers that are here today and thrown into the fire tomorrow, he will certainly care for you. Why do you have so little faith?

MATTHEW 6:28-30, NLT

IN TIMES OF EXHAUSTION, grief, or trial, holding on to a sense of order and loveliness is essential. Though many trials of life cannot be easily fixed with a pat answer, the difficulty of walking through them is often eased if it can be experienced in a lovely environment.

This idea stems from being made in the image of a creative God. Just as God looked into the void and created our orderly, lovely, magnificent universe—the cosmos—so we are able to look into the messiness of our lives and create spaces of meaning and beauty. We all feel the weight of our humanity and our ability to dissolve into chaos. A simple way to combat chaos is to focus on creating small spaces of beauty.

Lighting a candle or setting a vase of fragrant flowers, using beautiful dishes or an interesting centerpiece—any of these little acts can soothe a soul overwhelmed with life.

Framed photos of memorable moments adorn the small tables and shelves in my own home. Candlesticks and candles appear in almost every area where there is a chair. Framed calligraphy of favorite quotations and verses adorns our walls, and at least three water pitchers full of flowers garnish our sitting areas. Interesting and beautiful magazines and books are piled high in baskets and bins in every room. I rarely hang curtains because I prefer seeing outside views while sitting in the chairs I've positioned next to the windows.

Looking back, can you see ways that God has provided for you in the past? How can remembering His past providence help you to cultivate beauty, even in difficult times?

MARCH 12

The LORD bless you, and keep you; the LORD make His face shine on you, and be gracious to you; the LORD lift up His countenance on you, and give you peace.

NUMBERS 6:24-26

"Mama, will you squish into my bed with me so we can talk just for a little while tonight?" my young-adult child begged with wistful eyes.

"How can I resist time with one of my best friends in all the world? What's on your heart, Tookies?" Tookies was a nickname that had somehow evolved during her early years and could certainly be used on her birthday after she had been duly celebrated.

"You know, I didn't even know how emotionally empty I was. It seems there are battlegrounds everywhere in my life—at college, at work, with friends, everyplace. I feel alone and sometimes battle with doubt—you know me!

"Today, when everyone told me what they appreciated about my life, how glad they were that I was their sister, and when you and Daddy invested your words of faith in who I am, the woman I have become, my heart just soaked it in. All day I've been reviewing all the things that were said. I've thought about the round-table prayers for my life, and it all seems sweeter to me than ever before. It's as though the love poured into me on my birthday is an anchor that keeps pulling me back to what we all believe together."

When my children were growing up, I didn't know if they were listening or paying attention. Yet today I'm beginning to see the fruits of our years of deliberately speaking forward into their lives. Reminding them that they are uniquely special to God, that His fingerprints are on their lives and on the story they will tell through their own days, has shaped the individuals they're becoming.

What elements of blessing can you find in today's Scripture?
Reword the passage so that it becomes a blessing you
could speak into the life of someone you love.

Encourage each other and build each other up,
just as you are already doing.

I THESSALONIANS 5:11, NLT

I HAVE LEARNED OVER THE YEARS that if I want my family and friends to feel they are a priority in my life, I must regularly set aside time to invite them into my space. Preparing myself with an expectation of being interrupted has helped me host many at my teatime table who needed to feel the touch and hear the words of God in their moment of need.

There's a limit to what I can do to protect those I love from what the world throws at them. But I can listen and help them sort out their thoughts and feelings—if I choose to make myself available when they need me.

Availability became a habit of my life over many years. Making myself available to my loved ones when they needed me was a choice I learned to make again and again—a choice that helped forge a deep connection with each of them. I became the confidant for my children and others, so that as they grew older, they would know they could come to me at any time.

Who taught me this? Jesus did. Immediate availability was the way He operated. He answered questions when they were asked. He made a point of going off alone with His disciples to provide them with focused attention. And often He did this over food. In fact, He gave the most strategic talks of His life as His best friends and most devoted disciples were filling their stomachs with warm food (what could be better than fish over an open fire?), and they sat listening to His wisdom as their ease and comfort opened their hearts.

We would do well, I think, to follow His example.

Encouragement means to give courage to someone, which is important
if we are to stay strong in the Christian life. What does today's verse
reflect about our responsibility to invest in our loved ones?

MARCH 14

*Once I was young, and now I am old. Yet I have never seen
the godly abandoned or their children begging for bread.*

PSALM 37:25, NLT

THANKSGIVING IS INTIMATELY TIED to remembering. If you can't remember what someone has done for you, how can you be thankful? The Bible uses various forms of the
word *remember* more than 150 times, and very often the idea of remembering is tied
to thanking God. The Psalms in particular make this frequent connection. Over and
over the psalmist encourages the Israelites to remember God's covenant to them and
to remember what He has done for them, so that they might know His faithfulness
and in turn live faithfully according to His covenant.

Take, for instance, Psalm 66. The psalmist calls the people to "shout joyful praises
to God" (NLT), then engages in a jubilant recollection of what God has done for the
house of Israel—delivering them from Egypt through the Red Sea, testing and purify-
ing them, giving them leaders, bringing them "through fire and flood" to "a place of
great abundance."

Why all the reminders?

Because, quite simply, people forget. And when they forget or don't notice, they
tend to whine or complain.

The Israelites forgot again and again about God's faithfulness and His plans for
them, and they complained a lot. We all do. So many times in my life I have seen God
work, felt His presence, heard Him speak directly to the desires of my heart. And then,
only a few days later, I have found myself pouring out my exasperated heart, feeling
like my prayers are hitting the ceiling, wondering if there is a God in the universe.

When it comes to God's work in our lives, we fall so easily into spiritual amnesia.
This is why, from time to time, we need to stop the busyness in our lives and remember.
Even better, we need to create reminders of God's faithfulness.

*Take a few moments today to remind yourself of God's faithfulness throughout
your own life. Consider writing a list of all the times you can think of!*

As for the days of our life, they contain seventy years, or if due to strength, eighty years. . . . So teach us to number our days, that we may present to You a heart of wisdom.

PSALM 90:10-12

STATISTICS HAVE SHOWN THAT the vast majority of mothers feel severely stressed and overcome with anxiety due to poor time management and difficulty prioritizing. I think we were simply not designed to multitask to this extent. We often try so hard to juggle a million ideals, and when we drop even one of them, we feel defeated.

As mothers and wives, we must learn to breathe, relax, and focus in on what should be our true priority. Do the people who should have priority in your life (your husband, your children, your friends) feel that you are often distracted by all the other things you do? Do they comment on how much they appreciate your ability to give full attention to them, or complain that you are not listening?

Are you so stressed about making your home squeaky clean that you don't make time for game night or a stroll at sunset? Is your mind so preoccupied with getting back to the kitchen to wash the dishes that you forget to actually *enjoy* dinner with your family? Do you fill your day with so many errands that you run out of energy to extend a kind word, an affectionate kiss, and a warm greeting to your husband? Are you so busy correcting the immature antics of your toddler or the noisiness of your teenager that you have forgotten to really look at them and see the wonder of their unique personality and heart?

Worst of all, busyness can lead us to neglect our relationship with the Father. He is so ready to give peace and guide us in wisdom through His gentle voice. But if we do not still our souls, we will surely live in frustration.

What is causing you the most stress and depleting your life?
What can you do about it?

MARCH 16

Two are better than one because they have a good return for their labor. For if either of them falls, the one will lift up his companion. But woe to the one who falls when there is not another to lift him up.

ECCLESIASTES 4:9-10

I REMEMBER WATCHING the sun rise with one of my best friends when I was a young teen. We bundled up and took flasks of coffee to keep us warm in the early morning chill. Picking a soft spot of grass, we watched in awe as the sun rose in all its golden glory. Something about it caused us to think about true and beautiful things, and we ended up sharing our dreams of what life might be.

While the sunrise would have been just as lovely had I watched it on my own, it would not have been as meaningful. Having someone to share the moment with sealed the experience as a moment of significance in my life.

I believe this is how true friendships impact our lives. In friendship we share beauty, acknowledge significant moments, and cherish memories that sustain us through life. We become companionable witnesses to God's goodness, witnesses who can later remind one another who we are and to whom we belong.

We are so much more vulnerable to attack when we are alone. It is easier to become depressed, defeated, or prideful without friends who cheer us, correct us, and fight for our good. When we reach points of deep discouragement, convinced we can never progress, true friends lift our heads and say, "Remember who you are! God has worked, and He will again."

Write a list of what you wish for in a kindred-spirit friend. Do you have such a friend? Is it a desire of your heart? Write down how you would be that sort of friend to another person. Pray for God to bless the friendships you have, or ask Him for a kindred-spirit friend.

David was greatly distressed because the people spoke of stoning him, for all the people were embittered, each one because of his sons and his daughters. But David strengthened himself in the LORD his God.

I SAMUEL 30:6

I HAVE WORKED IN MINISTRY FOR forty-two years, raised four children to adulthood, and navigated thirty-six years of marriage. All this has meant learning to pace myself in life's journey. Learning to listen to myself has helped me to identify the danger signals when I am running low on resources and in need of refueling. Sudden outbursts of anger, feelings of impatience, or quickly building frustration are sure signs that I have exceeded my body and mind's capacity to live life well.

Here are just a few habits I have found essential to sustaining myself for the long haul:

1. Eating nourishing, healthy, sustaining food is foundational.

2. Getting physical exercise helps build strength and burn off tension. Walking outdoors especially is therapy for my whole self.

3. Getting sufficient sleep is essential to lasting well.

4. Having private quiet times each day gives me the opportunity to center myself and "fill my cup."

5. Setting aside the Sabbath for rest or building in some restoration spots helps me keep going. So does getting away from normal responsibilities by taking a weekend with a friend or family member or going on a weekend trip alone.

6. Planning regular table times with friends who fill me up and bring me joy is an investment that is necessary to keep going over many years.

7. Making time to laugh, play, and celebrate life with my family and friends (ideally over a delicious meal) keeps me thankful and relieves stress.

What rhythm of life do you prefer to set up so that you can invest in time with the Lord?

MARCH 18

While we have opportunity, let us do good to all people, and especially to those who are of the household of the faith.

GALATIANS 6:10

How I TREASURE THE GIFTS OF time I've had with my children! Thanks to having three older ones before Joy came along, I knew that my wide-open window into her heart was going to close sooner than I could imagine. The fact that her older brothers and sister had made it through our household and still loved us and loved the Lord gave me grace, freedom, and peace in the midst of her varied days, since I knew all would turn out well. I didn't worry about the result; I just enjoyed the time we had, knowing God would be at work.

It is wonderful to see her grow and stretch her wings.

She is currently studying for her doctorate in another country, and as she matures, I am becoming a guide as she builds on the foundation she has been given. But I also know her movement in that direction has provided me with another adult best friend. So even though I hate the thought of her growing up, I love the idea of seeing her flourish and spread her wings to carry off and share the messages of her heart and mind—and to build that legacy, hopefully, into the lives of her own children, that the baton of righteousness may be passed on faithfully to my grandchildren.

Today will bring highs and lows, difficulties and joys. There are tasks to be completed and deadlines to meet, meals to make and laundry to wash. But my day is more than a to-do list; it is an opportunity. How will I spend these twenty-four hours? The choice, to quite an extent, is mine.

Do you see each day as an opportunity to do good to all people? How can you especially seek to do good to those actually living in your own household?

MARCH 19

Strength and dignity are her clothing, and she smiles at the future.

PROVERBS 31:25

In Lucy Maud Montgomery's book *Rilla of Ingleside*, the heroine, who has spent two years of her young life living through the hardships of war, is asked whether she'd like to change those difficult years.

> "No," said Rilla slowly, "I wouldn't. It's strange—isn't it?—They have been two terrible years—and yet I have a queer feeling of thankfulness for them—as if they had brought me something very precious, with all their pain. . . . I suppose I had a soul then, Miss Oliver—but I didn't know it. I know it now—and that is worth a great deal—worth all the suffering of the past two years. . . ."
>
> "We never do [want suffering]," said Miss Oliver. "That is why we are not left to choose our own means and measure of development, I suppose. No matter how much we value what our lessons have brought us we don't want to go on with the bitter schooling."*

Though we sometimes find a feeling of dread at having to face difficulties, we can still choose to be spiritual and godly! We were made for rejoicing and happiness. If we rightly understand that trials cause us to suffer and we find that we don't want to suffer, we are only feeling what Jesus felt when he went to the cross. Hebrews 12:2 tells us, "For the joy set before Him [Jesus] endured the cross, despising the shame."

It helped me so much to realize that Jesus despised the shame of the cross, just as I despise difficult times in my own life! But because He knew He would redeem mankind and be seated with the Father, He went to the cross despite those feelings.

Looking back, can you see times of trial that led to growth in your life? How might you thank God for those difficult times?

* Lucy Maud Montgomery, *Rilla of Ingleside* (Frederick A. Stokes Co.: New York, 1921), 250–51.

MARCH 20

Those who wait for the LORD will gain new strength;
they will mount up with wings like eagles, they will run
and not get tired, they will walk and not become weary.

ISAIAH 40:31

MANY YEARS AGO, I juggled three-year-old Sarah, six-month-old Joel, and all the accompanying baggage through multiple security checkpoints and transportation transfers on my way back to America from our home in Austria. I was the only parent, as Clay had stayed behind in Austria to deal with the movers and would follow in a few days.

By the time we'd landed and settled into my mother-in-law's home that night, however, I knew something was wrong. Joel was lethargic and wheezing and had developed a fever that wouldn't come down even with medication. I found myself in the emergency room with a deathly ill child and a very concerned doctor.

"Lord," I prayed in tears as I watched my baby, "let me know that You are here and that I am not alone. Please help me." I waited in the darkness, yearning for comfort. Gradually, the darkness of the room began to fade as I sensed that somehow, even in this despair, I was not alone.

It was as if the Lord was saying that He felt the same way about me that I felt about my baby boy:

I love you as you love your son. I created My children to know My love.
I love you. I am with you. I will never leave you. Even as you actively love
Joel, though he is unconscious and unaware because of his grave illness, so I
have loved My children, though their grave illness of sin and rebellion has
created a temporary sense of separation from Me. Don't worry; trust Me.
I will take care of Joel. I will take care of you.

Do you know—really know—how much God loves you and longs
to care for you? Can you wait upon Him for strength today?

"We went in to the land where you sent us; and it certainly does flow with milk and honey, and this is its fruit. Nevertheless, the people who live in the land are strong, and the cities are fortified and very large." . . . Then Caleb quieted the people before Moses and said, "We should by all means go up and take possession of it, for we will surely overcome it."

NUMBERS 13:27-30

When the Israelites were going from Egypt to the Promised Land, twelve spies were sent out to see what the land was like. They did indeed find it to be a great land with fruit and cultivated pastures. Yet they also saw that there were giants in the land, and so they became "like grasshoppers" (Numbers 13:33) in their own sight.

Instead of focusing on God's provision and His ability to open the doors to this land, ten of the men focused on their fears and what seemed like impossibility. Joshua and Caleb were the only ones who reported back to the people that God would surely help them to overcome it.

The Israelites chose to listen to the voice of discouragement. They grumbled and complained and even wanted to appoint a leader who would take them back to Egypt—the land where they had been slaves! Because of their grumbling and whining spirits, God condemned them to forty years in the desert—a year for every day the men had spied out the good land and had chosen not to believe.

There will always be giants in our lands too. There will always be things threatening to overwhelm us. We have to make a choice to believe in God's ability to provide, or life will demoralize us and we will instead model for our children an attitude of complaining and grumbling.

When you look at your life circumstances, do you see God's provision, or all the obstacles in your way? How might a change in perspective change your life?

MARCH 22

O LORD, who may abide in Your tent? Who may dwell on Your holy hill? He who walks with integrity, and works righteousness, and speaks truth in his heart.

PSALM 15:1-2

How DOES A MOTHER WALK with integrity and work righteousness?

We follow the example of God before us. In Genesis 1, we read that in the beginning, the world was formless, void, and dark. But God is the Creator. It is part of His divine nature to create and bring forth something new. So He, in His goodness, spoke light, beauty, color, form, meaning, and love into the darkness and void.

What is our role, then? It is to follow His example. With His grace in our hearts, we partner with Him. We dispel our own darkness by choosing to walk in the light. We bring the living, resurrection power of Christ into the moments of our lives so that our children can learn how the Christian life is lived by watching us.

In situations when we are unjustly hurt, we choose to forgive and love unconditionally. In situations where we feel abandoned, we choose to believe in God's goodness and live in hope.

We practice telling the truth. We give back money when someone has inadvertently overpaid us. We ask our children to forgive us when we have wronged them, teaching them humility through a relationship with us. We seek to bow our knee to God's will, even when it doesn't seem pleasant, so that they learn how to bow their will to God. We live with the Holy Spirit working visibly through us, producing love, joy, peace, patience, kindness, goodness, faithfulness, gentleness, and self-control.

What attitudes are keeping you from becoming a person of excellence? In what way do you need to conform your heart to the image of Christ so that you may reflect righteousness to your children?

The Mighty One, God, the LORD, has spoken, and summoned the earth from the rising of the sun to its setting. Out of Zion, the perfection of beauty, God has shone forth.

PSALM 50:1-2

ONE SUMMER, my girls and I decided it was time to take a long-dreamed-of vacation to Prince Edward Island, the setting of the Anne of Green Gables stories. On a quiet, late afternoon a couple of days into the trip, we all agreed we needed a long ramble down the quiet beach.

We scrambled up the last few slippery steps of the sandy slope and turned our eyes to the ocean just in time to witness one of the most spectacular sunsets I have ever seen. The sky was awash in a rainbow of rich rose light with swaths of purple and blue running through it, and the sunlight was turning the edges of the sky gold.

Certainly, this was perfection of beauty if I had ever seen it. The colors softened gradually, melting into muted pinks, light purple, and pastel blues, slowly fading into darkness. We sat in silence, fearing words would break the spell. Finally, after the chill of a sunless sky swept over our shoulders, we began to shiver and reluctantly decided to go home.

Just as we were slipping and sliding down the sandy slopes of the dunes, we turned to glance up at the last light in the sky, and there, to our delight, hanging low on the horizon, was a blazing moon of burnished gold, lighting up the darkening sky so that it was almost as bright as day.

I suddenly felt as if we had been literally immersed in the light and goodness of God. This evening of tangible light, this symphony of beauty, did something to my heart. I felt overcome with His goodness.

Think back to a time you were amazed at the beauty God has created. Let that memory bring light into your own heart, banishing any worry and fear you might be carrying.

MARCH 24

*How blessed is the man who does not walk in the counsel
of the wicked, nor stand in the path of sinners, nor sit
in the seat of scoffers! But his delight is in the law of the
LORD, and in His law he meditates day and night.*

PSALM 1:1-2

THE MORNING LIGHT PEEKED into my window and woke me earlier than usual. I gingerly tiptoed out of our bedroom and tried to close the door as noiselessly as possible, heading down the stairs and into the kitchen. I filled the electric kettle with fresh water and turned on the switch, then rummaged through drawers, where I finally found a box with one match left so I could light two small candles. Somehow when I establish a serene, adult atmosphere, my heart aligns with the surroundings.

I sat down in the chair I'd bought years before, where countless sacred hours of life-changing proportions had been celebrated. I always kept a basketful of books next to my chair, so that I could feed my mind with devotional thoughts of writers from various places and times. My beloved, worn, red-leather Bible was in the basket, too, along with a couple of favorite journals where I recorded what I was learning and feeling, what Scripture I was praying, and any thoughts that came to mind.

As I began yet another time of study, I was vitally aware of the legacy of these morning times. I had invested literally thousands of hours at the feet of my greatest professor and teacher, Jesus. His words had made the difference between a wasted life and one focused strategically on the issues of eternity. This time was where I received His strength, wisdom, and direction for all the moments of my life—as a woman, wife, mom, daughter, and believer—here Christ had met me daily, shown me His path and His ways, and assured me of His constant companionship.

*Are there any changes you need to make in your life to
ensure that you have time to study God's Word?*

MARCH 25

Surely I have composed and quieted my soul;
like a weaned child rests against his mother.

PSALM 131:2

As I climbed into bed with a racing mind one night, I realized how desperately I longed for someone bigger than me to soothe my ruffled soul. I suddenly missed my mother. Where was my person to soothe my fears, kiss me, and assure me that all was well, to tuck me in peacefully after taking all my worries away?

I suddenly remembered a season when Joy was about three and was having terrible nightmares that woke her up just before dawn. Often she would quietly pad into my bedroom, crawl up onto my side of the bed, and snuggle in next to me. Throwing one of her little legs over my back, she would quickly fall deeply asleep. It was precious to feel the warmth of her soft body. She seemed to know that her place was with me, next to me. Just being with me was enough to give her the ease she needed to fall back to sleep.

She never asked permission. She knew that she belonged with me. As a baby who had nursed for two years, she had grown up being comforted by me. Now, familiar with the close affection of snuggling next to my warm body, she felt secure and fell fast asleep.

In the late-night darkness of my present night, I was brought back to those sleepy, sweet mornings. The Lord had given me a picture of what He desired for me to do. Joy, my sweet little baby, had been such a picture to me of what a child I was to God and how deeply He desired for me to wrap myself into His presence. I could fall asleep in His peace and protection, because that was where I belonged.

List any areas of life that cause you anxiety. Give them one by
one to God, remembering He wants you to be near to Him.

MARCH 26

We are His workmanship, created in Christ Jesus for good works,
which God prepared beforehand so that we would walk in them.
EPHESIANS 2:10

ONE OF OUR GREATEST RESPONSIBILITIES is to walk through the days of our lives seeking to love our King and promote His Kingdom. One of the primary ways we do this is in teaching our children and modeling for them what it means to be a devoted servant of the King. We show them what it means to enter into the battle, to be willing to serve and give of ourselves. We are the ones who paint them a picture of the great battle, the great King, and their parts in fighting for redemption.

God has designed all of us with the purpose of being a part of His redemptive Kingdom work. Our children's hearts long to be a part of a great cause. Serving God is not about knowing all the right rules and keeping them; it is about joining God in His plans to reach the world. Mothers can cultivate compassion for a lost world in the hearts of their children and show them how they can practically be a part of God's Kingdom work.

In the secular world, everyone's attention is turned on who is the most famous or powerful or has the biggest salary. By the world's standards, the call is not to service in the fight for redemption; it is to self-protection and self-fulfillment.

But from God's point of view, history is the account of human souls joining into the battle for the righteous Kingdom. Each of us is given a unique opportunity to live out a story in which we employ the moments, money, talents, and relationships of our lives to promote the priorities that are on the heart of the King, the Lord Jesus.

As you consider your life and the life of your family, what
"work" has God given you a heart for? In which areas does your
family have compassion to invest in the lives of others?

MARCH 27

*It was for freedom that Christ set us free; therefore keep standing
firm and do not be subject again to a yoke of slavery.*

GALATIANS 5:1

I REMEMBER READING A BOOK about being a godly woman that a dear friend had recommended. Some of it was useful, but as I continued to read, I found pressure mounting in my heart and tension pounding in my mind. The pinnacle came when the author said a sign of godliness was if a woman organized the inside of her dressers. The implication was that if a woman was orderly in the way she kept the insides of her drawers, then her character would probably also be in order, and thus she would be godly! Which Scripture defines this rule? I have searched and searched the Bible and have yet to find that one.

I spend a lot of time straightening my house and attempting to keep a peaceful, orderly environment that soothes and blesses my family. However, I am a passionate, philosophical, artistic person. I am very relational but love to have time to think, read, write, and drink lots and lots of tea and coffee. It would probably never even dawn on me to use my rare spare time to straighten out the inside of my drawers. I would be too busy planning how I was going to change the world or be deep in conversation and counseling with someone.

I don't have to feel guilty for not being good at everything. God gave gifts through His Holy Spirit so that the whole body of Christ could accomplish His purposes. We are free, not subject to a yoke of slavery.

*Are there any ways in your life as a mom that you are trying to live up
to the false expectations of others? In what ways does God want you to
release any areas of bondage so that you may live in His freedom?*

MARCH 28

If anyone is in Christ, he is a new creature;
the old things passed away; behold, new things have come.

2 CORINTHIANS 5:17

WHEN SARAH WAS A LITTLE GIRL, she was mesmerized by butterflies. She made an amazing collection with species of every size and color: huge swallowtails and little blue butterflies, moths with dull brown upper wings that hid a gorgeous underside, and every kind of small butterfly to be found in our Texas fields.

As we pursued this interest through a variety of books and nature stories, I was captured again by the story of the butterfly. Every butterfly and moth begins as a lowly caterpillar inching its way across the ground until it reaches the transforming shelter of its chrysalis or cocoon. Once inside, the old miracle happens again; the creeping, wormlike caterpillar gives way to a creature that is almost otherworldly in its beauty— a fragile and lovely butterfly.

This is such a poignant picture to me of the transformation that takes place in our own lives. When we were once simply creatures who had the burden of sin and condemnation to drag around, Jesus came and transformed us into beautiful new creatures who can fly freely through life in the power of His resurrection and love. A wormlike life as a sinful human being in need of transformation is an accurate picture of me apart from Christ, without His grace. Entering the cocoon is a picture of me dying to myself and my limitations. The newly emerged butterfly, beautiful and strong, is a picture of me living my life in the love of Christ.

I am indeed a butterfly—free to be new and perfect in Him.

Make a list of some things that have been transformed in your life
since Christ began to renew your soul and spirit. Old things have
passed away, and all things are new—you're a butterfly too!

Your lovingkindness is before my eyes,
and I have walked in Your truth.

PSALM 26:3

WHEN WE LIVED IN VIENNA LONG AGO, there came a point when the early dark on winter evenings, the reality of a charming yet leaky old house, a language I didn't entirely understand, ministry pressures, and distance from family and friends became overwhelming to me. When a desired trip home fell through, I finally broke down in tears.

The next morning, I made my way to a small café nearby and sat down with an apple strudel and hot cup of coffee. As I sat in the soft contours of the chair that morning, a sense of indignation bubbled up in my soul. *Lord, how can You treat us this way? We gave up everything to come here. Do You know how lonely I am? Couldn't you at least provide a few friends? Is it such an incredible demand to ask for Joel to sleep through the night? A little rest is all I'm asking for, Lord, even a teensy bit of affirmation.*

I glanced heavenward and sighed as I thought all of this, then opened my Bible. Finding myself turning to Genesis 3, I read and reread the passage where Satan tempts Eve. And as I read, I observed that the first recorded temptation in Scripture came as a result of Satan casting doubt upon God's character. His temptation was to make Eve doubt God's goodness and the rightness of what He had wrought in her life.

Oh, how quickly conviction comes. Doubting God's love for me and His goodness in my life was the root of my worry and despair. Now, I had to choose which I would believe: the lies of Satan as he tempted me to look at my struggles and doubts, or the eternal, life-changing truths of God's overwhelming love and entirely trustworthy goodness to me as His child.

Are you keeping God's lovingkindness before your
eyes? It's the only way to walk in truth.

MARCH 30

Be imitators of God, as beloved children; and walk in love,
just as Christ also loved you and gave Himself up for us,
an offering and a sacrifice to God as a fragrant aroma.

EPHESIANS 5:1-2

OUR LIVES AS MOTHERS ARE often filled up with hurry and demand: chores, lists, and a multitude of responsibilities. There are so many ideals we feel we absolutely must live up to: clean houses, ordered lives, and children who accurately know math and Scripture and play their instruments perfectly, besides having just the right number of friends and activities. In the face of so much urgent need, our "Martha" lives often take over as we contemplate how to get it all done.

Yet these demands and ideals, the constant busyness and bustle, are not what will actually reach the hearts of our children and shape them into beautiful souls.

Christ did not create disciples who would literally die out of their love for Him by giving them a list of moral rules or commandments on how to live. What He gave them was the gift of His own very present life. He lived with them so that they experienced His love intimately throughout the moments of their days. He showed them what it meant to be a servant leader by healing, comforting, and compassionately sharing His loving redemption with needy and humble people.

Jesus showed us mothers how to disciple our children by being a model Himself. He laid down His life, not just in death, but also day by day with the souls He was shaping. This is what mothers do as well, laying down our lives for our children in order to create disciples for Christ with deep, rich souls.

In what ways do you communicate love to your children?
Is there a specific way you can change your schedule
in order to better show them intentional love?

*Since we have so great a cloud of witnesses surrounding us,
let us also lay aside every encumbrance and the sin which
so easily entangles us, and let us run with endurance the
race that is set before us, fixing our eyes on Jesus.*

HEBREWS 12:1-2

I STARTED OUT ON THE JOURNEY of motherhood assuming it would be a lovely adventure I would be able to accomplish with vibrancy and grace. I did not understand how truly long this walk would be, or about the blisters, hot sun, rough pavement, and curves I would face on the road ahead.

I hadn't counted on the weariness of the years of growing my family—being pregnant, giving birth, nursing babies, and having miscarriages. I didn't know the many challenges of motherhood that would demand all my strength—asthma, ear infections, tantrums, messes and fusses, thousands of mounds of dirty dishes and clothes, and countless days to fill with meaningful occupation, not to mention the training, correcting, and instruction of my children in righteousness.

So many times, when I was tempted to quit taking so much time from my own life to give to my kids, when I felt like I simply couldn't go on, I would creep away into my quiet corner to spend a few minutes with the Lord. Without fail, He would use those stolen moments to show me how important my role was in the spiritual life and heritage of my children. In those times, I glimpsed the goal of righteousness I was working toward and realized that I must reach it step by weary step.

I kept going by sheer faith and resolve because I could not ignore the ideals and calls of Scripture. With God's help, I chose to follow them and trust that they were blessed and right and would bring blessing to me and my family.

*Motherhood is a marathon, not a sprint! Have you fixed your
eyes on Jesus, determining to be in it for the long haul?*

APRIL 1

Love covers a multitude of sins. Be hospitable to one another without complaint. As each one has received a special gift, employ it in serving one another as good stewards of the manifold grace of God.

I PETER 4:8-10

WE PILED ONTO THE COUCH, juggling plates of cheese, fruit, and bread, anxious to watch the movie we'd chosen for this year's pre-Easter friends gathering: a word-for-word depiction of the Gospel of John. As the story played out on-screen, I found myself profoundly moved once again. As I watched Jesus with His friends, the message from His Spirit became clear: if I am to understand my God, I am to imitate Jesus' life, His love, His generous forgiveness and mercy, and His pattern of pouring Himself out for others who were undeserving. No more room for the pointing of fingers or critical attitudes or the pettiness of hateful thoughts that rob my soul of grace!

In order for a muscle to be built, it must be torn and then repair itself—the ending result is strength. Similarly, soul strength comes through the same process. Jesus loved unconditionally, served others, and laid down His life for the unlovely. As I do the same, I am being chiseled into His likeness.

In this place, there is no room for bitterness, accusations, hate, or anger to overpower, because the light of His forgiving love overcomes all darkness. Choosing to love others who have sinned with a face of forgiveness, my soul is transformed by His grace, and light begins to pour into my being.

Remember that Christ's reckless forgiveness and love has been applied to your own account, and ponder the ways you can hand that same grace to those around you.

God is our refuge and strength, a very present help in trouble.
Therefore we will not fear, though the earth should change and
though the mountains slip into the heart of the sea.

PSALM 46:1-2

"MAMA, THE WORLD SEEMS LIKE a very scary place, and it makes me feel powerless. I am afraid I will be so lonely and insecure without friends and family around me."

Joy, my daughter, would be leaving the next day to study in Oxford, England, and we had just finished zipping her last suitcase shut. She'd been listening to the news about terrorist threats to England and the United States, devastating reports of earthquakes and war, and immorality among Christian leaders. Joy was understandably feeling overwhelmed.

"Can we have one last time together out on the grass, under the stars?" she pleaded. "I need some peace before I go to bed."

In our last moments together, I wanted to lift Joy up to God, to leave her with courage, and to assure her of the One who would care for her. "Joy, this vast display of stars and all the galaxies beyond have been held in place by the sure, strong hands of God for thousands of years. You will always have a choice to make. If you look at the darkness and fear, you will grow dark in your soul. But if you look to God and trust Him with your days, you will reflect His reality in all of your words, your relationships, your work, and your celebrations. Keep the memory of this night and His power and beauty always before your eyes and ever in your thoughts. And, of course, you know that you will be in my heart and in my prayers constantly."

In what areas do you find yourself facing fear?
How does knowing God's power encourage your heart?

APRIL 3

Keep yourselves in God's love as you wait for the mercy of our Lord Jesus Christ to bring you to eternal life.

JUDE 1:21, NIV

WE ONCE HAD A FRIEND WHO was very pious. Her attempts to be spiritual and "work" for God came from a heart that was striving to know God and serve Him sincerely. Yet all her self-denial, pious speech, and work, work, work left most people in her life feeling guilty and distant from her. Since she had not experienced the grace and peace of God, she could only give out of a soul of performance, which brings death to relationships. She often spoke in religious phrases and with each passing month seemed more cold and drained of life—just the result she wouldn't want.

In contrast, when I am in the presence of someone who really walks with God, there is evidence of life, joy, goodness, well-being, grace, and faith. When one is washed with the unconditional love and grace and mercy of God, the result is peace and thankfulness of heart and humility. Of course, those who really exhibit the life of the Lord aren't above discouragement or humanity, but there is a palpable sense of walking with God and having made a decision to please Him and trust Him through the ups and downs of life. There is a security I feel in being with them, because I know their sails have been set toward the King and His Kingdom, and I can trust in their integrity to continue journeying in the right direction with Him at the helm. I feel a rest in my relationship with such people because I know I am safe in the hands of mature, seasoned lovers of God who will love me and accept me and point me to Him gently as we walk this road of life in fellowship.

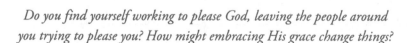

Do you find yourself working to please God, leaving the people around you trying to please you? How might embracing His grace change things?

There is now no condemnation for those who are in Christ Jesus.

ROMANS 8:1

MOTHERHOOD IS VERY PRECIOUS to the Lord. It is not an easy journey. I kept feeling that I needed to have more children so I could do it right at least once!

When I had my first baby, I did not know how to hold a baby. I had never even changed a diaper. I also did not know how selfish and self-absorbed I was. And I have to admit that over the years, there were many times when I did not feel loving or like a good mother or even like I wanted to *be* a mother. I was always committed to my children and always committed to loving them, because I knew God wanted me to. But I did not always like them, and sometimes that made me feel guilty.

I just put one foot in front of the other because I thought that was what God wanted me to do.

So if you feel that you are not a "natural" mother, or you enjoy doing things outside your home, or you have other ambitions, please do not condemn yourself. I felt all of those feelings and had to learn how to balance the different pulls on my life. But God has loved me and led me through it all.

I know that there are so many precious ones with deep scars. Perhaps you came from an angry family, where you were criticized or rejected. Or maybe you were ignored and you still wish someone would notice you and love you in those places that only you can feel. Perhaps you made some bad choices morally that have deeply injured your own heart. Or you have a passive and indifferent or mean and abusive husband.

Know this today: you are not defined by any of these things—not by what people have said to you, not by your flaws (we all have them), and not by your past failures or present difficulties.

God loves you so very much.
God is with you. God is your champion.

APRIL 5

Be of sober spirit, be on the alert. Your adversary, the devil,
prowls around like a roaring lion, seeking someone to devour.

I PETER 5:8

SOME YEARS AGO, after we had a great time with our children over the holidays, Satan came out unexpectedly and whapped us full force. It caused some havoc and lots of deep, abiding sadness in our family. This attack caused one of the saddest days I have known in many years. It was a strike against one of my children, which especially broke my heart.

Yet we must not be surprised in such situations, but rather on the alert, remembering there is an enemy who hates for us to keep faithful to our ideals for our families and for the Lord. Satan, Peter tells us, is our adversary. He prowls through the earth—like he did when he asked God if he could seek to destroy Job; as he did when Jesus said to Peter, "Satan has demanded permission to sift you like wheat" (Luke 22:31). Peter, who was so personally experienced at this, because of Satan tempting him to deny Jesus before His crucifixion, warns us to be on the alert. He is seeking, Peter tells us, to devour us!

We are, after all, in a battle that rages in this world—a battle for hearts and souls giving allegiance to the one true God. We have an enemy who is the enemy of God, and he wants to destroy us. Resisting him is the only way to cause him to flee.

I have learned to ask myself questions in the midst of my own dark times, and also to ask these questions of other women:

Who would like for you to remain bitter? Discouraged?
Who would like for you to give up on your ideals,
to say, "I can't do this anymore"?
Who wants you to be angry at your spouse?
To be resentful of your children? Your family? Your in-laws?
How can you resist your enemy today?

APRIL 6

He who has found his life will lose it,
and he who has lost his life for My sake will find it.

MATTHEW 10:39

To FOLLOW JESUS, we must carry our cross. We must give up our lives, die to ourselves—our expectations, dreams, and rights—in order to be surrendered to His Kingdom and His work. This, of course, goes against the world's priorities and is not understood by most people. We must be single-minded, as all good soldiers must be in a war, and to remain faithful to Christ.

We are not of this world but rather waiting for the time when we will spend eternity with Jesus in heaven. We must prepare our children for this and model to them the type of sacrifice it requires from Jesus' followers to lose their lives for His sake. Serving in love is the bottom line, even if it costs us our lives.

Moms, God is calling us to a work that is quite important—He will give us the strength and supply us with wisdom one day at a time. He will listen to our prayers. But most of all, we have to be willing to bend over backwards to meet our children's needs, to encourage them, to help them figure out a new game plan when necessary, because we are God's guards in a fallen, tempting world. We are His hands, His words of comfort and wisdom, His voice to tell our children that we love them and believe in them because God loves and believes in them, even in the midst of their immaturity. May you feel His grace to you today.

Remember, God has promised that those who lose their
lives for His sake will find them. That's you, mama.
Ask the Lord to show you His pleasure in your sacrifice.

APRIL 7

Watch over your heart with all diligence,
for from it flow the springs of life.

PROVERBS 4:23

OVER THE YEARS, a number of moms have asked me about how to keep the hearts of preteens and teens when they start drifting away. I have definitely not been a perfect mom, but Clay and I have learned so much and have seen so much of His grace to keep us going along the way. I truly love my children as best friends and companions, and though so many days were irritating, the fruit of remaining under the load of cultivating patience with our children has paid off so much more than we could have imagined!

I think it is of the utmost importance to focus on the hearts of our children, rather than on their behavior. There is a reason that God uses the word *heart* over eight hundred times in Scripture.

Every child has a different personality, with different capacities and abilities. If we really believe we are supposed to study our children and seek to release the passions and personalities and drives of their hearts so that they can pursue God's call on their lives, we will seek to be winsome, gracious, lifegiving, and encouraging. If their behavior is our only focus, we can force them to submit to us when they are young simply because we are bigger than them! However, the short-term "success" could lead to long-term failure if this control causes us to lose their hearts. The goal is for them to love and obey with joy, not out of compulsion.

If, when your children are young, in the midst of training them and holding up God's ideals, you also serve them and love them unconditionally, then you will be laying a foundation for them to be willing to listen to you when they are older.

What can you do to strengthen your ties to your children's hearts?

He Himself knows our frame; He is mindful that we are but dust.

PSALM 103:14

APRIL WAS ABLOOM WITH tiny buds beginning to burst, daffodils pushing through the cold ground, and all the promise of spring pulsing through our home. The Saturday before Easter found my girls and me working together to prepare our traditional feast for about twenty people. Teenager Joy had decided to make the deviled eggs, so she'd hard-boiled two dozen. Then she got a bright idea of how to make it easier to fill them.

Her effort to stuff a flimsy, plastic sandwich bag with egg filling resulted in a mess everywhere. My first reaction was frustration. Suddenly, the Lord poked my heart and gave me eyes to see this hormonal young woman—my sweet little girl—in the throes of growing up. Insecurity and frustration flashed from her dark eyes as she watched me clean up her mess. When I was finished cleaning and pondering the situation, I took her to our den couch and gave her a cup of tea.

"Joyness," I began, "you have been so exceedingly helpful and thoughtful today. The table you set looks lovely; the groceries are put away, and you have labored by my side for hours. I don't know what I would do without your help. Many times I have baked bread and then burned it, or grilled something outside that ends up tough as nails. So, I know how you must have felt when the bag kept breaking and the mess just poured out. You are such a treasure to me, and I know you were trying to do a good job. Thanks so much for all the ways you have helped me this week!"

Suddenly, a sheepish grin crossed her face. She climbed into my lap; long, gangly, teenage legs and all, and said, "I am so thankful that you always love me, Mommy." A kiss on the cheek . . . and she was gone.

How might God want to offer grace to you, knowing your limitations, today? How might you receive it?

APRIL 9

Treat others the same way you want them to treat you.

LUKE 6:31

THERE IS A MYSTERIOUS POINT when a child no longer wants to be "mommy-ed," but will turn away toward the process of becoming an adult. (All of mine have.) No amount of seeking to retrieve the innocent years will make this new phase go away. Suddenly, it is God's time for your children to begin growing up! Until that time, there is a window of opportunity to pour in foundations of morality, truth, values, habits, and character, but then, suddenly, your whole relationship with your children will hit a roadblock, and you know that there will be a detour ahead—a different route to go!

So if you find yourself in the stages of new hormones and feelings expressed through your children, now, for a moment, ask yourself the question, "When I am having a bout with hormones and anger or rage or emotions come upon me with no warning, how do I want others to behave toward me?"

When I'm grouchy, I want people to treat me gently and to give me grace, understanding that this is not my real self or my usual behavior! And so my teens want this from me, that I would take seriously Jesus' admonition to "do to others as you would have them do to you" (Luke 6:31, NIV).

During this phase, it is important to gently hold their hearts in respect, rather than treating them as small children and focusing on their failures.

Do you remember what it felt like to be a young child, with everyone else making your decisions? Or a teen bandied about by wild emotions you couldn't control? How can you ease the way for your own children today?

While I was with them, I was keeping them in Your name
which You have given Me; and I guarded them.

JOHN 17:12

OCCASIONALLY, I make an effort to take each of my children out for a date alone. It gives me the opportunity to share a passage from Scripture and discuss issues. I try to avoid approaching them to produce guilt, but rather keep painting God's purposes for them as young men and young women in a winsome way—"You are such a treasure. I see you making good decisions. I think God has a real purpose for your life." I tell them of my trust in them, my belief that God will use them as a light.

Keeping my children in Christ's name means staying close to them, praying for them, being available for them, even at odd times. When they want to talk (usually late at night!) I need to be there, so when they find themselves in any trouble, temptation, or danger, our line of communication is already established. My children have a habit of telling us everything—everything! This way, we don't doubt when they report on where they are or what they are doing, because we know they will tell us the truth.

It is so tempting during the preteen and teen years to tire of these pushy and sometimes irritating kids, but don't give up. Most especially, don't hand them over, in your weariness, to this culture. Polish your ideals and get back on track—have a rest if you want, but this is not a time to abandon ship. The stakes are high as to what kind of scars will be made on their lives if you leave your post. Don't battle the small issues, but make your battlegrounds the things that really matter.

How will you develop a personal, discussion-filled time with your
children now, so you have a forum for big conversations later?

APRIL 11

I satisfy the weary ones and refresh everyone who languishes.

JEREMIAH 31:25

I HAVE SEEN SOME BOOKS AND articles going around that suggest that moms don't really need a break from their children and that it is possible to be around them all the time without going crazy. Now, I love my children and am very committed to my family, and I hope I don't step on anyone's toes, but it is statements like this that put lots of burden and law on women and make them feel guilty unnecessarily. Motherhood is a very long-term calling, and I think all moms need breaks and the encouragement of other women, without having to feel guilty for taking some time for themselves.

There are lots of pieces of parenting advice around that sound wise, but in the end, I have to say, "Is this law? Is it an unshakable truth that applies to all moms at all times?" Or is it possible that there is grace for each mom to conduct her own symphony, so to speak, with her family, circumstances, and children in mind? I think this is far more likely! Paul tells us in Galatians, "It was for freedom that Christ set us free; therefore keep standing firm and do not be subject again to a yoke of slavery" (5:1).

Stand firm in your ideals before God without letting someone else's yoke slip around your neck unnecessarily.

---

*Are there areas in which someone else's translation of how God wants
you to behave is pressing upon you—and choking the life out of you?
Ask yourself, "Where in Scripture is this idea actually given as a command?"
If you can't find it . . . consider shaking that piece of advice (or yoke) off!*

"It is enough; now, O LORD, take my life, for I am not better than my fathers." [Elijah] lay down and slept under a juniper tree; and behold, there was an angel touching him, and he said to him, "Arise, eat."

I KINGS 19:4-5

ONE NIGHT MANY YEARS AGO, after we had been reading a book out loud, Joy said, "Mom, I have a surprise for you. Go take a hot bath and before you get into the tub, I want to put an avocado mask on you that I read about." So I obeyed gladly, and she smoothed avocado all over my face (with extra for the wrinkles!).

After I got out of my bath, she made me close my eyes and led me by the hand into my bedroom. When I opened my eyes, I saw she had gathered candles and lit them all over my room, put on instrumental music, and laid out towels and a pillow for me to lie on. She then gave me a hand massage and filed my nails, gave me a wonderful foot massage with great-smelling lotion, and followed up with a back and shoulder massage. I cannot tell you how the stress went out of my body. I felt like I had been touched by an angel. I slept so soundly that night, and every time I awakened, a smile came to my face as I remembered the service of this precious thirteen-year-old and her last words before she left my room: "Mom, I love you so much, and I just wanted to show you my love."

Sometimes when I am exhausted or drained, I really don't need anyone to settle my problems or bring answers. I just need sleep or rest. There is a healing power to touch and affection, and Joy's touch literally melted me that night and ushered me into rest.

Today, hug those you love, touch the disgruntled, kiss and scratch weary backs, and if you are weary, get rest and sleep.

APRIL 13

The light shines in the darkness, and the darkness has not overcome it.
JOHN 1:5, NIV

GWEN TODD WAS THE FIRST FRIEND who taught me the value of commitment and love as I worked alongside her in ministry. We are indeed like sisters. Some years ago, I had flown to Nashville a day early when scheduled to speak at an event, so we could visit at her home in Kentucky.

Except . . . Gwen didn't meet me at the airport. I found out she was snowbound with her elderly mother, who was suffering with Alzheimer's and quite frail, requiring Gwen's constant care. They had been without electricity, lights, or heat for the past three days because of the storm! Another dear friend loaned me a car, and I began the drive to Kentucky. It was like a ghost town—no working stoplights, no store or streetlights anywhere, trees fallen in the road . . . As I finally reached her street, I saw a candle in the window of one house amidst a sea of darkness—a candle my friend had lit for me! So I eased into her driveway, knocking countless icicles off the bushes as I climbed out of the car. When I went to the door, there was my sweet friend, with candles aglow in the rooms beyond. She had found out I was coming through a very short cell phone message that had finally gone through after two days, and had some chips and cheese waiting for me—the last fresh package of cold food to be had.

What a fun memory we made eating by candlelight, storing up one more memory of adventure. How thankful I was to be of encouragement to her in the midst of feeling alone in the dark—as she has helped me through my own crises. We felt blessed to sit in our gowns, cuddled under piles of blankets, enjoying the candlelight and just being together.

*How might you light a candle for someone today
and enjoy its brightness together?*

Let us not lose heart in doing good,
for in due time we will reap if we do not grow weary.

GALATIANS 6:9

As I LOOK BACK OVER my thirty-some years of mothering, I can remember so many times in which I was by myself in my bedroom, pouring my heart out to the Lord—searching for strength when I was so tired from sleepless nights; asking for wisdom as my children and marriage presented me with so many mysteries and dilemmas I did not know how to handle; hoping for friendship and community in the midst of so many moves. I begged Him, my heavenly Father, to meet with me and to hear my cries. By faith, I would leave my room not always changed in my emotions, but resolved in my heart to move in the direction of faith and toward loving Him more and serving Him as I served my family day after day, year after year.

Sometimes, I felt invisible—did He see me? Did my prayers matter? Did my obedience make a difference? Did my day-in, day-out choices of faithfully serving and cultivating life in my home matter? Every mama, I think, has these questions.

You never know how eternity may be changing because of your decision to be faithful to God in your home. He has plans to bring light and beauty to the whole world, and He delights in using very normal people like you and like me to do it! Perhaps a word from you will spark a chain reaction that will have implications throughout the world as one person shares what you have shared with them, or as you share a book or send a note or give words of life and love. Perhaps one of your children will change history and affect thousands or millions because of your faithfulness today. Your labor is not in vain!

Think over your life and ask God to show you whose faithful
labor was a blessing to you. Determine to be the person
someone else will one day remember the same way!

APRIL 15

If you love Me, you will keep My commandments.

JOHN 14:15

A SWEET MOM ONCE WROTE me a letter to say she and her friends were reading through *Ministry of Motherhood* together and really enjoyed it, but it was a little overwhelming because it seemed I was consistently positive about my children and acted loving toward them. Then she asked if I truly always felt that way!

We all go through seasons when we wonder if some of our children came from another family. Sometimes we wonder if we even like them, and sometimes we just wish we could escape!

I learned very early in my Christian life about the concept of obedience. Jesus said, "If you love me, obey my commandments" (John 14:15, NLT). So, obedience is a response that comes out of love, not feeling. Many times I do the right thing even though the feelings don't match. In other words, I know it is right to act in a loving, patient manner toward my children or to respect Clay—even when I don't feel like it! Because I want to love Jesus well, I obey. What I've found out is that my feelings follow my actions. In other words, the more I obey the Lord in serving my children and encouraging them, the more of an investment they become to me, and the more I cherish them.

Growth is a long process. My deep love and reverence for my children has grown through many, many years of cherishing them, sometimes because I truly felt loving and enjoyed them—and sometimes purely out of faith! As in a garden, whatever you water and nourish most is what will flourish. If you water the garden of family and children and love and lifegiving words and beauty, it will grow and flourish—it is a long-term work.

Are you practicing obediently cherishing your children?
Do you see loving them well as part of your obedience to God?

Let us hold fast the confession of our hope without
wavering, for He who promised is faithful.

HEBREWS 10:23

It seems to be a hallmark of mature Christians to have a story of having to wait years and years on God and then seeing Him come through with beauty, wisdom, and grace. But the Bible is full of people who took matters into their own hands when they thought God needed a little help, and it created havoc.

When Abraham got tired of waiting, he got his maidservant pregnant and caused all sorts of problems (Genesis 16:1-16; 21:8-21).

Saul was terrified by the approaching Philistine army, and instead of waiting on God for how to proceed, he consulted a medium—something God had explicitly warned against (1 Samuel 28).

Others, who made up their minds to wait with patience, have better stories: Joseph had to wait twelve years before he became the assistant to Pharaoh and head of all Egypt (Genesis 37; 39–41).

David had to wait decades from the time he was anointed king until the time he was finally crowned king over all the houses of Israel (1 Samuel 16; 2 Samuel 2).

Waiting and persevering seem to have an incredible value to God. His timing never seems to be as soon as mine—but He is so good and always faithful, just in a different way than my impatient heart wants Him to be.

Waiting proves (or disproves!) the strength of our hearts and our convictions. If we do it well, it strengthens our faith. It increases our capacity to long for heavenly answers instead of just being satisfied with earthly, immediate fixes.

How are you doing with whatever you're waiting on today?

APRIL 17

Another also said, "I will follow You, Lord; but first permit me to say good-bye to those at home." But Jesus said to him, "No one, after putting his hand to the plough and looking back, is fit for the kingdom of God."

LUKE 9:61-62

GOD'S WORD IS CLEAR: He values dedication and perseverance, as they are part of His own character.

Yet, daily, people are tempted to give up on their ideals—giving up in marriage, in relationships, on a child, on a commitment. People capitulate all the time to Satan's wily and clever messages encouraging them to compromise—"You can't expect anyone in this time of the world to be moral. No one else is doing this hard thing you're doing. You deserve better than this."

There are so many messages he sends to try and make us want to quit. However, if we persevere and wait on God, we will receive the reward of a holier character and the grace of seeing Him work in our lives.

So, today, if you are weary, discouraged, or downhearted, look up—God sees you, God is at work. Don't quit before He accomplishes His will. You will be greatly fulfilled if you keep going and wait for God's grace and for His work in His way at His time. When I look back I see His wisdom and how He was always in control—even when it didn't seem like He was.

Take some time today to search your heart and ask God to remind you about the commitments you've made that He most values. What does He want to encourage you to rededicate yourself to? How has the enemy tried to discourage you and convince you to give up? Determine to listen to God's voice.

The kingdom of heaven is like a merchant seeking fine pearls,
and upon finding one pearl of great value,
he went and sold all that he had and bought it.

MATTHEW 13:45-46

A COUPLE OF WEEKS AGO, Sarah invited friends to our home, where she shared with them some things she'd been studying about beauty. Beauty is one of the attributes of God we see in creation. There is something in God's very nature that must express itself in beauty.

Both mothers and daughters attended, and we all had lots of fun together. Each person had to bring something she thought was beautiful and tell a story about it. One of my favorites was a beautiful piece of framed embroidery that the husband of one of the moms had made for her when they were in high school! Under each woman's luncheon plate, Sarah had placed a slip of paper bearing a quotation about beauty, which we shared with one another.

Finally, Sarah read a beautiful passage from *The Secret Garden*. When Colin, the crippled protagonist of the story, is finally wheeled into the secret garden his two friends have prepared for him, he marvels breathlessly at the beauty of it. Then he says, "I shall get well! And I shall live forever and ever and ever!" Sarah then talked to us about the intrinsic beauty God has placed in our souls—the way we are all able to reflect Him in our lives; the way we live, the way we serve, the way we dress—along with a reminder that when we subdue and create an atmosphere of beauty and creativity in our homes, we give one more testimony of His reality in our lives. The end of the gathering was even better than the beginning, because Sarah had made a lemon cake with raspberry filling for dessert!

She also gave each daughter a real pearl necklace. Jesus, the Author of beauty, is the Pearl of great price—the only One worth giving up everything for.

Think about planning a day to celebrate beauty and inspire your own friends!

APRIL 19

Who is God, but the LORD? and who . . . girds me with strength and makes my way blameless? He makes my feet like hinds' feet, and sets me upon my high places. . . .You enlarge my steps under me, and my feet have not slipped.

PSALM 18:31-33, 36

YESTERDAY MORNING, my birthday, I lit candles in my bedroom, got some strong tea, made blueberry muffins for myself, and climbed back into bed before anyone else was up. I had the luxury of over an hour to read and have a quiet time without interruption.

I am at the age where I am gaining perspective. I can see the pathways God led me on were intentional. Since it was my birthday, it was a good time to reflect on where I had come from and where I was going. I was born two and a half months early and spent two months in a special unit in the hospital afterward, long days in which my mother spent many hours without me, worrying about whether I'd make it (as many premature babies at that time didn't) and how I'd progress if I did survive. I have indeed lived a life of battle, and yet God Himself has led me through. Since my birth, God has been building me all along, shaping my soul, and then building our children, our ministry, and our messages one day, one decision of faith, one twenty-four-hour day of work at a time.

How grateful I am that His Spirit kept me going forward, holding on to ideals, living by faith while not seeing the end, sometimes barely taking one step forward at a time. Yet, how privileged to have been in the race for righteousness and to have passed the baton to my children so that they could run their race and carry on righteousness in their generation.

Can you see both difficulty and grace, too, in your life? Thank God for your past, and place your trust in Him again today for your future.

APRIL 20

Learn from Me, for I am gentle and humble in heart.

MATTHEW 11:29

EZEKIEL 28:12-16 TELLS US THAT God created Satan (Lucifer) as one of the highest angels in heaven. He was crafted in beauty and clothed in precious jewels—ruby, topaz, diamond, and emerald set in gold. His beauty and splendor were magnificent. God created him blameless (Ezekiel 28:15). And yet Scripture tells us Satan's heart was lifted up because of his beauty. As Satan looked at himself, he became exalted in confidence at his own glory and lifted himself above God in his mind. This extreme esteem of himself became the ground in which sin would grow.

Satan said in his heart, "I will ascend to heaven; I will raise my throne above the stars of God . . . I will make myself like the Most High" (Isaiah 14:13-14).

And so it was Satan's pride in himself, his arrogance, that was the seed for all corruption and sin and wickedness in the world, the starting point for sin to grow and flourish.

In precise, striking contrast to Satan, who would exalt himself above all at any cost, crushing and killing the souls of all people in order that God would not have their allegiance, Jesus comes to bow His knee before the Father and willingly lays down His life for all—even the very lowly—to serve, wash their feet, heal their diseases, and forgive their worst deeds.

So all pride and exalting of myself makes me less like Jesus. Any time anything I have done or accomplished makes me think, *I am better than you*, I'm heading in the direction of Satan's attitude rather than that of Jesus.

Have you ever thought of pride as being dangerous because it mimics Satan's original step away from God? Lay down the burden of pride today.

APRIL 21

[Jesus] did not regard equality with God a thing to be grasped, but . . .
humbled Himself by becoming obedient to the point of death.

PHILIPPIANS 2:6-8

ONE YEAR I DETERMINED TO teach Joy the attributes of God, beginning our study with a look at His humility. Jesus touched lepers, spoke with prostitutes, ate with tax collectors, rubbed shoulders with sinners, and felt compassion for all of them. He humbled Himself literally to the point of death.

As we studied, I was reminded that my daughter would not believe the words I taught unless I modeled them to her by humbly serving all in my home, accepting the limitations of all in my life as Jesus did, becoming more of a servant leader, seeking to wash the feet of those He brought my way. Only through this example would my student believe that I believe the words of my exalted Teacher: "Learn from Me, for I am gentle and humble in heart" (Matthew 11:29).

If I want to be like Him, I must take His posture. And in my pursuit of offering the best to my student, Joy, the very windows of heaven were opened up to my soul.

As I prepare and then teach truth, I am discipled by the One who is true, and I am hopefully changed forever.

Teaching is taking responsibility for informing the mind, heart, and thoughts of my student. When I seek to present truth, knowledge, and wisdom—the best thoughts, the most soul-gripping ideals, the foundations of truth and insights of understanding—it forces my own soul to broaden in the preparation of my presentation.

What's your goal for your own student's learning about God this year?
How might taking Jesus' posture enhance your own presentation of the gospel?

Hear, O Israel! The LORD is our God, the LORD is one!
You shall love the LORD your God with all your heart and
with all your soul and with all your might. These words, which I am
commanding you today, shall be on your heart. You shall teach them diligently
to your sons and shall talk of them when you sit in your house and when
you walk by the way and when you lie down and when you rise up.

DEUTERONOMY 6:4-7

DO YOU EVER HEAR VOICES IN YOUR HEAD?
  A good mom would (fill in the blank).
  I potty trained my children by twelve months, and if you were disciplined,
      you would do the same.
  My children never whine; what's wrong with yours?
  If you were really committed to your home, your house would be cleaner.
  You are too lenient on your children. You need to discipline them more.
  Your children are probably rebelling because you are too harsh.

Formulas don't always work, but they can sure make us feel like we are accomplishing something! I used to hear voices in my mind, echoing things other people said to me. Almost all of them made me feel condemned, as though I wasn't mothering the right way or doing enough of the right things.

Then there were these four children of mine, differing in personality, heart issues, and developmental time frames. We had so many issues that I thought if I just knew the right rule or had a better day-planner or the right book or curriculum, I could get it right, and everything would be easy!

It seems to me that Scripture gives many wisdom principles, but very little advice of an exact nature. God is surprisingly, intentionally vague on so many issues. He gives us great freedom to live into our own personalities, our own puzzles, and to apply wisdom in our own creative ways.

Do you struggle with "the voices"?
How do you replace them with real wisdom?

APRIL 23

They heard the sound of the LORD God walking in the garden in the cool of the day, and the man and his wife hid themselves from the presence of the LORD God among the trees of the garden. Then the LORD God called to the man, and said to him, "Where are you?"

GENESIS 3:8-9

I HAVE ALWAYS LOVED THE PASSAGE in Genesis when, after creating a breathtaking, dazzling, wondrous world full of life, color, sounds, scents, and pleasure, God, the master Artist, was strolling in the Garden of Eden looking for Adam and Eve, the ones for whom He had created such a personal gift.

He was walking along in His Garden, surely admiring it and wanting to know what His children thought—if they were happy, if they appreciated it. He went looking for them in the cool of the day. "Where are you?" He called out, but they were not looking for Him. Sadly, they were hiding from God because they had sinned and felt ashamed.

I receive such pleasure at providing for my own treasured children—cooking, decorating, loving, serving—hoping to be God's very hands and breath and words to them so that they can better perceive what He is like. I look for them in the garden of my own life: "How do you like what I have provided?" I want to be with them, to enjoy their companionship.

I realized very early in knowing God that the miracle was that He was always looking for me, wanting me to be His companion and friend; to talk, to commune, to live together hand in hand, to delight in the pleasures He had prepared for me.

Just as I desire the companionship of my own children, that is what—amazingly!—He desires of me.

Do you know how much God wants to just live life with you?
Even now, He is calling . . . "Where are you?" I pray you'll answer today.

Jesus said to him, "The foxes have holes and the birds of the air have nests, but the Son of Man has nowhere to lay His head."

LUKE 9:58

GOD'S WILL IS VERY CLEAR AND straightforward—rejoice, pray, and give thanks in everything. A heart that is grateful is a heart that is satisfied and content.

At this juncture in history, we have more material goods available to purchase, more entertainment, more food options than at any other time. Yet, "having more" has created a culture that is never satisfied, often in debt, and dependent on pleasure and self-gratification while neglecting the greater needs of people less fortunate than themselves. As a result, the development of a strong character in children has often been neglected. Children are coddled, entertained to death, and spoiled with expectations that can never totally be assuaged, which creates a complaining spirit and self-pity if every desire is not promptly met.

Worse, many parents have come to think they are supposed to provide all these things for their children so they can be happy, instead of understanding God wants them to cultivate children who have learned to be content.

Jesus came into the world with no stately form or majesty that would cause us to look upon Him. Having no title, and few possessions, He chose fishermen, tax collectors, and common men and women to be His companions. He lived a simple, common life, with "nowhere to lay His head." In this, He modeled to us a thankful heart.

Simplicity is one of the keys to gratitude. For children, how important it is that they learn to be satisfied with playing at the beach or walking in a forest or digging in the dirt, carrying a notebook around so they can draw a tree or flowers, singing and dreaming under a shade tree.

The fewer choices people have, the more likely they will be happy and grateful for what they have been given. Are there ways you might simplify your life and cultivate gratitude?

APRIL 25

*The Spirit of the Lord GOD is upon me, because the LORD has anointed
me to bring good news to the afflicted; He has sent me to bind up the
brokenhearted, to proclaim liberty to captives and freedom to prisoners;
to proclaim the favorable year of the LORD and the day of vengeance
of our God; to comfort all who mourn, to grant those who mourn in
Zion, giving them a garland instead of ashes, the oil of gladness instead
of mourning, the mantle of praise instead of a spirit of fainting.*

ISAIAH 61:1-3

INTERESTINGLY, when Jesus went to the synagogue in Nazareth, it is this passage that
He read. He was on a mission—to heal, to save, to encourage, to proclaim God. When
we love Jesus, we will be overcome with His compassion toward others, as He was. Our
words will be full of power and lifegiving. No one will leave our homes without having a sense of His hand of love, His voice of truth, His arms of comfort, His strength
and calling.

Jesus was a servant-king. He held and blessed children, loved the downcast—the
lepers, the prostitutes, the poor, and the sick—served meals, washed feet. Love was
His message.

Our homes are the arena immediately available to us, the place in which we can
build the life of Christ. They become a sanctuary for those who need to feel His life
by being welcomed and receiving a cup of cold water, a home-cooked meal, a focused
conversation, a healing touch. We celebrate the traditions of home not because we want
to be busier (no one needs that!) but to make the life of Christ come alive, to show the
beauty of God, to give our children a live picture of His beauty, His reality, His truth,
His words, and His outreaching love.

---

*This declaration of Jesus from Isaiah applies to you, too! How might your
home become a stage for you to show Christ's love to others today?*

APRIL 26

Take My yoke upon you and learn from Me, for I am gentle and humble in heart, and you will find rest for your souls.

MATTHEW 11:29

EVERY DAY, we have twenty-four hours to invest our lives in what will matter for eternity. It is in the seemingly insignificant moments of our lives when nobility, civility, and graciousness must flow from our hearts. We will often be tempted to act in a manner that is harsh, impatient, unloving, judgmental of others, quick to lash out when we feel attacked . . . Yet, the only way to overcome these temptations and end life with a wise, peacemaking, loving, gentle heart is to invest in our spiritual lives every day by spending time with the Source of all goodness and lovingkindness, the Lord Jesus Himself. Hebrews 1:3 tells us that He is the exact representation of God—He speaks God's words, He shows His heart, He manifests His wisdom.

Jesus said, "Learn from Me, for I am gentle and humble in heart." This seems to be my pondering of the year. Learn from Him. He didn't revile when He was reviled. He loved and gave grace to Peter when he fell. He washed 120 toes the night before He was crucified, serving those for whom He would die.

The more I regularly invest my heart, my commitments, my faith, my love in my relationship to my Lord, the more my own heart will be noble and pure. And the place where reality marries truth is in my obedience, each second, each moment, each day as I seek to emulate His life, choosing to obey, against my feelings, those things He spoke to my heart in the privacy of my time with Him.

How do you make time to learn from Jesus? Are you growing in humility?

APRIL 27

Consider it all joy, my brethren, when you encounter various
trials, knowing that the testing of your faith produces endurance.
and let endurance have its perfect result, so that you may
be perfect and complete, lacking in nothing.

JAMES 1:2-4

I AM NOT NATURALLY A VERY NOBLE or valiant person. And so when I read this verse over the years, I would flinch and go through it quickly, because I didn't relish trials. Our lives have been full of them, and I have, at times, learned to dread another day in case it might have some new trial in it!

Having four children, homeschooling, moving seventeen times, and all the difficulties in relationships, criticism for my ideals, financial struggles, health issues, loneliness, marital tensions, the ever-changing phases of my children's lives, ministry challenges, and an overload of responsibilities—just keeping up with all the work that never ends was so very much harder than I ever realized life would be. Though in my early twenties I became serious about the Lord and truly committed to going anywhere and doing anything for His Kingdom, I no more had an idea of what that would mean than a little girl who dresses up as a princess and pretends to know what it would mean to become a queen and rule a country.

Yet, I can look back now and see that God had such great plans for my life, and the only pathway to these plans of His was through many trials. I had pretty much committed myself to becoming a warrior for His Kingdom in this life, not realizing that in order for someone to become a general to lead others into battle, he must first begin with basic training.

Do you ever feel incapable of doing what God might have planned for
you? Have you considered the idea that perhaps the very difficulties
you're facing right now are part of the way He is preparing you?

You therefore, my son, be strong in the grace that is in Christ Jesus. The things which you have heard from me in the presence of many witnesses, entrust these to faithful men who will be able to teach others also. Suffer hardship with me, as a good soldier of Christ Jesus.

2 TIMOTHY 2:1-3

AFTER PASSING SUCCESSFULLY through basic training, a soldier must prove worthy in real battles to earn the right to humbly and wisely lead others into victory in bigger arenas. Because God delights in us entering into the fray of this world, to bring light, beauty, and truth and to stand strongly and boldly for His purposes, He sends us trials and training to prepare us for the platform He would have us stand on.

I know this because my own victories through trials became the very platform on which I saw the grace of God, His goodness, and His love, as I saw He had a better plan for me than I had for myself. My integrity was won in the seemingly invisible places, where He was testing and strengthening me for bigger arenas.

Each of us has this same opportunity to live a faithful story as we walk through the difficulties of life. How can we encourage others in this fallen place if we do not see God's faithfulness in our own stories? As we hold His hand and move forward, we will have a story to tell, a way to encourage others from the integrity of our own lives.

Today, don't resist the trials—they will be the making of your character, the galvanizing of your integrity, the defining of a great story of your King working on your behalf in the history of His redeeming the world back to Himself—your opportunity to show forth your true love for Him.

What trials are you facing right now? How would it change your perspective to view those trials as the training ground for something God may be calling you to in the future?

APRIL 29

"For I know the plans that I have for you," declares the LORD,
"plans for welfare and not for calamity to give you a future and a hope."
JEREMIAH 29:11

SOMETIMES WHEN my two girls and I get together, we share our dreams for the future. It can be a bittersweet time for me to listen to their hearts, as I know we all have dreams that have not yet come true. But how precious it was to hold in my memory this time when hearts were open and deepest desires shared.

A sweet mama in tears once asked me, "How long do you keep praying for your dreams to come true, and when do you quit and accept God's response as no?"

Well, I can't answer God's will for her life, but the older I get, the more childlike I seek to be. There is a temptation in life to become jaded and lose hope. Yet Scripture instructs us to pursue childlike (not childish) faith. When we trust His character, we can keep believing our God can do anything, and we can continue coming to Him in prayer.

So, I commit the future of our family to Him. I pray for miracles. I pray for Him to do great things in and through the lives of my children, Clay, and me. I ask Him to knock down walls and to stretch our sphere of influence—because I want everyone to know how personal, responsive, and gracious He is. I want to believe in Him and trust Him—just like a child.

Today, write down some of the things He has put on your heart to
keep dreaming. Then, place them into His capable hands.

Whoever causes one of these little ones who believe in Me to stumble, it would be better for him to have a heavy millstone hung around his neck, and to be drowned in the depth of the sea.

MATTHEW 18:6

WE ARE CALLED TO GIVE UP OUR LIVES, as Jesus gave up His life for us, for the purpose of training, loving, and preparing our children for life—eternal life. Jesus had a pretty strong opinion about what we would face if we willingly put our children in harm's way! We are not mature Christians if we're seeking to get rid of the "burden" of having children by handing the training of them to others. It is our responsibility to care for our children's souls, presenting Jesus to them in hopes that they will choose to follow Him.

It seems that these days, women are not being taught that choices have consequences—that their children's hearts, minds, morals, and future lives are dependent on the vision and faithfulness of mothers in this generation.

"What does it profit a mom to gain the whole world, and lose her children's souls?" (my paraphrase of Mark 8:36).

I believe that if mothers do not take initiative now to be personally responsible for their children, we will never see a future generation of adults with excellent character, biblical convictions, and leadership qualities. We will not have children who have learned that family is important, that marriage is of great value to God, and that we are responsible for the world hearing the truth in our generation.

And yet, these truths are foundational to society! There is no better use of our time than to pour our lives out for God, both within our homes and without.

Is there anything about the way you are living your life that might cause a little one to stumble? Confess it, turn away, and ask God to show you what corrections must be made.

MAY 1

Where no oxen are, the manger is clean,
but much revenue comes by the strength of the ox.

PROVERBS 14:4

OH, THE MESSES WE'VE MADE IN our home over the years. This verse always makes me giggle as I picture all the oxen tromping through my house!

Thousands of Legos, dress-up clothes from the thrift store, an old tape recorder, swords and capes, a play kitchen with real pots and pans and plastic food, garden tools, wood and nails, blankets and card tables for making indoor tents, colored pencils, paints, butcher paper by the yard, Play-Doh, cups of tea—all these and more were the building blocks of my children's playtime.

They were not allowed to use any screens more than thirty minutes during daylight hours unless they were sick—they knew not to ask. All because I had read article after article that said how important play, discovery, and creativity were to the growth process of children's brains.

Building a "real" culture of life in your home may require planning, and it also probably means lots of kids will spend time at your house—because yours may be one of the only places where children are still encouraged to be creative and play and run wild and have free time and fun! We always enjoyed local parks when we lived in small apartments overseas, and found various hiking trails, too, so we could take a good, long walk each day.

In everyday life, nature, and home, God has provided all that our children need to develop intelligence, great vocabularies, and healthy minds and bodies. Mamas need to be protectors and promoters of that provision so children can gain all that's possible from it!

Consider your own home and your children's free-time activities.
Is there room for creative play, both in the house and on the calendar?
See what you can do to promote imagination in your house today!

*Do not fear, for I am with you; do not anxiously look about you,
for I am your God. I will strengthen you, surely I will help you,
surely I will uphold you with My righteous right hand.*

ISAIAH 41:10

A SWEET YOUNG COUPLE HAD decided to kayak from Maine down to Florida. They planned their trip, got sponsors to support them, and blogged about their journey. It took them a year to complete the itinerary they had planned.

Storms of great magnitude arose during their journey, sending waves crashing all around them. Often, the rain would pelt continuously on their weary bodies and soak them to the bone. Discouragement would overwhelm, and they would think, *Why did we undertake this? We will never finish. It is too difficult. No one could do it!*

One time, however, in the middle of one such moment, they made a pact with each other. "We will never make a decision to quit when we are in the midst of a storm."

Such a simple but profound commitment—one I believe is worth emulating!

So many dear friends are surrounded by storms in their lives right now—financial, physical, social. They face weariness, loneliness, lack of support systems, difficult marriages, prodigal children, fear of the future, despair because of the times we are in . . . The list goes on and on.

Yet, it is in the midst of the storms of life that our faith is most precious. It is in these times when we can say to Satan, "You would have me fear, but I choose to believe in the goodness of God and in His provision."

*Do you need to make a similar commitment to not give up during
a time of storm? Take a moment to write down your intention
today, and pray for strength to maintain the course.*

MAY 3

The LORD is my light and my salvation; whom shall I fear?
The LORD is the defense of my life; whom shall I dread? . . .
Though a host encamp against me, my heart will not fear;
though war arise against me, in spite of this I shall be confident.

PSALM 27:1, 3

WHEN I WAS WORKING IN Communist countries many years ago, where there were constant persecutions and imprisonments, I was surprised to see the fervor of so many Christians in their worship of God and their delight in His reality. Their praise of Him in music was heavenly. I asked an old woman about it, and she said to me, "You Americans have had so much heaven on earth, you have not known what it is to long for and hope for the heavenly Kingdom of God where righteousness will rule, where our real longings will be satisfied, and where we will see our precious Lord face to face."

We are told very clearly in Scripture that difficult times will come. Scripture tells us at the end of the times, earthquakes will increase—and so they have. We know that many Christians will be persecuted all over the world—and so they are. Great economic troubles, shaking our foundations as we know them, have been predicted and are coming true before our eyes. Paul has told us immorality, wickedness, and godlessness will be rampant (2 Timothy 3:1-5). We know from Revelation that Satan, knowing his time is short, will be pouring out great wrath (Revelation 12:12).

This, then, could be one of the finest hours for Christians to stay true, faithful until the end, enduring hardship, rejoicing in His reality, and living by faith.

Is your heart surrounded with fear and discouragement in the
storms of life? Look to the face of Jesus, your King, Savior, and Lord.
He is with you. He will not abandon you, but carry you.

MAY 4

You shall love your neighbor as yourself.

MARK 12:31

WHEN I LOOKED INTO BABY Sarah's deep blue eyes for the very first time, my heart was astonished at the vast love that overwhelmed me. I am so grateful for that love, as it seems a key factor for reaching children's hearts is how greatly loved and connected to their family they feel.

When babies start out being loved, touched, sung to, nursed, and cherished, their heart needs and physical needs begin to be connected in the brain in the right way. However, when babies are left to cry for long periods and not cherished and touched and cuddled and enjoyed, an essential chemical imbalance is created in their brain that makes them more apt to be irritated, fussy, and less responsive.

Loving a child, to me, means loving who your child is—his or her God-designed personality. It means delighting in your child and communicating that with words, gestures, and tone of voice. It means spending time playing with them and listening to them, and affirming them in front of others.

This did not come naturally to me, but I followed this love principle obediently by faith and saw the results in my children's lives. I always thought of myself as more of an "adult" person than a "kid" person, as I had never been around children much at all before mine were born! But as I read many books about babies and researched Scripture and studied Christ, I knew that love would be the foundation for reaching the hearts of my children with the messages and truth of God, so I sought to cherish the essential design of who they were.

Does loving your children come easily to you? Or do you have to make an effort to appreciate your children as they are? (Remember, everyone has to put in extra effort sometimes!) Ask the Lord to help you see what He sees when He looks at them, each one a unique creation.

MAY 5

Hear, O Israel! The LORD is our God, the LORD is one! You shall love the LORD your God with all your heart and with all your soul and with all your might. These words, which I am commanding you today, shall be on your heart. You shall teach them diligently to your sons and shall talk of them when you sit in your house and when you walk by the way and when you lie down and when you rise up. You shall bind them as a sign on your hand and they shall be as frontals on your forehead. You shall write them on the doorposts of your house and on your gates.

DEUTERONOMY 6:4-9

SCRIPTURE IS VERY CLEAR THAT we are to discipline and train our children. Discipline is not really an area I know how to write well about, though, because it's such a personalized issue in which other people's directives probably won't help us much, because they aren't written for our specific children! For me discipline was an overarching journey and relationship. I would approach each day, each minute, each child with my grid of expectations, knowing the way I wanted to train them. I developed an internal filter clearly focused on the results I wanted to accomplish with my children, and then all day I was with them, operating from that filter.

I had two main themes in parenting: honor, which focuses on attitude, and obedience, which focuses on behavior.

Both were a part of what I knew I needed to secure with age-appropriate expectations. Children need to know what is expected of them before we discipline them for not obeying. Yelling may be needed at the moment a child is in danger, but usually a child should know to obey ahead of time. Children must also know a parent will surely take action if they do not obey.

What have you found to be the most productive way to train your children toward obedience in advance?

I have set before you today life and prosperity, and death and adversity; in that I command you today to love the LORD your God, to walk in His ways and to keep His commandments and His statutes and His judgments, that you may live and multiply, and that the LORD your God may bless you in the land where you are entering to possess it.

DEUTERONOMY 30:15-16

I HAVE NOTICED THAT MANY young parents neglect to listen to their children, then wonder why their children do not obey them. Little children need to be attended to and taught and instructed often so they have a learned pattern of obedience and know how to follow.

For instance, before we would go to someone's house, I reminded my children of using their best manners. We'd talk about being a blessing and sharing, and they knew if they did not behave, they would lose the privilege of playing with the others. Follow-through is a must, and getting down to their eye level, talking to them calmly, and listening to their part of the story is also very important.

In Deuteronomy, God gave Israel a choice—life and prosperity, or death and adversity. God told Israel He would bless them if they would obey Him and that there would be consequences if they chose not to obey Him. So we taught our children that—we wanted them to learn to obey us so that we could bless them, but if they chose to disobey, they were choosing to be disciplined by our consequences.

Do you remind your children, before you arrive somewhere, of your expectations for their behavior? Do you find it hard to follow through with consequences? Ask God to help you be consistently diligent in training today.

MAY 7

To each one of us grace has been given as Christ apportioned it.

EPHESIANS 4:7, NIV

GATHERING PASSPORTS FOR our family in advance of a mission trip often proved easier said than done. Once I found myself on hold with the passport office multiple times, spending hours trying to find out why Nathan's passport hadn't arrived when we had ordered it months before the trip we planned. Before I left to go overseas the first time, I envisioned missionaries as very spiritual people who talked in biblical phrases and saw daily miracles. When I arrived on the field, I found very normal people who struggled with administrative details and the difficulties of a new language, while missing familiar things like M&M's, chocolate chip cookies, and English. They, like me, had to live through the stress of getting visas, packing, and adjusting to a new culture.

Many others who aren't on the mission field have a heart for the Kingdom of God. Their work is not so noticeable or honored, though just as precious to the Lord. Some are taking care of a parent with Alzheimer's; others are holding and rocking sick children who cry throughout the night with an ear infection or stomachache. There are young single men or women keeping faithful to a pure moral standard and putting up with the loneliness of being a part of the small minority who hold biblical ideals; homeschooling moms patiently serving children at home without a break while daily hoping for progress in each of their children's educations; single mamas working hard and wondering how they will meet all their children's needs and daily depending on God to fill in the cracks. All are so very precious to God—all seen by Him—each tiny act of faith, love, and perseverance.

Do you know that God's grace has been given to you, too? Take a moment to close your eyes, breathe deeply, and remind yourself of this great gift, available for whatever task lies before you.

Wisdom has built her house, she has hewn out her seven pillars; she has prepared her food, she has mixed her wine; she has also set her table; she has sent out her maidens, she calls from the tops of the heights of the city: "Whoever is naive, let him turn in here!" To him who lacks understanding she says, "Come, eat of my food and drink of the wine I have mixed. Forsake your folly and live, and proceed in the way of understanding."

PROVERBS 9:1-6

JASON IS THE HERO IN a classic tale from Greek mythology in which he leads a ship of men in a quest for the golden fleece. As all good stories go, there are many adventures, battles, and catastrophes. One particularly dangerous trap is that of the Sirens, described in Homer's epic poem about Odysseus. The Sirens have the ability to sing beautiful songs that entice sailors to their island, causing them to crash their ships on its shore, meeting death and destruction.

Orpheus comes to Jason's and the crew's aid, having the ability to play more beautiful songs, more loudly—thus drowning out the Sirens' bewitching songs so they can pass by safely.

This story is a paradigm of what we need to consider for our children. When they are young, we not only build foundations of beauty, truth, love, and goodness, but we also saturate them with the celebration of life and the joy of Christ, so they will always consider our homes the most comforting, beautiful, peaceful places to be.

In this world, at this time, the Sirens sing an alluring song. It is our responsibility to figure out how to sing a more beautiful one.

Have you thought of yourself as a singer of beautiful songs for your children, drawing them toward truth? How might this picture inform the ways you interact with them?

MAY 9

The woman of folly is boisterous, she is naive and knows nothing. She sits at the doorway of her house, on a seat by the high places of the city, calling to those who pass by, who are making their paths straight: "Whoever is naive, let him turn in here," and to him who lacks understanding she says, "Stolen water is sweet; and bread eaten in secret is pleasant."

PROVERBS 9:13-17

TODAY'S PASSAGE DEPICTS A VOICE of foolishness. Her name is Folly, and she is calling out to those who are passing by "who are making their paths straight." She wants to bring these, our children—whose lives we have sought to put on the "path of life" for our Lord Jesus—to destruction. She calls out to them with lies, deception, and promises of love and fulfillment, through the world's ways.

Earlier, Solomon depicts the other voice that is crying out—that of Wisdom. She sets her table, cooks her food, and makes her place one of life and beauty, an atmosphere where love has prepared a meal. She then calls out to the sons of men and invites them to her home to learn from her (Proverbs 9:1-6). She is there to call these youth to excellence, beauty, and truth to help them safely go through the passage of teenage years unscathed. She sings a beautiful song!

And so, as we reflect the image of God through our lives in our homes, it is a necessity of our spiritual warfare that we provide and cultivate havens of comfort for our families: shelters in the storms of life, filled with wisdom, love, pleasure, and deep satisfaction in an atmosphere of showing God's reality through it all. God was a creative artist—in His image, we create the art of life and so sing a beautiful song that will be louder to our children's souls than the song of culture.

In what ways does the voice of Folly call out to your own children—or even to you? How can you silence her today?

Only give heed to yourself and keep your soul diligently, so that you do not forget the things which your eyes have seen and they do not depart from your heart all the days of your life; but make them known to your sons and your grandsons.

DEUTERONOMY 4:9

As I LOOK UPON THE LANDSCAPE of our culture, I believe that more than anything else, adults who love God with all of their hearts, practice righteousness, have a heart to reach others, and stand strong against the moral battles of this day are what is most desperately needed in our world. God intended for righteousness to be passed on from one generation to the next by discipling those children who would become these adults. He wanted parents to effectively pass on Kingdom messages and values and loyal allegiance to Him to those in the next generation. The key to building healthy, godly souls is providing a home where this life of Christ is lived, breathed, and taught.

Parents were God's finest idea of how such a legacy would be passed on to each generation. Mothers were designed to shape and influence the hearts of their children. We have the capacity to inspire messages of truth and hope, to model love and servant leadership, to build mental and academic strength by overseeing the education of our children, to lead in faith, and to build a haven of all that is good, true, and beautiful.

Satan would love to obscure such an important calling, so that generations would not be so well built. He works to diminish ideals of marriage, having children, family, our walk with God, and loyal love, the glue that holds all these relationships together.

My prayer for you this Mother's Day is that you will embrace your eternally significant role. I pray that every day you will have vision for understanding how much faithfully serving as a mom matters to God, your family, and the world.

MAY 11

As he thinks within himself, so is he.

PROVERBS 23:7

WHAT ARE THE MESSAGES YOU PLAY OVER and over in your heart and mind? Your life will reflect the voices you are listening to and the messages you are believing and rehearsing.

If you feel condemned, inadequate, or judged, perhaps you are hearing that God is disappointed with you, or that He is a God ready to condemn, a rule keeper—expecting more of you than you can give.

If you live in bitterness or anger, you are listening to voices that say life is unfair to you and God has not heard your prayers. Or perhaps you believe that no one really loves you and He is not really good.

On the other hand, if you are living with a real sense of His love and goodness, perhaps you are listening to messages that say, "There is now no condemnation for those who are in Christ Jesus" (Romans 8:1). Or perhaps this one: "Just as a father has compassion on his children, so the LORD has compassion on those who fear Him" (Psalm 103:13).

Maybe you are living in hope and peace of mind, and the message in your heart is, "We know that God causes all things to work together for good to those who love God, to those who are called according to His purpose" (Romans 8:28). Or it could be, "I know whom I have believed and I am convinced that He is able to guard what I have entrusted to Him until that day" (2 Timothy 1:12).

You are what you believe, and your actions show those beliefs to the world.

What are your actions telling those around you about what you truly believe? What messages do you need to start listening to?

In the beginning God created the heavens and the earth. . . .
God created man in His own image, in the image of God
He created him; male and female He created them. . . .
God saw all that He had made, and behold, it was very good.

GENESIS 1:1, 27, 31

IN GENESIS 1, we read that God created the heavens and the earth, and it was good. We can see the handiwork of the Lord—the intricacy of design—from snowflakes to zebras, an iris to a mimosa tree, the starlight at night to a rainbow after a storm. All of this speaks to the magnificence of our transcendent Creator God.

Family was thought up by God to give all people a place to belong. The family and home were to be a haven—a place where celebration would take place; a port in the midst of the storms where one could come for peace, strength, help, and security; a place of comfort amidst the demands and stresses of life. The rhythm of eating together, playing together, working together, and loving together was to be a circle of God's presence as seen through those made in His image to extend His love on the earth.

A mother and father were to be the inspirational leaders, providers, teachers, counselors, cheerleaders, spiritual guides, and friends to usher their children through life with emotional, physical, and spiritual health.

It is no wonder that Satan has sought to break up the family. If a person is isolated from all support and love and accountability that God intended to be his strength and foundation through his family, then he will be an easy target for the enemy.

A family, a home, a heritage is all worth fighting for. It is God's design, it is His way, the way of His best blessing—even in a fallen world—worth the cost for a future that is secure.

Do you see your family as a foundational part of God's design?

MAY 13

Above all, keep fervent in your love for one another,
because love covers a multitude of sins. Be hospitable
to one another without complaint.

I PETER 4:8-9

ONE OF MY FAVORITE CHILDHOOD memories is of the parties my parents hosted in our home. It was not unusual for us to have over a hundred people at a time for celebrations. We just opened up our whole house—the den, living room, dining room, kitchen, porch, yard—almost anywhere my parents could find room.

The week before a party, my mom and dad would put all of us to work. The boys would mow the yard and pick weeds and make everything outside beautiful. My mom and I would clean the house and begin cooking. On the day of a party, we would have to dress in our very best, and then we were instructed in how to greet guests and ask them interesting questions. We were also sent out during the evening to offer trays of cheese and crackers or cookies or deviled eggs or mini-sandwiches.

We grew up with lots of unusual people and learned somehow to love and enjoy the company of people of all different ages and personalities. My mom had come from a Southern home where people would put shared dishes on a table (potluck style) and stack plates high, then spread the love with adults sitting on chairs and porch swings and kids sitting on the steps or floors. In the South, in her little town, welcoming friends was just what you did.

My mother passed on the heritage to me. I sometimes have time to plan, and get to clean up everything ahead of time, but other times I just straighten a bit and hope no one will notice the dust!

Have you learned to enjoy offering the gift of hospitality in your
own home? Think about choosing a date in the future, and plan
a time to invite your friends to enjoy one another's company!

Listen to this, O Job, stand and consider the wonders of God.
Do you know how God establishes them, and makes the lightning
of His cloud to shine? Do you know about the layers of the
thick clouds, the wonders of one perfect in knowledge?

JOB 37:14-16

THICK PURPLE AND BLACK CLOUDS, sparkling crystal drops dangling from tree limbs, and mist dancing in the shadows of the trees met me this morning as I had my quiet time in the wee morning hours—it was a visual feast as is reputed here in the Colorado mountains.

I was thinking about how this kind of beauty sometimes calls to a deep longing in my soul for more—more of God, more of love, more of purpose and adventure and life. I think that these longings are here because we were created by God to experience deep intimacy, profound beauty, and heartfelt satisfaction. Yet Paul tells us that in this world we see as in a mirror dimly (1 Corinthians 13:12). These shadows of reality here are but a taste of what is to come. Our longings are there because God made us to have them fulfilled—and so they will be in His new heavens and new earth.

Before I awakened Joy, I lit the candles, prepared food and tea, and put on an old Celtic album that we love so that my little princess could come down the stairs to a few moments of civility and delight, devotion and prayer before beginning her normal day.

I have seen that when the atmosphere and table are set, as God had done for me in the beauty around me this morning, God shows up in special ways for my children, too, and allows us to have great moments of conversation and devotion together.

Have you enjoyed some of the beauty God has placed all around
you today? If not, stop now to take a moment to find it!

MAY 15

God created man in His own image, in the image of God He created him; male and female He created them. God blessed them; and God said to them, "Be fruitful and multiply, and fill the earth, and subdue it; and rule over the fish of the sea and over the birds of the sky and over every living thing that moves on the earth."

GENESIS 1:27-28

AFTER THE LORD HAD MADE A perfectly beautiful creation that expressed His artistry, craft, and design in magnificent ways, He created a perfect social system that would further show His design and wisdom. God wanted us to have our social needs met—the need for deep love, for overarching purpose and fulfillment. And so He created love, marriage, family, children, and heritage as the beautiful place in which human beings would find all that they needed to live abundantly and well in this gorgeous world God had created for them to enjoy and to rule over.

God was concerned that Adam would be alone, so He created a helper, suitable to companionship—both made in God's image—to look like Him, to reflect Him. God is intelligent, so they were made with intelligence. God manifests love and righteousness and authority, and so they were made to love and pursue righteousness and authority.

Then, of course, He blessed them and the first blessing out of His mouth was, "Be fruitful and multiply." Having children, as it says in Psalm 127, is a blessing from God, a good thing. We Clarksons are to ask, "What will our family do to bring God's image and messages and righteousness to bear on the earth? How will He use the Clarksons to bring His Kingdom work to reality?"

Take a moment to ask God what His specific plans are for your family. How does He want you to reflect Him in the world?

The seed whose fruit is righteousness is sown in
peace by those who make peace.

JAMES 3:18

SLOUCHED DOWN IN MY SEAT in a crowded railway car, I was being gently rocked to sleep by the rhythmic swaying of the old train clattering across the Polish country-side. I was returning from a student conference in the mountains that had left me a bit weary and depleted. I remember riding along in the car, wondering if I would ever not feel lonely.

Suddenly, the train took a small bend, and in front of me were fields of thousands of bright red poppies, gently swaying in the wind. I began to imagine the invisible hand of God intentionally spreading seed generously over the many fields, so that in a country where there had been so much division, war, and darkness for so many generations, there would still be a picture of His beauty, creation, and life to comfort those who would see it.

This has become to me a sort of picture of my place in the world. I desire that there be a harvest of righteousness in and through my life as big and expansive as the poppy fields of my memory. Today's verse would indicate that righteousness is sown by peacemakers. Jesus' whole being is focused on redeeming, buying back that which was lost, bringing life where there is death. I am most like Him when I, too, become a peacemaker, a redeemer, establishing peace where there is hostility, life where there is death. But the reason I so like the verse in James is that it gives us a picture of what we must do to bring this harvest of righteousness about—we must sow the seeds of righteousness, seed by seed, so that our harvest will be plentiful.

How can you sow seeds of righteousness and peace in your own home today?

MAY 17

Trust in the LORD and do good; dwell in the land and cultivate faithfulness.

PSALM 37:3

CLAY AND I SLEEP WITH OUR WINDOWS open throughout the summer, and in the early morning, cool breezes fill our room, inviting us to snuggle under our covers for just a little longer. One sweet summer morning I took a few moments to write down some thoughts that sprang to my mind.

"Fret not; it leads only to evildoing" was first on the list.

Now, "evildoing" sounds really bad—like robbing a bank, committing adultery, or murdering someone. Yet, my fretting's results seem much less extreme. When I am fretting, I am putting lots of effort into worrying about something that might happen, or worrying about a problem that has happened and doesn't seem to be going away!

I am a well-practiced fretter. It's as if I think, *Maybe if I fret a little bit more passionately, He will work more quickly!* And there are so many things about which to fret—finances, the kids' futures, ministry, health—the list goes on and on.

God is transcendent—outside of time and able to see the behind and before. He has already planned to be with me and available to me every step of the way. He has a plan, but I have a choice to make. I can either rest in that plan, accepting the limitations of this husband, child, family trouble, or life circumstance and trusting in God's ownership of my life and times. Or I can worry, fret, beg, stew, advise—and find more strife, emptiness, and frustration. This is what is precious in His sight—my loyalty, deep inside every day, when He knows what trusting Him costs me, and how hard it is to trust. I can make the decision to abandon it all unto Him or choose to fret about it for a few more days.

Choose to dwell in the land and cultivate faithfulness today— no matter the issue, the relationship, or the problem.

*I am the vine; you are the branches. If you remain in me and I in you,
you will bear much fruit; apart from me you can do nothing.*

JOHN 15:5, NIV

EVERY SPRING, I find myself itching to get my fingers into the soil to plant something! I don't want to be too hasty, for fear I will lose precious seedlings in this unpredictable Colorado climate. One fall I added about fifty to sixty tulip bulbs to my front yard, covered them with mulch and a prayer, and waited hopefully for spring. Each year they seem shy, barely poking their heads out of their protective leaves for the first warm week or two, but soon I have a colorful display with which to make beautiful bouquets.

As a gardener, you become a big part of giving life to a garden. Much work goes into it, from preparing the soil to planting the bulbs or seeds, watering everything as it grows, pulling weeds, pruning, nurturing, protecting . . . and the list goes on! All of this and more is needed to maintain life. What a huge amount of energy and responsibility it takes to maintain a living garden!

Gardening is a lot like our relationship with the Lord. When I think of the words that Jesus spoke in John 15:1-8, I understand that we need a Master Gardener in our lives. Jesus says He is the true vine and His Father is the gardener; we are unable to produce fruit on our own merits—just as my bulbs and tomatoes cannot thrive without the help of my gardening skills.

This spring, while out in my garden, I will continue to be in awe of the correlation between gardener and garden, God and mankind. I am so thankful that I have a Master Gardener in my life! I need Him every day to help me to grow, learn, and produce the fruit that glorifies Him.

*Do you garden? Ask the Lord what task may need
to be done in the garden of your soul today.*

MAY 19

It is vain for you to rise up early, to retire late, to eat the bread of painful labors; for He gives to His beloved even in his sleep.

PSALM 127:2

AFTER MY LAST CHILD WAS BORN, I found myself almost constantly in a state of exhaustion. Joy was my third child with nocturnal asthma, and I was up with her most nights as she gasped for breath. I was full into homeschooling my older children, having a ministry, and busy, busy, busy all the time. I suddenly came to a point where I was gaining weight, fighting to avoid depression and burnout, and I didn't know exactly how to get off the merry-go-round. When I went to a doctor, he said, "You can die early if you want to, but if you don't figure out how to get some rest, you will surely have serious consequences in your life."

It was a wake-up call for me. I realized that I needed to take hold of my life and make a plan.

I began to ask myself, *What things am I doing that are vain—creating too much work and stress and "painful labor"? Which activities are really not necessary or beneficial? How can I eliminate some of the "hurry up and get in the car so we won't be late" times that really add stress to all of us?*

I began to realize God had not given me more than I could do, so I needed to rest within the limitations of my season of life at that time. I began to say no to the expectations of other people that stole my energy and attention but did not build my core priorities. I had to ignore the false expectations and voices in my head that were telling me what I should do, and focus on my true desire to pursue what was best for me and my children.

How's your own emotional and physical health?
Are you, too, hearing a wake-up call? What might you
do to eliminate painful labor in your life?

*By the seventh day God completed His work which He had done,
and He rested on the seventh day from all His work.*

GENESIS 2:2

AFTER THE WAKE-UP CALL from the doctor I mentioned yesterday, I realized that God valued and modeled rest to us, and that I needed to begin organizing my life in a way that recognized rest as strategic and necessary.

So, not only did we establish our own weekly Sabbath rest day, but I instituted rest in the midst of every day at home.

On Sundays, we put away the work of the house—the typical Monday through Friday tasks. We established an afternoon teatime, so I would prepare or purchase something wonderful in advance. Around three on Sunday afternoons, after everyone had napped or played for a while, we would gather for a cup of tea and a delectable snack and read story or picture books, or perhaps just sit and talk, go for a walk as a family in the mountains, or watch a fun afternoon movie. We still do this every Sunday we are home.

I also established a rest time every day. Everyone would go to their rooms around two and have an hour of quiet time. I piled baskets of books and magazines in their rooms, and they could take a little snack with them to eat while they read during that hour. I would usually manage a cup of tea and thirty minutes or so by myself, which was a delight.

This became a parenthesis in my day, a time to sit just for a few minutes to regroup and to rest my mind, my emotions, and my body. Of course, no family is perfect, and there are always exceptions and interruptions, but it created space in my day and also contributed to turning my children into readers!

*Do you have plans for Sabbath and daily rest for everyone in your
house? How might you incorporate these ideas in your own way?*

MAY 21

A large crowd was following Him and pressing in on Him.

MARK 5:24

ONE SUMMER, we had sixty-two nights of overnight guests. That meant weeks on end of kids giving up their beds, washing stacks and stacks of dishes, laundering loads of sheets and towels, babysitting other children. One day, when one of my children looked out the window and saw a strange car drive up, he said, "Quick, everyone hide, and maybe no one will see us and want to come in!" I realized at this point, my kids needed a rest and a break from so much work!

One morning that summer, I got up at six to have a quiet time and a half-hour walk. Before I'd even settled into my chair, Nathan, who was preparing to leave for work, called up to me and said, "Hey, you wanna have eggs with me, and then we can talk? You make them, and I will eat them!"

When we finished, I realized it was time to awaken Joy and make her breakfast, as she is helping with the three-to-five-year-olds at VBS. Then Joel came in and said, "I will go shopping for you if you make a list."

As I got Joel and Joy out the door, Clay came in and said, "We really need to make a decision about some ministry issues." Forty minutes later, he left for work, so I took a walk in the heat rather than the cool, as the sun was fully risen by that time!

The moment I stepped in the door from taking the dog out, Sarah came in and said, "Can I just have a few moments of your time?" By then, it was almost eleven, and my whole morning had been taken up by everyone else. I had gotten none of my own plans accomplished—yet I'd done what I truly was supposed to do.

When this type of craziness happens in your life, do you see it as interruption or redirection? How might reframing it change your attitude?

*Just as we have many members in one body and all the members
do not have the same function, so we, who are many, are one body
in Christ, and individually members one of another.*

ROMANS 12:4-5

SOMETIMES I AM SO INTENT on keeping my head down and hand to the plow that I don't even recognize my need for other women. In days of old, people were born into and lived in their communities their whole lives. They knew their neighbors, and when they hung the laundry out to dry, they chatted over the fence with them. When they needed to borrow a cup of sugar, they went next door to that same friend they had known for years. Parents often lived in the same house as their adult children, and aunts and uncles and cousins would live nearby too.

Now, we live apart. Many of us attend churches of thousands, which are not in our neighborhoods. We don't usually know our neighbors, and we often have no values or background in common with those neighbors, anyway. So, we become used to fending for ourselves, until eventually we find ourselves exhausted, wanting to give up, and wondering where God has gone.

God's design was always for us to live in community. The family was to be a large group living together, loving each other, and sharing life and traditions together. There would be lots of children with similar values and close relationships, so moms could actually have a few minutes alone while the children played and ran and had whole-some fun.

No wonder Satan works so hard at creating isolation among us—because when we are alone in our homes, we naturally compromise our ideals, become discouraged, and listen to his voice of discouragement.

---

*Is there any way you can make changes in your life so you might
experience more of this community God designed you for?*

MAY 23

Mary . . . sat at the Lord's feet listening to what he said.
But Martha was distracted by all the preparations that had to be made.

LUKE 10:39-40, NIV

WHEN I HAD LITTLE BABIES, I had the illusion that someday, life would settle down and I would have more personal time to myself. Most moms find themselves saying, "Life will be easier when . . . the baby sleeps through the night/there aren't any more babies/all are out of diapers/all are reading/all can drive/all are through with these hormonal teen years . . ."

Yet, if we are not careful, we can fritter life away waiting for an elusive time in the future when we think all will be well and we will have more time to read, have quiet times, savor moments with our children, be sensitive to our husband's needs, or pray about what is on the heart of Jesus.

By doing that, we miss living today to its fullest and for God's glory. We miss the life that was the will of God.

We would all agree that we do not want to live the Martha life—always busy, busy, busy and a tad upset and grumpy, feeling sorry for ourselves, overwhelmed with the lists, having negative thoughts about our children, husband, and life. We do not always take the time to evaluate and see ourselves as we really are.

Mary dropped everything she had to do, sat at Jesus' feet, engaged her heart, listened intently, and worshiped. She was seeking and choosing what Martha was too distracted and busy to choose. There is evidently only one good path to choose, and it would not be taken away from Mary since she chose it.

What are you distracted by? What are you focusing on that is
stealing from your time? Your soul? Your emotions? Your body?

It is written, "You shall be holy, for I am holy."

I PETER 1:16

WE DON'T HEAR IT VERY OFTEN, but the Bible is clear that God wants us to walk in holiness. So what does it mean to be holy—set apart for God?

It means we have learned to view our lives in light of eternity. It is to live by scriptural principles—seeking first the Kingdom of God, laying up treasures in heaven and not on earth, numbering our days to present God with a heart of wisdom, loving God and our neighbors.

We must put away the sin inside our hearts. We root out idols in our lives, anything that we look to for our primary source of value or joy, whether money, television, social media, food, popularity, or any areas of sin we have not repented of.

Holiness means we must spend time in His Word. Will we truly listen to the voice of God?

A holy person is humble: meek, compassionate, and gracious to others. A proud person cannot be used by God, who gives grace to the humble but is opposed to the proud.

We must be committed to growing in love, because this is what pleases God. Loving means putting away anger and harshness and seeing the other person through the eyes of serving and encouraging them, not looking for what the person can do for me.

Holiness requires us to believe in God's presence, purpose, and attention, every moment, every day. Without faith, it is impossible to please Him. We believe during the dark times of life. We worship and sing to Him every day. We wait as long as it takes to see His answer to our prayers. We wait on God and God only.

What commitments to holiness have you made that keep you going?
No one can make you be faithful or strong, but God is cheering for you,
hoping you will stand fast, hold on, choose Him, and desire in your
heart to be holy and faithful to Him. What will you choose today?

MAY 25

Behold, I stand at the door and knock; if anyone hears My voice and opens the door, I will come in to him and will dine with him, and he with Me.
REVELATION 3:20

SOME DAYS I FIND MYSELF snapping at my children or feeling upset with someone over petty things. Later on in the day, I may realize that I haven't had my daily meeting with God. Without the investment of time with Jesus, of course, it is impossible to be spiritual!

Here are a few practical suggestions for meeting with God:

1. Find a time (or times) you can set aside to meet with God. Even five minutes is better than nothing! Do try to have a more leisurely time at least once a week. There is no specific time more holy than others—you can learn just as much at midnight as you can at early dawn. Whenever best suits you and your situation is the right time.

2. Read through the psalms, one each day. Circle or write down any truth it teaches you about God.

3. Do the same with the book of Hebrews. Look at Hebrews to learn the lessons of what pleases God, the attributes of Jesus, and His will for us to hold fast.

4. Read a chapter of Proverbs each day, and keep a list of what this book teaches you about folly versus wisdom.

Allow me to pray for you as you seek to regularly meet with God.

Lord, I pray that You will raise up women who will love You, seek You, trust You, and serve You with their whole hearts. Speak to them in their needs and issues of life, and help them to learn from You. Comfort them and guide them in wisdom. Bless these precious ones, I pray, and thank You so much for Your generous, unfailing love. We love and worship You. In Jesus' precious and wonderful name we come. Amen.

Which of the steps above can you take today to meet with God?

A soothing tongue is a tree of life,
but perversion in it crushes the spirit.

PROVERBS 15:4

I HAVE MET SO MANY TWENTYSOMETHINGS who have scars from their parents, whether by parents who never encouraged them, were too busy, or were just always critical of what their children did. "My parents never listened to me. They never understood me. They were always angry at me," these twentysomethings say.

But if we were to look at the Word, Jesus Himself, we would see intentional encouragement. "Peter, you are the rock" (see Matthew 16:18). "Nathanael, a man in whom there is no guile" (see John 1:47). To the centurion: "No one has had faith like you" (see Matthew 8:10). "Mary, your story will be told for all time" (see Matthew 26:13). Jesus always took time to show love by speaking words of life. He even believed in Peter and encouraged him as he was about to rebel: "Peter, Satan has desired to sift you like wheat. But I have prayed for you . . ." (see Luke 22:31-32).

Kind words held back could keep a person from hope, faith, and affirmation. And how many cruel words have caused children to be scarred, dreams dashed, hope obliterated? Jesus tells us we should be very careful of our words, as we will be held accountable for them someday (Matthew 12:36).

Encouraging and affirming words—words of life, as I like to call them—have power to give hope and strengthen others. If I, a grown woman, need them to keep me going through hard times, my children need them even more. Positive words act as water and sunshine to our souls to help them grow strong.

In Proverbs 15:4, how is a soothing tongue a tree of life?
How do bitter words stunt growth?

MAY 27

Like apples of gold in settings of silver is a
word spoken in right circumstances.

PROVERBS 25:11

STOMP, BANG, SLAM. "Everyone in this family is always losing things. If they would just be responsible, we wouldn't waste so much time looking for things all the time!" My sixteen-year-old son was getting ready to take the car to a friend's house, but we couldn't find the keys. Finally, we found them behind the refrigerator—of course, no one had any idea how they'd gotten there!

The bigger issue to me was the yelling, stomping, and banging around the house my son had done in his search. Somehow in my heart, though I was frustrated, I knew it was a time for grace.

I went to the kitchen and loaded my tray with a pot of hot tea, chocolate chip cookies on a plate, and a lit candle. Then, I took the tray into the tiny special spot in the back of my bedroom and turned on some instrumental music. The scene was ready. I told this child that I wanted to speak to him, "In my room—now!"

Dread filled his eyes. When we sat down on my couch, I poured tea, offered cookies, and began, "I just wanted to tell you how much I have come to appreciate you lately. I know it is hard to live in this crazy family sometimes, and we do lose things! I wanted you to know I understand your frustration and I love you."

Relief came over his face. "Wow, I thought I was going to get a lecture or something. Sometimes when I walk out the door of my bedroom, it is only minutes until someone irritates me. Have you ever felt like that?"

We ended up having a great time of friendship together. He felt understood, I had a chance to speak into his life, and the Lord worked in our midst.

Have you ever responded to a grumpy teen, an overtired toddler,
or overworked husband with tea and cookies and
an understanding word? You might try it sometime!

The LORD passed by in front of him and proclaimed, "The LORD, the LORD God, compassionate and gracious, slow to anger, and abounding in lovingkindness and truth."

EXODUS 34:6

OUR CULTURE IS FORMULA DRIVEN and impatient. We want to know what to do, how to do it, and when we can expect results so we can move on to the next issue. Surrounded by false teachings that offer "five steps to make your child obey," no wonder so many moms are tired and stressed and feel they have failed when their less-than-perfect children continue to act like children! Some children are out of control because they've been treated as objects of discipline and punishment instead of unique children with gender, personality, and maturity differences.

For many years, I have pondered Scripture regarding the ways God parents the Jews, as well as noticing how He parents me. Our heavenly Father is loving, gracious, and the Creator of beauty. His timetable for my life seems to be slower than I would plan if I were in charge. He doesn't seem to mind at all letting me suffer through circumstances, but instead He encourages me to hold fast, obey, stay strong, and wait for things rather than getting what I want immediately.

As I look at how Jesus worked with His disciples, I see He was patient with them and put up with their personality differences. He often observed that they didn't understand, and He allowed them to fail.

Aren't you thankful God loves you enough to stick with you, gently pointing out areas of your life that need work and allowing you ample opportunities to grow in those areas? I know I am!

With this kind of a patient, loving, accepting Father, I have no other choice but to be like Him as a parent to my children.

What qualities of God listed in today's verse from Exodus stand out to you most? Ask Him to make you more like Him in those areas.

MAY 29

The LORD appeared to Abram and said, "To your descendants I will give this land." So he built an altar there to the LORD.

GENESIS 12:7

DELIGHT SWEPT INTO MY HEART as Sarah and I sat on the couch, poring over an old Victorian magazine. Sipping tea, we delighted in the pictures of green, rose-covered English countryside, reminding us of so many memories from past wanderings there. I wish I could stay in those happy moments, or at least that they lasted longer.

But by morning, the sink of life is piled again with dirty dishes to be done. There is a never-ending pile of dirty dishes in my life because everyone insists on eating and drinking at least three times a day! And so with the stress of life . . . bills, a child's parking ticket, illness, the dog being sick, financial issues, doctor's appointments, cars, computers . . . it never ends!

One morning I was discussing these dirty dishes of life with a friend. She said, "You know, God doesn't want us to yell at the dishes or complain about them or cry over them or throw them across the room; He just wants us to take them in course, deal with them, and move on—and maybe even decide to have a good attitude about them every day."

Abram was a regular man, approached by God in the midst of his normal, daily life. He responded to God's call by making an altar and praising His name, right there in the sandy, weedy, spider-ridden piles upon which his sandals trod: those daily, messy places became altars, places of worship.

So, as I faced my sink this morning and also the dirty dishes of my life, I turned on one of Joel's CDs and danced and sang and made the place where I was standing an altar of my own praise, a place of worship and grace.

What are the dirty dishes of life that bother you most?
How can you make your own "sink" an altar today?

God is not unjust so as to forget your work and the love
which you have shown toward His name, in having
ministered and in still ministering to the saints.

HEBREWS 6:10

ALL OF US WHO HAVE LOVED and known Jesus have truth to share with those around us who are hungry and yet have no guidance or truth. Ministry means reaching out to those in our spheres of influence to share His words, His love, and His ways, knowing that when we see Him face to face, we will have to give an account for all that we knew and how we invested those truths for the benefit of those around us.

Studying the life of Jesus has set me on a different course in my ministry. God could have come to us as a king with miraculous powers and untold wealth, performing stunning spectacles for the whole world to see.

Instead, He came as a commoner. Down in the dirt with sinners, He washed their feet, put mud on their blind eyes, drew in the sand. Rejoicing in the joy of mothers, He caressed children, tousled hair, smiled into their shy little eyes. Sympathizing with the brokenhearted, He told stories of prodigals and accepted the touch of a forgiven prostitute as she poured out her gratitude upon His feet. He served meals, washed toes, gave words of life, and expressed His anger upon the self-righteous. His words, "Learn from Me, for I am gentle and humble in heart" (Matthew 11:29), continue to capture my imagination.

So, my life needs to characterize His life—as I learn to serve, love, give, and offer words of life, and as I invest in people one at a time, personally, face to face, life story to life story.

How are you offering the ministry of truth to others in your own life,
in order to follow the model Jesus gave of servant leadership?
Could there be something new the Lord wants you to begin doing?

MAY 31

The king gave the order, and they brought Daniel and threw him into the lions' den. The king said to Daniel, "May your God, whom you serve continually, rescue you!"

DANIEL 6:16, NIV

GASPING FOR BREATH, and turning blue at her lips, baby Sarah looked up at me with pleading eyes. "Please help me!" And so I held her in my arms, pleading for God's mercy and healing, not knowing what else to do after medicating, taking her to the doctor, and staying up with her for three nights.

"We have no money left. I can't find a job. I don't know what I am going to do," Clay said after working endlessly to get our ministry up and going, then coming to the end of our finances, many years ago. And so our family got down on our knees and sought heaven for an answer.

Do you desire to live a faith-filled life? Then you will come across great battles. When you are serious about God, you become involved in the spiritual battle between Satan and God, focused to see if there really is a remnant of faithful people who will believe in God, who will praise Him and wait for His provision like Daniel did in the lions' den.

How do we respond in these circumstances? It is at these times we are tempted to provide for our own needs, even as Abraham looked to Hagar, his solution to having a child, instead of waiting on God. Saul did not wait for Samuel's blessing and God's provision, and therefore lost his kingship and the blessing of God.

But this is our opportunity to say to the world, "I know whom I have believed, and I am persuaded that He is faithful and that He will answer."

Is today a lions' den for you? How might you take a step of faith?

Be still, and know that I am God.

PSALM 46:10, NIV

"I FEEL SO GUILTY! It seems I never have time with God lately," my sweet friend said. "With three children under five underfoot, when they finally go to bed, all I want to do is collapse. And honestly, I don't feel like spending the little time I have left studying my Bible."

When I had children of the same ages as hers, I thought someday my life would slow down and become more manageable, and then I'd have more time to study the Bible in a leisurely way. I am still waiting! While the intensity of the preschool years doesn't last forever, there will always be plenty of things vying for our time. That's why it's important to find a plan for meeting with God that works for each unique stage of our lives, recognizing that some days the best we can do is to talk with Him as we go about our tasks.

One day, when my kids were older and I thought I was on the brink of having more time, I was up early to have tea with Clay. I needed to take Joy to work by nine and Sarah to the doctor. Joel wrote to us about a big issue that he needed to make a decision about, and he wanted counsel. I had to pick up Joy after work and take her downtown to driver's ed, and then I was meeting with a friend. There were errands in town to run. At some point, I figured I should probably wash the previous night's dinner dishes, which were still in the sink because it was too late to face them when the activities of the day were over. Nathan asked me to do him a favor, which would take an hour in the middle of the day, and I still had articles to write, emails to answer, and . . . and . . . and.

See what I mean?

It is a choice of my will, a choice to worship Him, in the midst of my busy day— this day that He created for me to walk through. If I recognize this, then every minute is a minute spent with Him.

Your days may be overwhelming too. How can you be reminded
that each moment can be one spent with Him?

JUNE 2

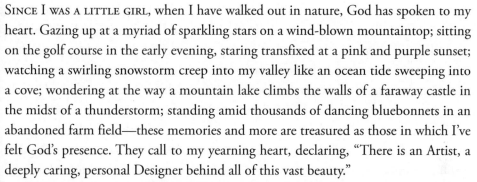

Behold, He who forms mountains and creates the wind and declares to man what are His thoughts, He who makes dawn into darkness and treads on the high places of the earth, the LORD God of hosts is His name.

AMOS 4:13

SINCE I WAS A LITTLE GIRL, when I have walked out in nature, God has spoken to my heart. Gazing up at a myriad of sparkling stars on a wind-blown mountaintop; sitting on the golf course in the early evening, staring transfixed at a pink and purple sunset; watching a swirling snowstorm creep into my valley like an ocean tide sweeping into a cove; wondering at the way a mountain lake climbs the walls of a faraway castle in the midst of a thunderstorm; standing amid thousands of dancing bluebonnets in an abandoned farm field—these memories and more are treasured as those in which I've felt God's presence. They call to my yearning heart, declaring, "There is an Artist, a deeply caring, personal Designer behind all of this vast beauty."

And so I became a walker, trekking miles and miles along mountain roads in Colorado, seashores on Prince Edward Island, city streets in Vienna, rivers and fields in Poland, all over the world, always finding new places to appreciate beauty and fellowship with its Creator. I learned that when fussing was inevitable and moods were tense, I could take my wee, precious ones out for a tromp in nature, where our ruffled souls would be soothed.

Even in the midst of my full days, I seek to walk or sit on my porch or find some way to bring beauty, nature, and peace into my home. It soothes my soul, supports creative and intelligent thought, and feeds and nurtures the life of my family.

Have you found solace and inspiration in God's beauty outdoors? Find a way to bring some inside today.

"Let him who boasts boast of this, that he understands and knows Me, that I am the LORD who exercises lovingkindness, justice and righteousness on earth . . . ," declares the LORD.

JEREMIAH 9:24

THE SMELL OF CINNAMON ROLLS fills the air as yet another birthday child comes down the stairs, ready for our well-worn tradition of a special breakfast to mark the day. I'm reminded that even as I take joy in planning for my children to feel loved on their birthdays with special treats and celebrations, I receive great pleasure when the child is blessed and responds to my preparations. God, too, delights in us coming to Him for provision and then responding joyfully when He gives it.

He has even provided things we don't "need," just to delight us—the reds, golds, browns, and oranges of fall leaves; the dark, steel blue of an ocean; the dark green or blue or amber of loved ones' eyes. He provided Adam and Eve with food with all sorts of tastes. He provided them with a garden of grand design to live in and clothing after they fell away from Him. Jesus provided the crowds with fish and loaves because they were hungry, and of course He has provided a way for us to be made right with God by offering His own body as the ultimate sacrifice. He has gone and is even now preparing to provide a place for us—a home in heaven—so we might be with Him in eternity.

Our children will learn how to recognize God as a provider as we provide for them—comfort during illness, food for feasting and celebrating life, music for dancing and singing. So these tasks we have in our homes are not meaningless, but filled with His very presence when we understand that in providing needs and desires, we are acting in the image of God.

God loves providing for you! How can you provide beauty or love or comfort to your family in the next twenty-four hours?

JUNE 4

I know that there is nothing better for them than to rejoice and to do good in one's lifetime; moreover, that every man who eats and drinks sees good in all his labor—it is the gift of God.

ECCLESIASTES 3:12-13

TODAY I HAVE BEEN BUSTLING around town, treasure hunting for anything that I think would add to soul-deep memories for my family. The Clarksons are traipsing off to the mountains this weekend, but this time, only the girls will be with Clay and me. I will miss my tall, young, idealistic boys who are out to make their way in the world. I was reflecting on what I would do if I had it to do over again.

I would stop unloading the groceries when my husband is talking to me and look deeply into his eyes and listen to what he is saying, communicating with my whole self, "You are such a treasure to me. I want to know what you are thinking and feeling and dreaming."

I would take the moment to tousle a head as I am passing through a room and say, "I am so blessed to have you as my very own child. You make me so happy, just being you."

I would stop what I am doing to go outside to look at a "treasure" when I hear, "Hey, Mama, come look!"

I would open my eyes to take a snapshot of the day just as it is, with children's noises, loud discussions, toys being played with intently, piano being practiced, thoughts being shared, messes coming and going.

I would laugh more, worry less, lecture only on rare occasions, overlook messes instead of wasting my time being neurotic, notice the fingerprints of my Maker in the moments of my days, and cherish those few years when we were all home, together, celebrating life.

What would you do differently? Why not start today?

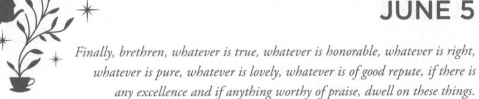

Finally, brethren, whatever is true, whatever is honorable, whatever is right, whatever is pure, whatever is lovely, whatever is of good repute, if there is any excellence and if anything worthy of praise, dwell on these things.

PHILIPPIANS 4:8

GRUMPY AND COMPLAINING, carrying around an Eeyore-type attitude, a woman in my extended family never failed to sigh deeply after almost everything she said. Though she was supposedly a mature believer who had been a Christian since childhood, her attitude always left me feeling discouraged when I would visit her home. I realized that this precious woman had high ideals, but her ideals did not include having a grateful heart! And so the spirit she cast on all who were in her wake was one of complaining and whining.

What we practice we will become. If we practice fear—being afraid of what life might bring our way or what could happen to our children at this point in history, worrying about our income stopping or slowing down, wondering what we would do if our child has an accident of some sort—then we will become progressively more fearful and frozen in our ability to trust God.

If we practice criticism of others, complaining and seeing them with a judgmental attitude, we will become even more harsh and critical, unloving and self-centered.

If we practice living in guilt and inadequacy, we will become small in our own minds and not enjoy God's grace and unconditional love.

Whatever we water in the souls of our hearts will certainly grow. And if we water these "weeds" in the garden of our souls, they will certainly take over and devastate the crop of faith, love, thankfulness, grace, and joy.

Our children will certainly follow our lead and become immature in the same areas of their own lives. What we sow, we will indeed reap.

What do you cherish in your heart and feel the right to rehearse over and over? Is it healthy? Is it producing life and peace?

JUNE 6

Everyone, after he has been fully trained, will be like his teacher.

LUKE 6:40

EVERYONE WANTS TO KNOW just what to do to have good results with their children, yet there is no one-size-fits-all answer. There is, however, one important key: you! I believe the key to raising excellent children is for you to grow in excellence. You cannot give your children what you do not possess. Buying the best curriculum or the most expensive lessons cannot compensate for shortcomings in your own life; as the Scripture says, your children will be like their teacher. We, as teachers and models, do not need to condemn ourselves for not being perfect. Yet, even as we look for a heart of obedience in our children, a willingness to try to please us, so He is looking for that intention in us.

I have found out that I can always accomplish more than I thought with God at my side. I can always work harder than I thought I had the capacity to work. And most of all, God's grace carries me through each weakness, failure, and sin, but He is always calling me to live beyond the place where I am, to grow more fully into the me He created me to be. If I am growing, learning, loving more, living more intentionally, He will bring excellence and growth into the very fiber of my family life. For indeed, the most important resource to my children in their life education is me, as I submit to God's training and calling on my own life, fully committed to being like Him, my Teacher.

*How can you encourage excellence of character by portraying
it to your children, your husband, and yourself? How is your
witness growing in goodness, beauty, and truth every day?*

The eyes of the LORD move to and fro throughout the earth that
He may strongly support those whose heart is completely His.

2 CHRONICLES 16:9

GOD PROMISES THAT He will support us, give us strength, and help us know how to take action. Because of their love and knowledge of God, many people in the Bible— including Esther, Daniel, David, Moses, Abraham, Ruth, Peter, and Mary, the mother of Jesus—displayed strength and took action in their own times. These are our models who give us hope to think that all of us, when filled with the Spirit of God, might do the same.

How do you move in the direction of receiving God's strength?

1. **Find those who, when you are with them, cause you to want to be better and more faithful and who inspire you to walk with God.** Whether in books, or in person, do what you can to be with them.

2. **Read biographies of faith-oriented people God has used.** Corrie ten Boom, Brother Andrew, Amy Carmichael, Hudson Taylor, George Müller, Ben Carson, Andrew Carnegie, Mother Teresa, Jim Elliot—there are so many who are inspiring because they were moved to take action in their generations.

3. **To know God, you must invest in His Word and prayer.** You could not deeply know someone with whom you never communicated. The more you are with God, the more you will reflect His influence.

4. **Regularly get away by yourself and observe the details of your life.** What is draining you? Where have you ceased to believe God? Is there any sin habit that is building an invisible wall between you and God? What activities are necessary, and which might be dropped?

How will you put yourself in a position to receive more
of God's strength in this season of your life?

JUNE 8

If we live by the Spirit, let us also walk by the Spirit.
GALATIANS 5:25

As GODLY MOTHERS, we strive to make the best possible decisions, set the perfect boundaries, and uphold the correct rules, which we believe will somehow cultivate spiritual children. However, there is a mysterious process by which the Holy Spirit leads our children to see their need for Christ even as we seek to cultivate their hearts.

We put *so* much pressure on ourselves as mothers. Each time we find ourselves too busy to cook, too exhausted to clean, or so hectic in our lives that we didn't do a devotional with our children one week, we feel defeated and believe that we failed.

Often, I receive comments or letters from mamas who say, "How did you seek joy? How did you manage to live by faith?" Then they will tell me about their very difficult circumstances or exhaustion or loss of job or marriage problem. The truth is, the grace of God is given in spite of our circumstances. His peace comes when our difficulties would suggest otherwise.

While it is wonderful to set our standards high and live within these great ideals, we must hold ourselves to a standard of *grace*, not perfection. We won't be able to have grace for our children if we do not have grace for ourselves. In my home, we did our best, but our best was certainly not perfection. We just committed our hearts toward our kids with a desire to shape their souls to respond passionately to their Creator. He came with grace and truth to bring life and wholeness into our hearts.

*Are there any ways in your life as a mom that you
are trying to live up to the false expectations of
others, rather than walking by the Spirit?*

JUNE 9

*Watch over your heart with all diligence,
for from it flow the springs of life.*

PROVERBS 4:23

WHEN YOU ARE TAXED BY your children, your friends, or your husband, what flows out from the depths of your heart? What you are pouring in will surely spill out in your words, your eyes, your attitudes, your actions. Filling our souls with beauty, goodness, humility, faith, and the love of Christ must be intentional so His life will be what spills over onto others when we are "squeezed."

Jesus said it is not the outside—our performance for others or attempts to do righteous works—that determines what a man or woman is like. It is possible to fool others because of our behavior, but it is never possible to fool God. He sees what we are like on the inside.

The starting point for spreading inspiration and faith is cultivating our own hearts. If a mama is reading Scripture, pondering the heart of Christ, worshiping Him, and following His ways, her children will draw the love and sweetness of Christ from her every day.

If a mama is engaging her mind in great books, learning new ideas, and stretching her own intellect, her children will also benefit.

If a mama is developing her character and taking small steps to become more self-disciplined, more of a servant leader, more patient, and more generous with lifegiving words because of her obedience to Christ, her children's souls will be watered by the strength of her obedience.

If she engages herself in meeting the needs of others and reaches out with the redeeming message of Christ, her children will learn not just to hear words of the gospel, but to live the gospel.

*Don't worry primarily about having the right rules, the best formula,
the right books. Be concerned, instead, for your soul—what are you planting
there? What are you watering in the depths of your heart attitudes?*

JUNE 10

The land through which we have gone, in spying it out,
is a land that devours its inhabitants; and all the people
whom we saw in it are men of great size.

NUMBERS 13:32

As LONG AS I CAN REMEMBER, there have been giants in my life. All stand before me threatening my stability and security, and all seem greater than my ability to conquer them. A giant is a picture of those obstacles or issues that come into our lives and tempt us to live in fear or cause us to wonder whether God has left us.

My giants are of differing sizes and threats: financial need, fears of how a child will turn out, marriage stresses and pressures or misunderstandings, deep loneliness, medical problems, relationship issues, weariness, and often fear of the future.

The story of the negative report brought back by the spies Moses sent out is such a picture of what happens when we see giants and don't face them with God's strength. We become as grasshoppers in our hearts; we become small-minded, fearful, and ineffective. God gives us over to our faithlessness and we end up "wandering in the wilderness."

In Scripture, giants gave people a great opportunity to glorify God—to see His faithfulness, to believe in His goodness, and to conquer. I think it's the same today. We really can't walk with God and hold on to fear and disbelief at the same time! Our heart has only enough room for one or the other. Sometimes we say, "I feel like God is far off and doesn't even hear my prayers," when in actuality we have left His presence and companionship by disbelieving in the midst of our fears.

Caleb and Joshua saw the situation differently than the other spies. They saw the giants, but they saw God and His strength more clearly. They believed He would conquer and lead them in victory. Because of their faith, they were the only men who survived the forty years of wandering in the desert and were allowed to enter the Promised Land.

Which looms largest in your life—your giant or your God?

David said to the Philistine, "You come to me with a sword, a spear, and a javelin, but I come to you in the name of the LORD of hosts, the God of the armies of Israel, whom you have taunted."

I SAMUEL 17:45

YIKES—HOW OFTEN HAVE I SEEN God's faithfulness and then looked at the next giant with fear and disbelief, as though God had never worked in my life! Sometimes I just get tired of giants and want things to go easily for a while. Am I grumbling against Him when the giants come, or resting and waiting patiently for His solutions?

David shows me how I am supposed to face my giants. Though they mock the reality of God in my life, I must face them in the name of the Lord of hosts. I am learning that God is stronger than all of my giants. It is a waste of time to live by fear, because when I give my giants into His hands, I can find rest for my soul.

But where does this battle take place? In my heart. It happens when I am alone in my bedroom pondering my issues, feeling the darkness, yet knowing God sees me and all I am facing. He knows when I choose to say, "I will believe. Even though I don't feel faith, I will choose today to praise You, to put one foot in front of the other, to be grateful, by faith, for Your presence, for this child, this circumstance."

Old giants will be defeated. New ones will come. But, this life, these giants, are the only opportunity I have to live a story of faith and show God's glory. This is how I will model faith in my home, so that my children can learn how to face their giants.

Today, I will look my giants in the face and see God's shadow towering over them, the Lord of hosts fighting for me.

What are your giants? How are you facing them?

JUNE 12

This hope we have as an anchor of the soul, a hope both sure and steadfast and one which enters within the veil.

HEBREWS 6:19

"MAMA, ONE OF THE THINGS THAT most distinguishes you is that you are always a hopeful person. No matter what would happen, you always pointed us to hope." How surprised I was to hear Joy say this, as I have often struggled through the many challenges that threatened to overcome us over the years.

Many years ago, I realized children long to have a happy mother. They are growing up in a time when media spreads the gloom and doom of catastrophes, fears, and threats. When mama spreads light, thankfulness, and hope in the darkness, her children feel secure and safe. But when mama lives darkly, the children harbor fear and insecurity and blame themselves for their parents being angry or sad. Hope is not natural; hope is supernatural. It wells up from deep inside because of a belief that God is good, that He will win in the end, and that there is always hope when God is present.

Women who choose to hope and to trust God are those who, instead of cursing the darkness, light a candle. But it is a choice of the will. Hope is not a feeling; it is a commitment to hold fast to what Scripture reminds us is true about God.

We live in an imperfect world filled with disappointments, devastation, and difficulty. Without hope, our lives can feel purposeless sometimes. In my own life, I have struggled with hardships I never could have seen coming. My heart has been broken, my faith has been tested, and I have had to push myself in ways that I couldn't have imagined. Difficult circumstances will come our way, and we will always have a choice to make. We can choose to give up, or we can choose hope.

Have you understood hope as not a feeling, but a choice?

May the God of hope fill you with all joy and peace as you trust in him,
so that you may overflow with hope by the power of the Holy Spirit.

ROMANS 15:13, NIV

OH, TO ALLOW THE HOLY SPIRIT to fill me to overflowing with hope!

Hope is not just wishful thinking. Hope is an assurance that our King has ultimately won the raging battle. Hope teaches us that this is the broken place where we have the honor of believing Him who is fighting on our behalf. When we have nothing else to rely on, our hope in God is what connects us to what is true.

Faith requires us to relinquish our fears, doubts, and worries into the hands of God, like a child who says, "I will trust my mama and daddy because I know they are good and reliable." So we say, "I will give this difficulty into His hands because I know He is good and loving and reliable."

Hope gives us the strength to take on our future. No circumstance, no problem, no issue, no devastation is too large or too difficult for God to take on. However, we have to *choose* this hope. We must receive it. Sometimes, life can beat us down and make us feel absolutely defeated. But when we choose to carry the hope God has given us, we are able to overcome *anything*.

My hope rests in God's character and ability to see me through. In Him who answers prayer. In Him who is always good. In Him who has overcome the world. In Him who has forgiven every sin. In Him who will never leave me or forsake me. I can leave my issues in the file drawer of heaven and know that He has the ability to work them out and to cause "all things to work together for good to those who love God" (Romans 8:28).

What is the value of hope?
Where does it come from? How does it guide us?

JUNE 14

The hand of the diligent will rule,
but the slack hand will be put to forced labor.

PROVERBS 12:24

TIME CHANGES FROM so much travel had left me so exhausted, I thought I would fall asleep standing up. An unusual seven weeks straight of traveling had me coming and going constantly as I flew back and forth across the country. After my final trip home, Joel met me at the airport, whisked my bags away, and drove me home.

Home sweet home called my name as we pulled into the driveway. As I walked in the door, I saw that candles were lit, music was playing softly, and the table was set with warm bowls of soup and crusty herb bread. Fresh flowers and a "welcome home" sign greeted me in the sweep of entering the front door.

"Welcome home, Mama. I bet you are ready to sleep in your own bed for a long while," Sarah commented as she put the last bowl of soup on the table.

What a treat! Finally, my labor had come to fruition. My children had "caught" it!

The values I had in mind when I prepared my home this way day after day, month after month, year after year, have become their own standard of what a home should "speak" to people when they walk into it.

A mama has to be a servant leader who provides a wonderful sanctuary for her children, so they will want to be a part of continuing to make it a sanctuary. Sometimes, the laboratory of life is a mess and you can't quite see what is being accomplished except just existing. But building these homey ideals into the warp and woof of life as the children grow with you creates habits and gives them a solid foundation for building beauty and order and comfort in their own homes.

Are your children learning to work alongside you to make
your home comfortable? Or do you tend to do it all?
Remember, they need to learn these skills too!

JUNE 15

Everyone must be quick to hear, slow to speak and slow to anger.

JAMES 1:19

WHEN JOEL WAS LITTLE, he played with Legos for hours a day. He would design elaborate cars, towns, houses, roadways—whatever he could imagine. When he was nine, he worked for months on a town that became an elaborate creation, around five feet wide. One day we hosted a new family for lunch, who had a boy Joel's age. When they went to Joel's room to play, the little boy rushed into the room and began hitting and destroying the whole of Joel's creation before we could pull him away. The devastation was complete and broke the hearts of our whole family.

Joel seemed to have a cloud around him for several days. Time had taught me that he had a very strong sense of justice. Every time I sat down to talk with him, it was clear that he needed sympathy.

So I went into his room and sat down with him. "Joel, I can't even imagine how bad this made you feel. I would be so hurt. What bothered you the most?"

"It was the injustice of it all. He had no right to be so destructive. I had never done anything to him. It took me almost a year to build all of these pieces. I just thought it was so unfair," Joel ended with a sigh.

"I so understand and want you to know how very, very sorry I am. It was unkind and unjust."

Then I prayed with him and blessed him.

That night, he said, "Mama, I think I can be strong now and build a whole new city. I just wanted someone to listen to me and to understand. Thanks, Mama."

*Do you know your children well enough to discern
their needs when they are out of sorts? Ask the
Lord to help you see into their hearts.*

JUNE 16

Rejoice in the Lord always; again I will say, rejoice!
Let your gentle spirit be known to all men. The Lord is near.

PHILIPPIANS 4:4-5

LIFE IS A CONSTANT CHALLENGE, every day, all the time. Things quit working, someone makes a mess, a situation just isn't fair. But what can make it worse is children and adults who whine and complain all the time. The habit of whining and complaining turns quickly into an attitude of self-absorption, which destroys hope, light, and beauty.

Of course, it is not wrong to be sad or depressed because of a tragedy. God is the One who gave us the ability to have emotions. We all long for and need people who will sympathize with us, to comfort us for the pain, brokenness, and injustices in life. God Himself wants to comfort us, and we heal more quickly if we have someone to help bear our burdens.

We have the opportunity to work with our children in hard or unfair situations to help them learn to be strong and mount up over their difficulties. This is what character training is all about—helping our children become stronger one day at a time. It is our will that chooses to have faith in God, that learns how to persevere under trial, that chooses to love the unlovely, that shows generosity to the needy. The will is what makes heroes, strong marriages, and legacies of faithfulness.

As we gently enter into the recesses of our children's hearts and understand their feelings, we can then teach them to be strong inside, but with tender, grateful hearts. Our attitudes are the place where real strength and spirituality are expressed. When we approach our children with attitudes of gentleness and patience, we lead them to embrace these same patterns.

This week, look at your own heart. Is it joyful?
Are you modeling to your children an uncomplaining spirit?

He who is slow to anger is better than the mighty, and
he who rules his spirit, than he who captures a city.

PROVERBS 16:32

RULING OVER ONE'S SPIRIT is such an amazing concept. When you help your child to learn to control his spirit and to rule over his emotions, you are giving him a gift that will serve him the rest of his life. I had to learn right alongside my children!

In a culture that has fast food, air travel, and nearly instantaneous responses to communication, the value of patience has become lost. Yet, patience is the virtue that will cause us to grow spiritually like no other. Waiting for our prayers to be answered forces us to look to God, to humble ourselves before Him, to acknowledge our dependence on Him.

God has wisdom, and He has a plan. He works to build spiritual muscle slowly, because His focus is on building character and the likeness of Christ in our lives. Holiness does not come from a quick fix.

Satan prowls the earth to see whom he may devour. The earth is in rebellion against God. If we are to resist evil and overcome it with good, we must learn the value of waiting patiently in the midst of life's storms. Weeping is for the night, but joy comes in the morning, as the psalms say.

All of life in a fallen world requires us to be patient and to rule over our impatient spirits. We do not walk by emotions or whims, but we learn to walk in obedience to the path God has given. Then, His reward will be sure and generous.

The value of training and teaching our children to put off self-gratification is great. Gently helping them to choose patience, to will to be strong, to wait on God, is to prepare them to understand how to live their lives for Him rather than themselves.

Do you feel you are a patient person?
How might you build more muscle in this area?

JUNE 18

Whatever you do in word or deed, do all in the name of the Lord Jesus, giving thanks through Him to God the Father.

COLOSSIANS 3:17

THERE'S ONE THING CHILDREN want that we seldom consider: a happy mama. Happiness is not always a feeling, but a choice that comes from a heart that desires to please God. Happiness is an attitude that says, "This is the day the Lord has made! I will rejoice and be glad in it."

How to develop this attitude little by little is another thing altogether. These are some things I have done to cultivate happiness in my home which you might consider:

- Fix your eyes on Jesus and talk to Him before you even step out of bed.
- Greet your children or husband with a blessing when you first see them. Kiss your husband in front of your children—this makes them feel happy and secure. Take the time to tell him good-bye before he goes to work.
- Say things like . . . "I am the most blessed mama in the world to have you as my little boy." "Good morning, sunshine. I am happy to see you this morning!"
- Put on music at different points all day.
- Light candles a lot because they can make you feel civilized.
- Institute an afternoon teatime.
- Place things in your life that give you happiness or a sense of fun. Think flowers, walks at sunset, back rubs, sitting on the deck and watching the pines sway in the wind, etc.
- Practice being thankful every day—take time to look at the antics and into the eyes of your children and thank God that they are with you now.

Today, put some of these ideas into practice. And thank God when you see flowers, stars, color, sunsets, all the things He made every day for us to enjoy. May your days be happy and bright!

We are ambassadors for Christ,
as though God were making an appeal through us.

2 CORINTHIANS 5:20

EXCELLENCE OF CHARACTER CAPTIVATED my attention many years ago when, as a young missionary, I was challenged to move into Communist Eastern Europe to draw people to Christ. I accepted the challenge, and part of the preparation was a great deal of training. One of the pictures of ministry presented to us then has stayed with me all these years and influenced my parenting—the idea that I am to be an ambassador for Christ.

An ambassador is a diplomat of the highest rank chosen to represent his or her country in a foreign land. As such, ambassadors must represent the messages, values, and wishes of the country they represent. They must also maintain the highest character so that their position of influence will impact the people they serve in the most positive manner. In today's verse, Paul's description of us as "ambassadors for Christ" to the nonbelieving world beautifully captures the idea: "as though God were making an appeal through us; we beg you on behalf of Christ, be reconciled to God."

I caught a picture in my young life that as an ambassador for Jesus and His Kingdom, I was to represent His love by being generously loving and kind. As He is righteous, I was to be righteous; I was to practice godly integrity in front of the people I was seeking to reach. As an ambassador of Christ, I was to represent Him in every situation. Consequently, when God blessed me with children, I already had in mind that I would prepare them to become the best representatives, the best ambassadors for Christ, wherever He would lead them.

Are you aware that you, too, are an ambassador?
What might change to make you a more effective one?

JUNE 20

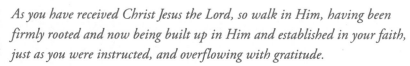

As you have received Christ Jesus the Lord, so walk in Him, having been firmly rooted and now being built up in Him and established in your faith, just as you were instructed, and overflowing with gratitude.

COLOSSIANS 2:6-7

IT WAS A SUNNY TEXAS DAY, and my children were laughing and fussing, squirming in their breakfast chairs. We had just decided to begin a ministry, which meant leaving behind a reliable salary, and when we came to prayer at the end of our devotions that morning, we told the children simply that we needed to see God provide financially for our family. Would they pray that too?

Their little faces grew very solemn (although this did not in the least stop their squirming). They squeezed their eyes shut and held hands tightly together where they sat at the table, and each of them prayed in their high voices that God would give us what we needed.

Clay went straight to his office after breakfast, and the kids and I finished the dishes and gathered in the living room to start our day. But before we could begin, Clay was back with news of an amazing discovery. On picking up the morning mail, he found in a national news magazine the story of a particular class-action lawsuit settlement. There was still one week left to file a claim before the lawsuit was closed. He did, and the amount we received would adequately meet our need for funds for months to come. When we told the kids, their eyes were wide with wonder at the fact that God had answered their prayers.

"Mama," said Sarah, "God really heard us, and it worked. Isn't that amazing?"

Have you invited your children into your own practical prayers, so they can see God move on your behalf?

JUNE 21

A friend loves at all times.

PROVERBS 17:17

As THE SUN SET, casting shadows around our kitchen as I made dinner, my little girl walked in slowly and sat at the kitchen counter. Tears welled up in her round, brown eyes as she put her elbows on the counter and held her face in her hands. "Mama," she started, and it all came tumbling out. "I thought that Christians were supposed to be different. I can't believe my friend would lie to me and then get mad at me for talking to her about it. It just doesn't seem fair!"

The whole story eventually came out through stops and starts of tears and sniffles. The cause of Joy's woe was a very close friend who had gotten angry, yelled harsh words, and stomped out when Joy tried to talk to her about a sensitive issue. I came around the counter and held my heartbroken daughter closely, helping her to wipe her eyes.

"How about we have a cup of tea together and talk about it?" I asked.

With candles lit a few minutes later, hot chocolate chip cookies ready to be dunked in milk, and tea steeping, I sat down with my sweet girl as she settled in on the couch.

"Mama," she started, "you've always quoted that proverb about 'a friend loves at all times.' I didn't really know what that meant until tonight. Gossip and fighting and drama are awful. I don't really feel like loving, but that verse means I'm supposed to be committed to my friend, no matter what, right? Just like Jesus is committed to us, even when we sin against Him."

I nodded and squeezed her hand as her tears flowed again. She smiled a wobbly smile and leaned close to me.

"It really costs a lot to be a good friend, doesn't it, Mama?"

Do you have a friend who is good at loving you at all times?
Ask God to help you maintain your commitment to friendship.

JUNE 22

The fruit of the Spirit is love, joy, peace, patience, kindness, goodness, faithfulness, gentleness, self-control; against such things there is no law.

GALATIANS 5:22-23

ONE OF MY GLORIES AS a mother was realizing that I had the opportunity to form the hearts and life habits of my children. Together, Clay and I had a never-to-be-repeated time to shape the faith of our children and to train them in godliness from their earliest years.

One of the ways we did this was to create a list of character standards for our home, family, and personal lives. Each of what we called "our twenty-four family ways" was backed with Scripture and a character quality definition. These became the language of biblical family values we wanted to instill in our children.

Clay was mostly responsible for the twenty-four ways and later turned them into a devotional and discipleship resource for families. *Our 24 Family Ways* included statements of biblical family values such as

1. We love one another, treating others with kindness, gentleness, and respect.

2. We serve one another, humbly thinking of the needs of others first.

3. We are thankful to God for what we have, whether it is a little or a lot.

4. We choose to be peacemakers, even when we feel like arguing.

There were also five days of family devotional outlines for each of the ways, which we would go through together as a family. Along with teaching our children the ways, we helped them memorize the Bible verse or passage for each way. We discussed the ways and used them as part of our discipline and training in the home, not only for confronting sinful attitudes, but much more for encouraging good ones.

What character qualities do you feel are the most important to pass on to your children?

Let your speech always be with grace, as though seasoned with salt,
so that you will know how you should respond to each person.

COLOSSIANS 4:6

ONE SUMMER, Nathan was invited to spend several weeks at a friend's home. He was deeply excited, as this presented an adventure all his own and would also be the first time he had flown on an airplane by himself. With a dozen motherly admonitions, I sent him off and told him to be sure to call me when he arrived safely. My phone rang that evening, and as I answered, his excited voice bubbled over through the receiver.

"Hey, Mama. It was so much fun to fly by myself. And you will never believe what happened! The flight attendant talked to me during the whole flight because I had a seat at the front. I remembered to ask her questions instead of doing all the talking. I thanked her when she served me. I told her I appreciated her helping me when I was looking for my seat. She said, 'You know, Nathan, you are one of the politest boys I have met in a long time. It was really a pleasure having you on my plane!' Can you believe she said that about me, Mama? I felt just like I was an adult!"

When I recovered from my shock, I smiled and congratulated him as heartily as I could. In the midst of that proud mama moment, I realized that all of those minutes, hours, days, weeks, and years of hard work and training had truly paid off. After all of those times when I wondered if Nathan was listening, I realized that he had taken it in after all. He actually knew how to be polite! Renewed in my resolve, I kept on with my training, and Nathan was ready for more when he got home.

Isn't it nice when someone else compliments your child
and they pass it along? Who might you encourage
with an unexpected word of grace today?

JUNE 24

The Son of Man did not come to be served, but to serve.

MARK 10:45

I ALWAYS FOUND THAT THE best way I could teach my children how to serve with a willing and joyous heart was simply to be a model of the kind of attitude I wanted them to learn. And I found that when I took the time to serve them personally, their hearts softened and they were willing to listen to my training.

Joy, my youngest child, has always responded to gifts of service. One year, when we were going to be out of town a lot, I had the idea of helping Joy pack her suitcase, something she usually did on her own. She had seemed particularly moody and unhelpful in the previous few days, but I just sat on the floor in her room as we worked together to select outfits and shoes and fit them all into her suitcase. The longer we sat, the chattier she got, and I watched her countenance soften. When I stood up at the end, she hugged me and said, "Thanks for serving me, Mama. I know you're busy, but it means a lot to me."

Companionship—having my children serve alongside me—was a way to teach my children how to serve. Clay and I involved the kids in almost every aspect of our ministry from the start. Sarah and Joel sealed envelopes and stamped newsletters, all of them babysat kids of the parents we counseled, they served at conferences and carried suitcases for the moms who came to our ministry events. "If it is God's will for us to be in ministry, it's God's will for you to be too," we said. We started every conference with an evening of training for our kids and the volunteers, talking about why we ministered and what kind of heart we wanted them to have for our guests.

If your children's actions and attitudes are at least in part
a reflection of you, are you happy with what you see?
Ask the Lord to change what He needs to change.

JUNE 25

Make it your ambition to lead a quiet life and attend to your own business and work with your hands, just as we commanded you, so that you will behave properly toward outsiders and not be in any need.

I THESSALONIANS 4:11-12

FROM THE TIME MY CHILDREN could do chores, they heard mom talk about work. I knew that one of the most vital qualities I could pass on to them would be a good attitude about work. A healthy, biblical attitude in this area would influence their chosen vocation in life, their relationships with authorities, and even the harmony of their own future homes and families.

A good work ethic is central to a whole and well-rounded life; embracing work, in whatever form it would take in their lives, would enable my children to flourish as adults. The apostle Paul said it clearly: "Whatever you do, do your work heartily, as for the Lord rather than for men" (Colossians 3:23).

Unfortunately, work is not a neutral term—it comes to us weighed down with negative associations and connotations. We've been taught by culture, and by our sinful and self-centered natures, that work is bad, an annoying distraction from our desire to enjoy the pleasures of life. It's something to be avoided and minimized, and, if necessary, endured.

But work was part of God's created order in Genesis 1 and 2, before sin's curse in Genesis 3 made it hard and onerous. When God called His completed creation "very good" (1:31), that declaration included work. God designed us originally to take pleasure in work—to create, subdue, and bring order and meaning to all that we are entrusted with by Him. God worked to create the world, and that quality of His image is also in us as His image-bearing creatures. As mothers, created in His image, it is our privilege to model and teach a healthy attitude about work to our children.

Sometimes I need to check on my own attitude about work! Does yours need an adjustment today?

JUNE 26

You ought to say, "If the Lord wills, we will live and also do this or that."
But as it is, you boast in your arrogance; all such boasting is evil.
Therefore, to one who knows the right thing to do and does not
do it, to him it is sin.

JAMES 4:15-17

WHEN I WAS JUST OUT OF college and a new staff member with Campus Crusade for Christ, one of my directors gave a powerful talk on the need for missionaries in then-Communist Poland. As he spoke, I felt conviction grow in my heart, and I heard a voice in my head saying, "Those people need us to help them!" When the talk was over and a general invitation was given to join the new team being formed to take the gospel to Poland, I rushed forward, sure I would be one of hundreds who wanted to apply. Instead, I found that I was one of only four.

Because of the great change that God's love had made in my own life, I was ready to do anything to bring that love to other people. God's love made me an initiator.

As I began to raise my children, I remembered the call to Poland and the few who responded. I resolved that my children would become first responders and initiators. I wanted them to be the ones who would hear the call and step forward to help. I wanted them to be active members of God's Kingdom. I knew that meant training them to take initiative in every area of their lives. As Winston Churchill said, "The price of greatness is responsibility."

Do you see yourself as an initiator? In what area might you know
a right thing to do . . . which you haven't yet begun doing?

Thus says the LORD, "Stand by the ways and see and ask for the ancient paths, where the good way is, and walk in it; and you will find rest for your souls. But they said, 'We will not walk in it.'"

JEREMIAH 6:16

TOO OFTEN TODAY, children are starving for real life and drowning in the midst of an empty one.

The old-fashioned way seems to be the healthiest way to raise emotionally, intellectually, physically, and spiritually resilient children. When they are constantly using technology for entertainment, children's brains have been shown to slow down because they are overstimulated, and their undeveloped eyes and brains cannot process what they are taking in. Because many children are deprived of what their bodies and brains are designed for—rest, play, curiosity, interaction with real people and real experiences, and problems to solve—there is a diminishing of their long-term emotional, spiritual, and mental health.

Children need to be outdoors. They need time to be bored. They need to be around books, have lots and lots of imaginative stories read to them, and then have time to act out the stories. They need lots of time with adults so that they can pattern their values and manners and relationships after mature people rather than always being in the company of immature children or exposed to digital images that display violence, foolishness, and questionable values.

May all children be blessed with the gift of play, imagination, free time, and the space to be outdoors to explore. May they wonder at the marvels of God's creation. May they have the treasure of real human beings who hold their hands while they explore the world, who rock them to sleep and sing them real songs and scratch their backs at bedtime and tell them their own love stories. And may they daily hear the words of their Creator God, marvel at His excellence, and grow to love Him with all of their hearts.

What can you do to ensure your children have the benefits of time for imagination and free play?

JUNE 28

I can do all things through Him who strengthens me.

PHILIPPIANS 4:13

NEGATIVE ATTITUDES OF the heart—whining, complaining, discouragement, defeatism—can affect our ability to endure. As I told my children, those are all natural responses to difficulty. Endurance requires the habit of faith, which you can intentionally train in your children.

The basis for a life of endurance is faith in a holy and good God. Your children need to have Scripture in their minds so that when they meet discouragement and fear, they can speak words of truth into their struggle.

Encouragement helps your children endure by faith; positive words will narrate steadfastness into their lives. Instead of lecturing your discouraged child, or verbalizing disappointment, articulate your belief in them. "I believe you can do this. I can't wait to see what God does with your life. I'm so proud of you. Keep trying. You're getting to be so strong. Don't give up." Your words of affirmation will become solid ground they can stand on to take the next step.

Narrate hero stories. One of the best and most delightful ways you can teach your children what enduring faith looks like is to read stories about heroism. Read to your children stories of biblical heroes, of missionaries, of historical people who lived their whole lives with an enduring faith in God. For Christian stories, we loved the Hero Tales series by Dave and Neta Jackson. We also read books about William Wilberforce, Abraham Lincoln, and many other historical figures—men and women who influenced their generations in heroic ways. We read biographies of great scientists, artists, inventors, explorers, statesmen, and teachers who endured with faith in order to change the world through their lives. Every story you read with your children feeds their imagination of what it looks like to be brave, to be gracious, to endure hardship, and to win the race.

What's your favorite method for encouraging your children (and yourself!) to endure?

WE ALL KNOW WHAT IT IS LIKE to be around a whiner or selfish person who has to be treated special, whose needs must always be met for them to be happy. Perhaps you are married to a selfish person—or maybe you are one! Most selfish adults come from homes where the selfishness was not curbed or trained out.

How do we teach our children to give up their belongings, their time, their lives to others?

1. **Teach your children to share and help one another from the very beginning.** "You are such a strong boy, and I can see that Joy needs your help. Would you please help her carry her box of toys to her room?" "More people came to this gathering than the hosts expected. Let's stay back and let the others eat first, so we can be sure there is enough for all the people who came. We can order a pizza on the way home."

2. **Teach your children Bible stories and hero stories about those who gave,** such as the little boy who gave his lunch so Jesus could feed the five thousand. Show your children that Jesus looked out on the crowd and had compassion, and say, "I wonder who needs our compassion. Let's look out for people God brings our way to encourage, or to give something to."

3. **Plan real ways for them to give and share.** Have them give up their rooms when company comes and sleep on the floor of your bedroom. Then praise them, of course! Let praying for, loving, encouraging, and serving others be the oxygen of your home.

Teaching them to live like this takes years and lots of time and planning, but you will give them the gift of an unselfish heart that serves and character that will give them contentment and self-control for the rest of their lives.

How might you offer your children an opportunity to share or give today?

JUNE 30

All the paths of the LORD are lovingkindness and truth to
those who keep His covenant and His testimonies.

PSALM 25:10

CLAY AND I, LIKE MOST PARENTS, had little conception when we started the journey what we were doing, and even less what it would require of us. We agreed that parenting was the best of all the ministry we've done in our lives, but we had no idea what that investment in our children would cost us physically, emotionally, spiritually, and financially. It is only now that we can begin to observe the dividends. Whatever lifegiving parenting we did is now paying out in the rich life of faith we see in each of our children.

However, did I also mention the speed bumps, potholes, blind curves, and other road hazards we encountered along the path of parenting? It was not a smooth ride. After all, every Christian family, ours included, is inhabited by sinful, selfish human beings called parents and children. The idea that Christian parenting should be a purely joyful journey through life is misguided at best and an illusion at worst. And yet, despite our own immaturities and weaknesses, we made it through with no casualties and with faith intact. We're all stronger than when we started.

But Christian parenting is more than just getting from one point to another by faith. We know intuitively we're made for something more than just crossing the finish line. We're made to be part of God's epic story of creation—the story He is writing not only for all of life but for each of our lives. As lifegiving parents, one of our most important tasks has been to help our children discover themselves in the story God is writing, to find their place in the unfolding tale of God's grand purpose and plan, and to know that we are all, as a family, in that story together.

When you first became a parent, did you feel confident in your choices?
How can you see God's hand in teaching you?

With You is the fountain of life; in Your light we see light.

PSALM 36:9

IN MANY PASSAGES THROUGHOUT Scripture about the life of God, the light of God also shines. The first words of God in the Bible are "Let there be light" (Genesis 1:3), for without light, there is no life. David says, "The LORD is my light and my salvation" (Psalm 27:1), the One who saves his life. Jesus, the incarnate Son of God, proclaims, "I am the Light of the world; he who follows Me will not walk in the darkness, but will have the Light of life" (John 8:12).

So when we give our children God's life, we are also giving them His light. It is the light of God that will shine in our hearts and our homes so that we can be a beacon of hope to the world around us. Lifegiving parenting must first be about helping them find eternal life in Christ and getting them on God's path so they can live in a way that's pleasing to Him. That is certainly the priority of lifegiving parenting. But it is also so much more than that.

On a much grander scale, lifegiving parenting is about becoming a part of the epic story of God breaking into our dark and dying world to bring light and life. It is about writing ourselves and our children into the overarching story of God's eternal plan. His life and light are what make us "the light of the world" so that we can "shine before men in such a way that they may see [our] good works, and glorify [our] Father who is in heaven" (Matthew 5:14-16). We're turning on that light in our homes so others who are overcome by darkness and death may see it and find the light and life in Christ that we have found.

---

*Your part in God's story is so important. Ask Him
to shine His light and life in your heart today!*

JULY 2

The wisdom of the sensible is to understand his way.

PROVERBS 14:8

As OUR CHILDREN WERE GROWING UP, we encouraged them to think about how they could follow God and grow in wisdom to please Him. Over time, they began to see the God who is "our dwelling place in all generations" (Psalm 90:1) as part of their own place of dwelling and their own generation. We were training them to think of God not just as an impersonal source of truth to be known or a maker of rules to be followed, but also as the living God in whom they would find real life and develop a real relationship.

As a family, we would gather to describe and discuss our goals, desires, and relationships with God. Whatever came out in those family times was wisdom borne of God's presence among us. It was a natural part of our life together as a family with God.

The apostle Paul makes this dynamic connection with God clear: "The mind set on the flesh is death, but the mind set on the Spirit is life and peace" (Romans 8:6). As we engaged with God through His Spirit living in and through us, we were bringing His life into our home. Paul goes on to say, "If Christ is in you, though the body is dead because of sin, yet the spirit is alive because of righteousness" (8:10). Perhaps the King James Version gets closer to the literal sense of the words: "The Spirit is life because of righteousness." The Spirit of God who "is life" brings life to our spirits. That is the goal of lifegiving parenting—to bring God's life to our children's lives in our home.

Most of us use some sort of planning device to "number our days."
Have you ever considered something similar for your
children? What might work best to help them begin seeing
their own lives as worthy of thought and planning?

JULY 3

We proved to be gentle among you, as a nursing mother tenderly cares for her own children. Having so fond an affection for you, we were well-pleased to impart to you not only the gospel of God but also our own lives.

1 THESSALONIANS 2:7-8

ONE MORNING I GOT UP VERY EARLY to take a predawn walk by myself. I tiptoed quietly to the front door, but before I could make my escape, eight-year-old Joel came down the stairs, saw me, and asked if he could go with me. For a moment I thought, *No, this is my time to be alone,* but of course my nurturing mama heart said, "Sure, sweetie." He held my hand as we made our way into the morning quiet and darkness and said, "I just love being with you, Mommy."

As we were talking and walking along the country road in the just-breaking dawn, the morning star was still visible in the sky. Joel noted how bright and beautiful it was, so I said, "Did you know that Jesus calls Himself the 'bright morning star'? That's what Jesus wants to be in your heart. He wants to be the brightest star in the sky of your life."

We talked a bit about it, and it was a nice moment—but soon we were back home, and life went on. All these years later, however, he still remembers that story of our early morning walk and tells it when he speaks at conferences. He still thinks about that image of Jesus as the "bright morning star" in his life now as an adult. This was just one moment of choosing to nurture one of my children—to feed Joel with God's life from my own heart—but that spontaneous object lesson from nature found a place in Joel's heart and mind that probably will be there for the rest of his life.

Do you have a fond affection for your children? Are you well-pleased to impart to them both the gospel and your daily life?

JULY 4

Watch over your heart with all diligence,
for from it flow the springs of life.

PROVERBS 4:23

FOR SEVERAL YEARS WHEN OUR children were younger, we had a friend living in our home. David, a ten-year-old boy, was so delightful that we would spend hours on the couch sipping hot chocolate and listening to his stories with rapt attention. (Oh, I should mention that David was not a real boy; he was a literary character, the namesake of the 1916 novel *Just David*.)

Clay and I thought young David was such an appealing literary model of a whole-hearted child that we searched out a first-edition copy of the book, put it back into print, and introduced thousands of other families to the story of David.

I mention *Just David* here because his literary life illustrates the concept of guarding a child's heart. The story opens in a secluded mountain cabin where David's father had moved with his son six years before with a very specific purpose in mind. Now David's father knows he is dying and that David will need to go back to the world from which he had removed him. Though ill, he begins to walk David down the mountain path to the village below, wondering if what he has done in those six years will mean anything.

The rest of the book is about David's new life in the village, with both beauty-deprived and beauty-filled townspeople who take him in after his father's death. It's about how David's guarded heart prepared him for the new life and people he would encounter and how his innocence and goodness brought needed beauty and life to the world he found.

Just David is only a story, a novel written a century ago, and yet it touches on hopes that are perhaps particularly distinctive to Christian parents.

Do you have any friends living in your home, joining your family through
the wonder of read-aloud stories? If not, consider adding a storytime
to your family rhythms. I hope you'll find a friend like David too.

JULY 5

*When they got out on the land, they saw a charcoal
fire already laid and fish placed on it, and bread. . . .
Jesus said to them, "Come and have breakfast."*

JOHN 21:9, 12

THE TABLE IS A UNIQUELY AND divinely ordered part of family life for the spiritual influence of children. Think about the family table for a moment. There is a physical unity when all sit at the table together, infused with the experiential unity of sharing a meal. That dynamic fosters a naturally interactive setting—looking at each other, engaging in conversation, serving one another. Taken all together, the table creates an anchor, a way for family members to be together. We tried to take full advantage of those times at our table to challenge our children's thinking, encourage their expression of ideas and opinions, talk about current events, explore theological views and Bible knowledge, talk about relationships, and so much more. Whenever there was food on the table, we also put food for the mind there.

And whenever we could, we ate at the table together. We simply refused to give in to the American norm that considers meals as little more than necessary fueling stops between other more important activities.

When we were at the table, we were talking. When our children were younger, we would read the Bible and talk about the characters and the meaning of the passages. We would talk about God, Jesus, the Christian life, faith, love, and whatever topics our children would find interesting. As they got older, we would talk about theological issues, books we'd read, stories in the news, biblical standards for relationships, and ministry ideas ad infinitum. There was also an abundance of lighthearted banter, debate about the best musical artists and songs, movie analysis, sharing of interesting or funny YouTube videos and blog posts, and so much more.

*Is your family table a place of food for the heart,
mind, and soul as well as the body?*

JULY 6

David said to the Philistine, "You come to me with a sword, a spear, and a javelin, but I come to you in the name of the LORD of hosts, the God of the armies of Israel, whom you have taunted."

I SAMUEL 17:45

WHEN NATHAN WAS A YOUNG CHILD, he was captivated by stories about heroes. He spent hours in his own costumes, doing battle with swords and shields against imaginary villains.

One night we were acting out the story of David and Goliath. Nathan wanted to be David, because he knew David was the hero. Clay, of course, was Goliath. He ad-libbed some taunts with his deep Goliath voice: "I defy you, men of Israel. Send out a man. Come and fight me!" And then, looking at Nathan, he bellowed, "Why, you're just a boy. Am I a dog that you come to me with sticks? Are you a coward?" To which Nathan straightened his back, raised his sword, and shouted boldly in his four-year-old voice, "Yes, I am!" He wasn't sure what a coward was, but if he was the hero, he would be one with all his heart. We couldn't contain our laughter, but we quickly recovered and went on to make sure the young hero David could slay Goliath.

I look back on that night over twenty years later and see more than just a fun family story. Even then, Nathan was putting hero stories into his heart. He would go on to inhabit other heroes in his childhood such as Audie Murphy, the World War II hero; Colonel William B. Travis of the Alamo; and his favorite hero, Superman. He told me once, "I think Superman is like Jesus because he came to earth to save people who needed help. That's what I want to do with my life." All those hero stories were cultivating in him a heart of faith.

Do your children have any specific heroes they identify with?
Do you? If not, consider going on a hero hunt—maybe together!

The righteous person behaves in integrity; blessed are his children after him. . . . Even a young man is known by his actions, whether his activity is pure and whether it is right.

PROVERBS 20:7, II, NET

WHEN JOY WAS TWELVE, one of my friends desperately needed help with the children at the Mom's Day Out program at church. I asked Joy if she would consider being the assistant, and she willingly agreed. When she got to the program, she found out she would be helping with sixteen toddlers. You can imagine all that entailed! She would come home and tell me stories of keeping the children entertained, clean, and under control.

Joy is very strong-willed in the best way, and even as a young girl she was self-motivated to accomplish whatever she had set her mind to do. So for this job, she planned what toys and special activities to bring; she knew each child's name, personality, and likes; and she threw herself into the job to do it the best that she could. The women in charge of the program had nothing but praise for her. The second year, they felt comfortable putting her, with an assistant, in charge of the toddlers and giving her a raise, because she was so diligent and capable and had earned their trust.

Joy worked there three years and put away a very nice nest egg for when she would later go to Biola University at seventeen. I think Joy's time of working in what others might see as a rather difficult and thankless job not only strengthened her will but also created in her a sense of the value of being diligent.

What opportunities are you encouraging
your children toward that might help them
become more responsible and diligent?

JULY 8

*The seed in the good soil, these are the ones who have
heard the word in an honest and good heart, and
hold it fast, and bear fruit with perseverance.*

LUKE 8:15

WHEN JOEL WAS ABOUT eleven years old, I thought he would enjoy being involved in a local boys' choir. He had been musical from a very young age, singing on pitch from around eighteen months and making music throughout childhood. I thought being in the boys' choir would give him an opportunity to receive some formal musical training and immerse himself in a structured musical experience.

As Joel got involved and received attention from the director, an older boy, who was about to graduate from the group, began to bully Joel. He was mean to him, pushing him around during breaks and telling him he wasn't really that good. Joel reported to us what was happening, and we made an appointment to talk to the choir director about it. One night when Clay was out of town, Joel came to talk to me about the boy. He'd found out this older boy's father had recently left his family and that they had been forced to move out of their house. He told me, "Mama, that would make me so sad and angry. Maybe that's why the boy is being mean to me. I think I just need to be patient and kind to him, because that's what Jesus would want me to do."

This was a moment when Joel decided to have character like Jesus so he could be a witness and help to this boy. Clay and I were ready to go to the director, but Joel wanted to handle the situation privately, a testimony to his developing Christian character that showed he'd been listening to our family devotions and discussions about humility and serving others.

*Do you tend to rush in to "fix things" when your children
encounter difficult situations? How might waiting on
God's timing allow for an even better result?*

You will keep in perfect peace all who trust in you,
all whose thoughts are fixed on you!

ISAIAH 26:3, NLT

SARAH WAS ALWAYS OUR "BOOK GIRL." She started reading on her own at five and had read all of the Chronicles of Narnia, the Little House series, and many other books by the time she was seven. She loved books and reading from the time she could turn a page, and she still does.

When Sarah was fourteen, we moved to Monument, Colorado, and she had no friends there. It was a lonely time for her at an age when girlfriends are an important part of growing up. She had read all of the Anne of Green Gables books when she was younger, but now that she was a teen like Anne, she revisited the series. She also read about the author, Lucy Maud Montgomery, and how her imagined stories about Anne Shirley and Diana Barry had been inspired by her own life experiences. Sarah dreamed of becoming a writer like Montgomery, whose stories about the kinds of girlfriends Sarah didn't have then encouraged her and fed her imagination.

What she couldn't see then is that this period of loneliness would create strategic and undistracted time for her to think about stories and writing. At sixteen, she completed her homeschooling senior project, "Journeys of Faithfulness: Stories for the Heart for Faithful Girls," an imaginative retelling of the stories of four single women in the Bible. She would later write other books, including *Read for the Heart, Caught Up in a Story*, and *Book Girl,* and she is now working on a novella.

When I look back, I'm reminded that imagination needs time and space to grow. By God's grace, those lonely years allowed the heart of a budding writer time to find her imagination and later release it as an author who will influence many through her words and stories.

Do you have a "bosom friend," as Anne would say? Thank the Lord.
Do you not? How might this lonely season be of benefit to you?

JULY 10

It was for freedom that Christ set us free; therefore keep standing firm and do not be subject again to a yoke of slavery.

GALATIANS 5:1

WE HUMANS ARE COMPLEX CREATURES, shaped internally by drives, fears, pride, ideals, hopes, and other unseen but influential forces. Even though they are not likely to be completely "in control" of us, let me suggest just a few representative negative influences that could affect our parenting.

When the sinful self, often called the flesh, is in control, we're not thinking about God or doing His will. Even though we are new creatures in Christ, we are still tempted by our sinful nature. And if we let emotions control us, strong feelings can affect how we interact with our immature children. Emotion-filled reactions such as anger, judgment, or criticism can replace thoughtful and reasoned actions. Also, we can let fear—of what others think, of doing the wrong thing, of angering God—control us.

Finally, there is formula parenting—uncritically following patterns we've been told are the best methods of parenting or just parenting thoughtlessly by habits and routines.

Those negative human forces, and many more, can influence our parenting, but only if we let them. The good news is that we have a choice; we can learn to let God be in control of our parenting. We can let Him become the controlling influence in our lives so our children will see the new person we are becoming in Christ, not the old person we were before. That happens through three positive influences by which God comes into our humanity—faith, freedom, and love. Much of parenting is simply learning to "walk by faith, not by sight" (2 Corinthians 5:7)—trusting in God for His wisdom, insight, and discernment to become the Christlike parents our children need. Faith, then, gives us the freedom to follow the Holy Spirit's ministry in our hearts and not be enslaved to man's laws and rules.

Are you walking in the freedom Christ died to offer to you in your life as a parent?

*If there is any excellence and if anything
worthy of praise, dwell on these things.*

PHILIPPIANS 4:8

WHEN JOEL AND NATHAN WERE around nine and seven, Clay and I were very aware of trying to cultivate an appetite for excellence in them. One decision we made was not to let them watch Saturday morning cartoons. One Friday afternoon, the boys and I looked at a lovely painting of two boys behind a barracks, playing cards while soldiers trained. We talked about what story the painting was trying to tell, what the boys might have been like, and what it means to be a soldier during wartime.

The next day, I let them spend some time with friends nearby. As we were driving home, Joel asked me, "Mommy, why aren't we allowed to watch Saturday morning cartoons like our friends?"

When we got home, I took out some paper and scribbled a simple stick-figure drawing of two boys. I asked, "What do you think of my drawing? Is it beautiful? Is it interesting? What kind of story is it telling?" Joel said, "Mama, it isn't interesting at all and doesn't have a story."

I asked, "Why was the painting we talked about yesterday interesting to you?" He responded, "Well, because it had real people and color. I could imagine the two boys in it being Nathan and me. It told an interesting story."

I said, "That's exactly right. And do you know why you were able to appreciate those things? Because I've tried to feed your mind the very best mind foods I can. I don't let you watch the junk food and sugars of Saturday morning cartoons because of what I know they will do to your mind and spirit. I want to feed your mind with good things so you'll have a healthy mind and imagination to create things like the painting of the two boys."

---

*God doesn't want us to let mediocrity crowd out excellence in
our minds; He wants us to train our appetites to appreciate
beauty and excellence. How do you do this in your home?*

JULY 12

He always lives to intercede for [us].

HEBREWS 7:25, NIV

THE FOLLOWING TALE FROM my Celtic prayer book has been a great comfort to me.

Two men sought wisdom from an educated, kind old monk who was reputed to be a man of great character, distinguished in his devotion to Scripture. Arriving at the seacoast town, they left their ship and climbed the long hill to the monastery. Several days were invested in spiritual conversations as the men pondered God's nature and presence and the essence of true spirituality. With full souls, they bid farewell to the wizened old monk, heading toward the ship that would take them back home. With hearts overflowing, they gratefully planned how they would apply such wisdom in their daily lives in their hometown.

Almost as soon as the giant ship left the small port, a raging storm gathered. Lightning flashed with thunder filling the air, and the ship swayed back and forth, the captain straining to keep it afloat amidst the crashing waves. In terror, the two men peered through the dark, blowing mists, searching for the lights of home fires burning near the shore. Suddenly, they saw a shadowy figure emerge from the door of the monastery and realized it was the old monk, looking out upon the ship at sea, and that he fell to the soaking ground on knees and began, in a posture of prayer, calling out to God passionately.

After a very short interlude, the sea softened its rage, and the sailors were able to come back to the safety of the port. The monk, it seems, had dedicated his heart and strength and devoted cries to God for the safety of those who had so recently been in his charge.

Let us follow the monk's example, as we devote ourselves to encouraging our children in the things of God, and also praying them though the storms of life that are sure to come.

Put on a heart of compassion, kindness, humility, gentleness and patience; bearing with one another, and forgiving each other.

COLOSSIANS 3:12-13

COMMITTED MOTHERHOOD IS a holy calling of God. I believe I am a steward of the children He has given me, and He trusts me to love, instruct, train, and provide for them in such a way that they may go into their adult lives emotionally healthy, loving God and serving His Kingdom purposes.

However, there are times when, seemingly out of the blue, I spew all over my children. The work of giving, serving, cleaning, cooking, and correcting consumes my patient feelings and slowly depletes my rational brain cells, causing frustration to build up inside until it suddenly takes over and spills anger on everyone in close range. I always feel terrible when I have thrown one of these fits.

I do not need a lecture from someone telling me I have been immature, out of control, unreasonable, and unloving. I already know that. What I long for instead is gentleness and patience—someone to tenderly place their arms around my shoulders, look into my eyes with compassion, understand how I feel, and say, "Grace to you, sweet one; you are forgiven. All will be well."

It is a comfort to have another mom who can say to me, "You are not alone. I am guilty of raging in the tempests of my own life too. Apologize, ask for forgiveness, and move on in love."

And then I need a maid, a waitress, and a day away to be an adult again, but that is not in the budget of my minutes and days. Instead, I will be comforted with compassion, kindness, humility, gentleness, and patience, as Paul so eloquently wrote in today's verse.

Can I be that mom for you today? If you've lost it with your children, can I assure you that you're not alone, and it's not irreparable? Apologize honestly. Ask for forgiveness. Begin again. God has already forgiven you and provided for a new tomorrow.

JULY 14

"Your words have been arrogant against Me," says the LORD.
"Yet you say, 'What have we spoken against You?' You have said,
'It is vain to serve God; and what profit is it that we have kept His charge,
and that we have walked in mourning before the LORD of hosts?'"

MALACHI 3:13-14

So MANY TIMES, feelings of fear or desperation or despair blew over my heart and soul. Often worry would strangle my heart, making it difficult to breathe in the reality of His freedom and grace. Too many children, too many bills, difficult relationships, an insurmountable workload, unanswered questions, and unanswered prayer often felt like too much for me to bear.

Feeling as though my "labor was in vain," or that God had forgotten me, I had to push through the darkness to sit still and picture Him as I read about Him. And then, in spite of my feelings, I would timidly offer Him my love gift: "I believe You, even though I can't see You right now. I want to thank You that darkness is not dark to You, but You are with me, working on these problems, loving me, and taking care of my worries, even though I can't imagine how. I love You, God. I have faith in Your faithfulness."

As I look back now, I can see that God usually had bigger purposes than just meeting the demands of my immediate prayers. He was building character, forming hearts, leading in a new direction, protecting me from my own temporal idol of the "quick fix," which would leave me empty. As a matter of fact, when I see where I am and where my children are now, I often think He was doing far more than I even asked Him.

Are you like me, sometimes doubting God's care for you when things
go wrong or life proves difficult? It helps to remind myself of ways
He has met my needs in the past. Determine to believe God's Word
about His love and care for you. Don't let your heart be arrogant.

Come away by yourselves to a secluded place and rest a while.

MARK 6:31

ONE MORNING AS WE SAT AT breakfast together, Joy said, "You know, social media just can't substitute for a real person. You can see words or a picture, but you can't see the movement of a nervous gesture, or smell the perfume of someone, or look into their eyes, or hear the tone of their voice. There is no substitute in a relationship for the real thing."

It struck me as she talked that it is the same with God. You can't just read words on a page, sit stiffly in a pew once a week while pondering what you are going to have for lunch, or read a five-minute blog post and imagine you have a healthy relationship with Him.

You can't just read God's Facebook profile and suppose you can be close to His heart. To be truly near to Him—understanding His heart, believing He really loves you, experiencing His personality—requires hours and hours of real life in His presence, knowing His words through the voice of Scripture, and then talking to Him, pouring out your heart in prayer. It takes engaging with Him in the privacy of your own room, all alone, believing He hears, and living through years of seeing His faithfulness.

If I am to find that place of quiet rest, it must be as a result of being with Him day in and day out, and then coming to better understand Him through all the moments of my life, through what He has made, what He has said, what He has taught me through His Holy Spirit, and what I have learned from being with other godly people who are filled with His attributes. It is a real live relationship—exciting, mysterious, an adventure. To be close to His heart will always bring confidence, peace, and security.

Have you spent enough time with God lately to feel
you truly are growing to know Him more and more?
Think about how you might build your relationship today.

JULY 16

The fear of man brings a snare,
but he who trusts in the LORD will be exalted.

PROVERBS 29:25

MANY TIMES THIS WEEK, I have been in conversation with different people whom I love and respect, who have expressed feeling inadequate in their lives.

"When I see what so-and-so is doing, I feel that I fall short."

"I think I am disappointing so many people. I can't seem to call everyone back, respond to emails, get all the housework done, and be patient—I always feel like I am falling short."

"My children seem to fight all the time. I just can't seem to manage them like other people do."

Even my children have felt this way lately.

"Compared to all of the other professional musicians around, I am not up to snuff."

"Mom, do you think she has more skills than I do? Will you be disappointed in me if I don't do as well as I thought?"

Comparing ourselves to others is an epidemic. Comparison will always be destructive. We will either find ourselves falling short of others, which will cultivate self-condemnation, or we will find ourselves better than others, and that will bring pride.

Proverbs tells us that "the fear of man brings a snare." When we look to others for approval, we make them idols. They become the standard by which we think we should live, instead of living by grace and freedom in Christ. When we look to others for our affirmation, we will never find enough. There will always be someone better at what we're trying to do, prettier, more successful, wiser, more mature . . .

How grateful I am that Jesus shows no favoritism! He reached out to the unlovely, the unpopular, the meek—children, prostitutes, tax collectors, lepers, Roman soldiers, bleeding women, and more—lifting them up and giving them worth.

Are you living under a weight of comparison?
It's time to lay it down. Today, He is reaching out to you.

Take My yoke upon you and learn from Me,
for I am gentle and humble in heart.

MATTHEW 11:29

I LOVE COMING INTO THE presence of Jesus. I am usually in my wrinkled pajamas, with sleep breath, no makeup, tousled hair, and a fearful heart—I am naturally a fearful person. But I light my candle and have my tea, and in His presence I find love and acceptance and hope.

He made me. He knows me, and as Psalm 103:14 says, "He is mindful that [I am] but dust." He formed me in my mother's womb. He redeemed me and made me part of His family. And He will always be loyal and accept me because I am His child.

In His presence, I am adequate, because He saved me so that I could live without pretense or performance.

I want to offer Jesus so much, yet all He asks of me is to give myself. I may not give perfection, or maturity, or prowess, but I can give Him my little-girl heart. The heart that sees His beauty, His unconditional love, the freedom He gives me to be me, just as I am. And that makes me respond with such love, appreciation, and gratefulness! How very glad I am that Jesus does not compare me to anyone else. He is my justification. He is my badge of honor.

Even the way our precious Savior came, as one of us, the common kind, with "no stately form or majesty" (Isaiah 53:2), shows us His preference. If we are to be pleasing and adequate, it must be with Him as our sole audience, the only One who can give us approval that will satisfy our souls.

Do you sometimes forget that the King of kings is "gentle and
humble in heart" (Matthew 11:29), not waiting to slap you
on the wrist but rather to draw you close and embrace you?
How can you offer Him your own little-girl heart today?

JULY 18

In the beginning was the Word, and the Word was with God, and the Word was God.

JOHN 1:1

JESUS WAS (AND IS) THE WORD—the message that brought life to those who were thirsty, love to those who felt unlovable, truth to those who longed for direction, comfort to those who were weary, forgiveness to those who were guilty.

Words have power to destroy or to heal. Even Peter, with all of his blunderings, got this right: "Lord, to whom shall we go? You have words of eternal life" (John 6:68).

Jesus said, "Out of the abundance of the heart his mouth speaks" (Luke 6:45, ESV).

Do our words bring life, hope, beauty, healing, comfort, inspiration? Words are as swords, wielded to bring power and influence. I have seen so often that my words are what go deep into the souls of my children, husband, and friends.

Lately I've been considering the fact that "the Word," Jesus, lives inside me. That means I have the power within to cultivate that which will bring the same life and truth that He brought. I am spending more and more time lately pondering His words, His heart, His messages, so I can be changed by them.

Today, I am going to be intentional about my words. I will write or speak words of life intentionally to each of my children today—face to face or on messages they will receive. I hope to hearten them, lift them, encourage them. I will invest words that Clay needs to hear. I will seek this week to give out those words to people He brings to my mind, that they might feel the wind of the Holy Spirit blowing through their lives.

May our words cause all who are around us to sense the fragrance of God lingering about them.

What words are forming your own heart today? How are they making you feel? How are the words you speak affecting those around you?

The eyes of the LORD are toward the righteous
and His ears are open to their cry.

PSALM 34:15

BABIES ARE DEPENDENT ON US for their very existence—our milk, our protection, our love and care, every moment of every day. When we answer their cries with tenderness and love, it helps them trust, and eventually they relate to the idea that God is also One who responds to their cries.

God has designed new babies to be fragile, so we can put an imprint of God's very hands and love and grace into their hearts and minds. In feeling our love, they become predisposed to know and believe in His love and touch when they hear stories about Him.

When we are new parents of young children, we have a sense that we are in control of their lives—that what we do and how we control them will determine what they will become.

However, as my children grew, I realized that apart from God's working deep in their souls, they will not follow righteousness. I cannot control their lives or their circumstances, and they must make their own decisions. There is a dark world of temptation, idolatry, despair, and immorality calling to them at every point. But I am not left helpless or hopeless. I can have a big impact on their lives and help shoulder their burdens every day.

Even as I read about how Jesus so often would pray all night, consider how He prayed specifically for Peter before he was tempted to deny Him, and reflect on the loving, tender words of prayer in John 17, I know that I must model my life after His. There is One who works directly within my children's hearts, One whose fingertips will mold and shape them: the Holy Spirit. My work is to mysteriously engage with Him before God's throne, and it is there that the life of my children will bloom afresh.

What are you praying for your children? Write down one
thing for each child, and commit to approaching God's
throne in confidence daily for the next few weeks.

JULY 20

Do not judge, and you will not be judged; and do not condemn,
and you will not be condemned; pardon, and you will be pardoned.

LUKE 6:37

My heart has been greatly troubled in the past year as I have observed the harsh and hateful ways Christians have blasted judgment of others—groups, politicians, leaders, broken people, immigrants, women in distress, nonbelievers, and those of different belief systems—over the internet. Often, they talk of those they are criticizing as though they are not real people with real lives and real feelings.

I understand many believe it is their "Christian duty" to espouse, with confidence, objections to those who do not share their values or beliefs. But in teaching our children manners, modeling how to minister to people, and seeking to understand that it is the kindness and mercy of God that leads to repentance, I believe we must consider how to offer our messages and convictions to the world in the same manner Jesus offered Himself and His teachings to the world.

There is a way to verbalize convictions without bearing emotional hostility and blatant animosity. When I ponder Christ, I see a different standard of relating to others. He speaks of love. He models love and sacrifices Himself for the sake of loving redemption of the many who are lost in brokenness.

Jesus, the holy Lamb of God, who was pure and spotless and had the right to condemn sinners, chose not to humiliate them publicly. So why would I think that I, one of the very sinners He saved, have the right to publicly condemn others?

He who bowed His knee to serve accepted the tears of a broken, adulterous woman washing His feet. He overlooked and did not highlight the many weaknesses or sins of those who surrounded Him, including His disciples. His modeling of love satisfies my heart's cry for a display of holy honor and propriety and self-control in all interactions—even those online.

Does your way of relating to others online honor Christ's example?

*Be steadfast, immovable, always abounding in the work of the Lord,
knowing that in the Lord your labor is not in vain.*

I CORINTHIANS 15:58, ESV

QUITTING JOBS, QUITTING SCHOOL, quitting on marriage, quitting on friendship, quitting on God—it seems all kinds of quitting have become acceptable and excusable these days.

Yet God gave us the capacity to "muscle up" in life, that we might be conquerors, defeat the darkness, and complete our work. How many times I have been sorely tempted to give up on some of my ideals! My children tested my patience and faith. Homeschooling challenged me to the core. Repetitive financial issues tempted me to believe God did not hear my prayers. People's negative voices caused me to second-guess my vision, tempting me to think ideals did not matter.

Yet, God's Word kept telling me to persevere, to be diligent, to overcome, to keep going. And by His grace, I am so very thankful He increased my capacity to work hard and remain faithful though it was difficult so many times.

Daily life is where diligence is trained and learned. As our children watch our faithfulness and experience our love, they develop a heart to be diligent. Giving them work to complete develops moral strength. Helping children to persevere in difficult relationships teaches them to be faithful in adult relationships.

Learning diligence is essential for fruitfulness. The world is in rebellion against God and His design, so our work is challenging, and our relationships are fraught with pain. But His spirit of redemption comes alive when we are diligent to complete the tasks we have been given. Diligence is the energy, the inner will of determination to keep going, that provides the power to overcome in life.

---

*A key to diligence is found in the second half of the verse above—
knowing that our labor is not in vain. Ask the Lord to renew
this knowing in your life, as you seek to grow in diligence.*

JULY 22

*At that time the kingdom of heaven will be like ten virgins
who took their lamps and went out to meet the bridegroom.
Five of them were foolish and five were wise. The foolish ones
took their lamps but did not take any oil with them. The wise
ones, however, took oil in jars along with their lamps.*

MATTHEW 25:1-4, NIV

SOME OF THE VIRGINS IN THIS parable were called wise, and some were called fool-ish. Why?

Because they had oil, which of course was because they had planned ahead for their priorities. They didn't let anything distract them from what was truly pressing, truly needful. The wise virgins took the time to put oil in their lamps—to be ready to meet the bridegroom.

What does it mean for us to be ready to meet God, to see Him face to face? And how does that play itself out in the warp and woof of our home life? There are times we definitely get distracted by dirty rooms, meals to prepare, and oh yes, definitely laundry! But do these things add oil into our souls? Likely not.

Focusing on the Savior who is the Bridegroom, the One who died on the cross and rose again, will definitely fill our souls and guide us in wisdom as we plan our days. All of our busyness will be in vain if it is not in preparation to see Him, to celebrate Him in our homes, to ready our children to place Him as their highest priority, as we await that wonderful day when He will come back to the earth. God wants us to be ready and anticipating His coming.

---

*Take some time today to evaluate your life in light of this
wonderful little story. Make sure you have the oil you
need for your lamp, so you, too, will be wise.*

It will come about after this that I will pour out My Spirit on all mankind; and your sons and daughters will prophesy, your old men will dream dreams, your young men will see visions.

JOEL 2:28

EVEN AS A YOUNG CHILD, I was a passionate dreamer, always questioning, challenging, wondering, and developing into an idealist. I remember one of my relatives saying to me once, "You always try to find the weirdest things to do, and then you do them just to embarrass us."

This nonconformity was evident when I became a deeply committed Christian in college. I shared my faith with anyone God brought my way. Later, I went on staff with Campus Crusade for Christ and had to raise support to go into missions in Communist Eastern Europe in the 1970s. I heard things like, "Oh my goodness, you are such a radical! Where do you come up with these strange ideas? There are plenty of nonbelievers in the United States. You don't have to leave the country and become a missionary to be committed!"

Eventually, I married another "radical," and we moved back overseas, where we dreamed of a different kind of discipleship for our own children, building them into godly leaders in our home, as we had been doing with others all over the world.

Finally, we made a faith step to leave the comfort of a job with insurance and a monthly check to start a ministry to families, going five years before we had a monthly salary. Over the next twenty years we started our own publishing business and hosted conferences, wrote books, moved several times, and sought to be stewards of the messages God put on our hearts.

What drove these dreams? I believe it was the Holy Spirit. It certainly wasn't the voices surrounding us!

Avoid, at all costs, listening to peer pressure. Do not measure your spirituality by rules or formulas. Don't live by arbitrary standards, but by faith in the living, active God. What dream is on your heart?

JULY 24

God is love, and the one who abides in love abides in God, and God abides in him.

1 JOHN 4:16

THE LOVER OF MY SOUL, the maker of beauty, the servant King is in our midst as a devoted Father. He is a bridegroom preparing a wedding feast. He is a wonderful counselor who has compassion on us when we feel lost. He is a shepherd who lays down His life for His sheep and leads them beside still waters.

As long as I keep my soul alive by dwelling in His presence, remembering the roles He plays in my own life, as long as I cultivate and practice a heart of love, I can overcome the darkness—including all darkness in my own soul—here on earth. But love and beauty and faith must be cultivated daily, in His presence, looking for His reality, so that my heart will be filled with His truth and His overcoming goodness and redeeming light.

The glory of a woman is her ability to stir up life in this dark world. We are born to civilize, to encourage, to inspire, to heal. Women are most beautiful when they are engaged in sharing the reality of His life and love wherever they go. But this love comes from intentional cultivation: I am created to be an overcomer, an artist who leaves beauty, a counselor who brings peace, a type of magician who brings hope and laughter in the very midst of despair.

So, today, I become a cocreator with Him who is the source of all that is beautiful and good, celebrating His reality into the midst of this puzzle that is called my life.

The strength of any woman is built on a foundation of what she cherishes, practices, waters, cultivates. Love is there, waiting to strengthen—the soul of a great woman depends on His love flowing in and through every day.

How is your soul today? Be reminded that He is walking alongside you, ready to pour life and love through you everywhere you go.

JULY 25

Beloved, let us love one another, for love is from God.

1 JOHN 4:7

"WE TREAT ONE ANOTHER with kindness, gentleness, and respect." This was one of the principles that our children heard and wrote down over and over again when they were young, so it would become a pathway in their brain, an ingrained way of behaving. We also came up with ideas over the years to help them practice taking initiative to extend words and actions of love towards people they cherished.

Once, we made a list of twenty friends who were special to our family. Together, we spent a whole day baking—cookies, bread, and cinnamon rolls. While we waited for the treats to bake, I provided doilies, markers, paper, ribbon, and glue to craft "I love you. I am so thankful you are my friend" and "I appreciate you and thank God for you" cards. Each was of the kids' own making, and each child chose which friends to present his or her cards to.

Finally, we all gathered our plates of goodies, ribbon-ed and card-ed, placed them gingerly into the car, and were off. It took four hours to deliver them all to the homes of those we had chosen to give our words of love to, and it delighted and filled all of my precious ones with memories of how much a tiny thoughtful gift can mean to someone who needs to hear the words "I love you."

These patterns we practiced are part of who my children perceive themselves to be now as adults—lovers of others. The habit of being thoughtful was a learned value, as we practiced it regularly.

The fruit of a soul that emanates love comes after that soul has been planted with seeds of intention that are then cultivated and watered with deeds of kindness.

*How might you encourage your children to love
someone intentionally and with effort today?*

JULY 26

Let not a wise man boast of his wisdom, and let not the mighty man
boast of his might, let not a rich man boast of his riches; but let him
who boasts boast of this, that he understands and knows Me.

JEREMIAH 9:23-24

IF THERE WAS ONE LEGACY I wish I could leave to women, it would be to help them think more biblically. When a woman knows Scripture—not just verses here and there taken out of context but a biblical understanding from Genesis to Revelation—she has more confidence and ease in her walk with God.

God makes it clear throughout Scripture that His priority is that we know Him and love Him with our whole heart and mind. And so the starting point for any arena in our lives must be God—our worship of Him and knowledge of Him, plus obedience coming from a heart that wants to please Him.

As we live the Christian life, God has given us a brain to think, a conscience to nudge our hearts, and most importantly, the Holy Spirit who lives inside of us to guide us. All He asks is that we live by faith in Him and dependence on Him. God always loves to lead us and work through us by faith in relationship to Him and what He is impressing us to do, within the beautiful design of our femininity and womanhood. That is why it is crucial that we are spending time in His presence and seeking to build a foundation of conviction on Scripture and knowledge of God.

Let me pray for you today . . .

Lord, I pray that each one who reads this devotional will be led by You.
I pray You will provide them with insight, skill, love, wisdom, and
the understanding of what it means to be filled with Your Spirit
and to walk by faith in this journey of motherhood. And bless
them with strength, joy, and a sense of affirmation in their great
calling as parents. In the precious name of Jesus, Amen.

Love the LORD your God with all your heart, and with all your
soul, and with all your strength, and with all your mind.

LUKE 10:27

OFTEN IN OUR TIME IN HISTORY, we think of worship as singing, praising, and lifting our hands up to God. But while all these may be part of worship, to truly worship God means to honor Him and to place Him as the lens through which we see and live our lives.

We are told to worship Him with our mind. Filling our minds with truth, pondering Christ, cherishing that which is holy is a part of this worship. God admonishes us to delight ourselves in His law in Psalm 1, which indicates we need to hide His Word in our hearts and minds and think true thoughts.

We are told to think only on things that are worthy of Him: "Finally, brothers and sisters, whatever is true, whatever is noble, whatever is right, whatever is pure, whatever is lovely, whatever is admirable—if anything is excellent or praiseworthy—think about such things" (Philippians 4:8, NIV).

I have never met a wise spiritual leader who did not think deeply, clearly, and well. My spiritual mentors are those who cause me to think more highly of God, who sharpen me with their ponderings of God, eternity, truth, and doctrine.

You cannot build your children into people who seek to be worthy of God and to be excellent in all their ways, unless you also invest in their minds. The foundations of their thinking patterns, vocabulary, and ideas must be cultivated. When you become a steward of what they think, your own life is enriched. And so worshiping God with our minds requires commitment, planning, and intention.

If we are to be worthy stewards of truth, we must mind our minds—that we might truly worship.

Evaluate your own thoughts today. Does your mind
cherish God and treat Him as holy? Do you regularly feed
your thoughts on truth, greatness, and beauty?

JULY 28

There is a time for every event under heaven. . . . A time to weep and a time to laugh; a time to mourn and a time to dance.

ECCLESIASTES 3:1, 4

LIFE CAN SOMETIMES BE STRESSFUL, overwhelming, exhausting, and demanding. Sometimes moms feel guilty admitting the variety of feelings they have. But feelings are just a reaction to the situation we are in.

Much of the stability of life depends upon us just doing whatever is in front of us that needs to be done, whether we feel like doing it or not! But there are times in life that seem overwhelming and too depleting to handle. A few years ago, Clay and I decided that when we got to this point, we needed to call a Sober Club meeting. It stands for

Sick
Of
Being
Responsible

On Sober Club nights, we always do something that we want to do just for us. We go out to dinner, see a movie, take a walk in the mountains, or go on a drive to see the city lights with music blaring and windows down, just cruising and trying to relax. We make it a point to do something different that takes us away from the stress, the kids, and the house. It's a rule that we can't talk about any problems or money or stress or ministry. We just get away, relax, and have fun!

The principle is similar to the idea of Sabbath. Get away from your responsibilities just for a while! Go to a park when your kids are driving you nuts. Or take a nap. Watch a movie instead of doing one more chore, buy some flowers when it has been snowing for ten days straight. You get the idea!

Life is still there tomorrow or whenever the Sober Club meeting ends, but we all have blown off a little steam and can face our responsibilities with a fresher outlook.

Do you need a Sober Club meeting? Who might you invite to join you, and what will you do?

Make your ear attentive to wisdom, incline your heart to understanding;
for if you cry for discernment, lift your voice for understanding; if you
seek her as silver and search for her as for hidden treasures; then you will
discern the fear of the LORD and discover the knowledge of God.

PROVERBS 2:2-5

BONE-CHILLING FOG WAFTED through the mysterious, ancient cobblestone streets as I made my way to school each morning in Krakow, Poland. Mists wrapped around the gray stone walls of the aged city, whispering of the hidden secrets of kings and queens who resided there through hundreds of years.

Living there under Communism meant meat was scarce and fresh fruit and vegetables were rare. Always, though, we could find beautifully carved wooden boxes of every size, shape, and style. I was particularly drawn to the treasure chests that had keys to lock away precious letters, secrets, journals, or jewels.

Years later, when my home became a reality and little feet pattered around, my treasure chests became favorite relics. Often, I would hide a verse scribbled on a piece of colored paper, some gold-covered chocolate coins, a tiny ring, bracelet, knight in shining armor, or small puzzle inside these boxes for my children to discover.

During a quiet time one morning, my eyes lighted upon one of my little chests, and the Holy Spirit impressed me to see the heart of each of my children as a treasure chest. Filling the treasure chests of their hearts with truth, beauty, love, great thoughts, books, ideas, adventures, memories, traditions, wisdom, music, art, lessons, and all the good things I could imagine became a purposeful goal. I wanted to fill them with such an abundance of relics of eternal value that they could draw beauty, strength, guidance, assurance, courage, and love from those deposits for the rest of their lives.

Have you ever considered yourself to be the filler of your
own children's treasure chests? What goodness can you add
to your own heart today that it might spill over?

JULY 30

By wisdom a house is built, and by understanding it is established;
and by knowledge the rooms are filled with all precious and pleasant riches.

PROVERBS 24:3-4

ALONG WITH THE REALIZATION that my children's hearts were like treasure chests came another: I could not give to them what I did not myself possess. If I wanted the souls of my children to be rich, then my soul needed to be rich, because it was my soul they would draw from. I became passionate about investing time every morning with the Lord so I could pass on what I'd learned when we gathered each morning over breakfast.

It seems rare that I find truly great people whose presence brings life and inspiration, causing me to want to be more excellent and trust God for more miracles or strive to be a better person. So I realized that I wanted to be that kind of person—where the living, sparkling, dancing Spirit of God was so much a part of me, that to be with me was to be in the presence of God. I see that in God's economy, it is possible to become a "great" person, because He is great and desires to produce in us His holiness, righteousness, and integrity.

If I am to become the kind of woman whom all can count on as a fount of life and inspiration, I must have a plan that utilizes every moment of every day to mold me into such a person. And so, I became a treasure seeker—I pursued all that was excellent and good, seeking to model myself after the most excellent, the most beautiful, getting rid of the garbage that was in my heart, as often as I needed to, so I could fill my soul with all that was good.

Filling our own souls with His character and grace does not happen
by accident. What does your plan to be filled look like?

In repentance and rest you will be saved,
in quietness and trust is your strength.

ISAIAH 30:15

So OFTEN, we give and give and give and then wonder why we have become grumpy or short on patience. In our 24-7 world, with false lights to keep us up and working all hours of the day, 24 hours of internet, 24 hours of television, cars with lights that can travel all hours, etc., we lose the concept of rest.

No wonder there are so many stress diseases—heart, obesity, and thyroid problems, as well as nervous disorders, mental disorders, and emotional disorders. We are busy all the time, feeling guilty for all we do not get done, and wearing ourselves out.

I realized many years ago that I was becoming ill from so much push, push, push and work, work, work. I also realized that no one else was going to take responsibility for my health and well-being but me. I have to stop, put everything aside, and rest on a regular basis.

As a woman who is attempting to grow in maturity in the Lord, I have to be intentional about being sure that I incorporate rest, refueling, restoration, and inspiration in my own personal life, not just once in a while, but regularly so that I can keep going.

So right now, though there are many letters to answer, piles to organize, rooms to clean, groceries to shop for, people to call back, ad infinitum, I will lay them all in the file folders of heaven for God to keep. I have learned that they will all still be here tomorrow, and that God wants me to leave my burdens alone—as He is the Father, I the toddler, and He will indeed work in all of my circumstances without my help. But if I take responsibility to take care of my own heart and soul, I will last much longer, much better, and even have peace and quietness.

How are you incorporating rest into your own life
so you can find strength?

AUGUST 1

I have chosen him, so that he may command his children and his household
after him to keep the way of the LORD by doing righteousness and justice,
so that the LORD may bring upon Abraham what He has spoken about him.
GENESIS 18:19

I HAVE A HEART TO TRAIN my children in righteousness, and my focus is on winning their hearts and instructing their minds. I want them to love God with their whole hearts, not just to obey rules, so they won't be obeying on the outside but rebelling on the inside. Works and performance are not my goal; a transformed and inspired heart is my goal. Jesus accomplished that by cultivating a deep, loving, and committed relationship with His disciples. They all loved and respected Him so much, as He served them so generously, that they wanted to follow Him even to death. They believed in Him and wanted to serve Him out of loving and transformed hearts.

I want my children to love righteousness and truth and beauty, so I come along beside them as an advocate, morning, noon, and night, to instruct and show and help them.

And so, when Joy called yesterday and I could understand that she needed my ear, my time, my encouragement, and my attention, I knew what to do. The grid through which I had learned to practice life told me she is my priority. I had to take that time, right then, that moment, because today is the day to parent. She will not be with me always, but I have her this day, to love and serve her and to point her to the God who will always be with her and who has a plan for her life.

Do you have a heart-grid created by God that is determined to put others
at the center of your priority list? How can you respond to your children in
such a way that they feel valued and loved by you, as they are by Him?

AUGUST 2

*Behold, children are a gift of the LORD,
the fruit of the womb is a reward.*

PSALM 127:3

ONE THING I'VE COME TO understand over the years is that all of us see our children through a grid. A grid is the lens through which we see life. It is created by what we are taught, what we experience, our own study, the surrounding culture, input from mentors, and hopefully prayer and the Holy Spirit! Our grid determines how we behave in relationship to our children.

Do you see your children through the grid of them being a blessing from God? To answer this question, consider this: how does one treat blessings and gifts?

We read in Mark 10:16 that Jesus took the little children into His arms and blessed them. Do you bless your children and see that as a part of being Jesus to them? He said of little children, "the kingdom of God belongs to such as these" (Luke 18:16).

It is written in Matthew 18:6 that Jesus also said, "Whoever causes one of these little ones who believe in Me to stumble, it would be better for him to have a heavy millstone hung around his neck." What would cause a little one to stumble? I think this could include attitudes as well as actions. Are any of those things part of our lives?

As in all great work, raising godly children requires so very much time, effort, work, fortitude, faith, and patience. But it is such an important work, as it will last throughout eternity.

So today, I leave you with these questions:

*What is the grid through which you see your children? What informs
your mind when you look upon their sweet faces? Do you see them
through the eyes of Jesus? Do you focus on them as people to police
or correct—or people to love and serve, understand, protect, and
instruct? Ask the Lord to shape your grid to match His own.*

AUGUST 3

*If anybody does sin, we have an advocate with the
Father—Jesus Christ, the Righteous One.*

1 JOHN 2:1, NIV

ONE SUMMER HERE IN COLORADO SPRINGS, several laws were passed that caused an increase in officers assigned to particular areas, as well as the number of tickets they were expected to be handing out. Just at that time, Joy started to learn to drive. She was at the wheel one day when we saw a policeman hiding behind a road sign on the highway.

"Oh, no, Mom, it's a policeman!" she said. "It makes me sick to my stomach just to see him because the police have been stopping so many people lately. I'm doing all I can just to drive in a straight line, going the right speed, without causing a wreck, but I know I will do something wrong!"

If we speed or drive wildly out of control or run a red light, we should feel guilty and deserve to be caught. We are grateful there are policemen to keep us protected and safe.

But when laws are many and there are eyes everywhere looking for a person to make a mistake, we all feel relieved to get out of the view of potential judgment. So young children will feel afraid of their authorities—their parents—if they feel they are being watched negatively. They will always be wondering what they will do wrong or how they will disappoint or how they will be punished.

---

*Do your children see you as an adversary, waiting for them to fail,
to do something wrong, or to make a mistake? Do they fear you
may be in their faces every moment, reminding them of these
failures and punishing every act of immaturity as well as sin?
Or do your children see you as an advocate, one who comes alongside
them, to love and correct gently, to keep them on the path of
righteousness, to motivate them toward holiness, to encourage them
when they are discouraged, to paint a vision for their lives?*

AUGUST 4

I will walk at liberty, for I seek Your precepts.

PSALM 119:45

MANY LIFE CIRCUMSTANCES HAVE taught me that fitting into the mold or expectations of others is not God's will for me. If, for example, I had followed all the parenting advice of friends, I could have easily cultivated rebellion or resentment in the hearts of my children. But because God gave them to me, it was for me to love, discipline, and nurture them according to their bent and the wisdom and intuition He gave day by day.

Each of my children had out-of-the-box tendencies. Sarah was a dreamer and introvert, and so many times people said we were too close to each other. Now she is my cowriter and dear friend—yet she travels all over the world in ministry, speaking and encouraging others. Joel was so abstract and artistic that at times my mom thought he was deaf because he wouldn't reply to me when I talked to him or asked him to do something. Now he is a creative composer and a brilliant, absent-minded professor who is always dependable and hardworking but not at all time oriented. Nathan didn't sleep through the night until he was four. He was also an extrovert and struggled with ADHD and other clinical disorders. A number of friends were critical of his behavior and immature bouts over the years. Yet I knew in my heart that harshness and spanking and criticism would have alienated him from me. He is now channeling that energy as an actor, an author, and a filmmaker. Joy was a firecracker, confident, always wanting to be doing something; she had a strong sense of personal justice and was ready to fight you about it if necessary! Today she is studying for her doctorate, writing a book, and regularly podcasting her thoughts to the world.

Each child was different; none of them fit anyone's mold—and it was just too much pressure to worry about what anyone else thought, anyway!

How would you describe your own children? Take some time to think about the ways they are unique individuals—and gifts to you!

AUGUST 5

I have loved you with an everlasting love;
I have drawn you with unfailing kindness.

JEREMIAH 31:3, NIV

I PICTURE MY SOUL AS A GARDEN that must be tended and cultivated and watered. If my own soul is healthy, then those who draw from my soul will receive true nurture and strength. All the great women I know have been very intentional about cultivating and building themselves into godly people. They invested purposefully to become who they are.

What are some ways to fill your own soul, so that you may have strength and love to give? Here are three areas to consider:

1. **Surround yourself with good and godly friends.** Find those friends: challenge a friend or two to be a prayer partner, to study a book together, or to meet with you on a regular basis.

2. **Spend time every day with the Lord. Find books, resources, people who can help you with this.** Some simple ways to do this: go through Psalms and circle or underline every promise or character quality of God. Read one chapter of John or Matthew a day and write down one lesson you have learned. Read through Philippians and note all the ways Paul tells us to follow Jesus. You get the idea!

3. **Clean out your soul on a regular basis.** Get rid of rubbish that has kept you from experiencing God's love. "If we confess our sin, He is faithful and righteous to forgive us our sins and to cleanse us from all unrighteousness" (1 John 1:9). Don't hang on to bitterness or condemnation—it will poison you. We must rid our hearts of lies that would keep us from experiencing the generous love of God.

How might you incorporate these three suggestions into your daily life?
Can you see them as ways the Lord is drawing you with His kindness?

Let your gentle spirit be known to all men. The Lord is near.

PHILIPPIANS 4:5

THE ONLY WAY WE CAN TRULY make it in this life productively is to tend to the garden of our own souls. The only way you can be a loving mother, wife, or friend is to have your soul filled with the deep, unchanging, unconditional love of God.

To continue with a few more ideas on how to have a well-watered garden within your soul . . .

4. **Be careful what you read! Surround yourself with books, blogs, and magazines that feed your mind on truth and encourage you to become a better self.** There are so many wonderful devotionals and autobiographies and classic fiction books that are encouraging and truthful, in contrast to others that stir feelings of insecurity or greed or even impurity. Choose well.

5. **Spend time in nature—His workshop.** When I see the artistry of God and rest in the glory of the canopy of His beauty, I find great peace. Creation was made for us. When I invest time in His works of art, I am inspired to reflect His art and beauty in my home as a picture of His reality in an otherwise dark world. Creation nurtures my soul when I take time to observe it.

6. **Restore, relax, recreate.** Moms need sleep! Sometimes grumpiness or depression goes away with just a couple of good nights of sleep or time away with a friend. Moms need to have a friend who understands them and still loves them! They need to laugh and lighten up. Cultivate times of breaks in your life, times of just getting away. Don't always be serious—it is exhausting.

When you look over your bookshelves and tables, are they full of encouragement or discouragement? Perhaps a trip to the bookstore is in order! How can you spend some time in nature today? And consider an earlier bedtime, especially if you're one who burns the midnight oil!

AUGUST 7

Peter got out of the boat, and walked on the water. . . .
But seeing the wind, he became frightened, and beginning
to sink, he cried out, "Lord, save me!"

MATTHEW 14:29-30

WHEN I LOOK BACK OVER OUR life as a family, I often picture a boat on the sea. Clay and I were in the boat, seeking to guide our children to a life of righteousness in the midst of constant storms and challenges. Our secret to surviving was always God and walking by faith with Him. Here are some obstacles we all face in parenting by faith:

Fear When we walk by fear, we say, "This is frightening! What if my children give in to cultural storms?" "What if we do not have enough money to make it?" "I am not adequate for this difficult task of parenthood." We look at the storm around us and find it threatening and discouraging. Yet we cannot live by fear in parenting, or we will fail to show our children the reality of God.

Formula A parent who is dependent on formula says, "If I spank this way, or follow these rules, or use this curriculum, then surely I will raise a perfect child." This kind of parenting depends on works. But formulas will disappoint. Following law will never equal the redeeming power of God, so no matter how much you search, you will not find the right formula because it doesn't exist.

Flesh Sometimes our mental recordings sound like this: "If I just get up earlier, have more quiet times, control my kids' behavior more, craft the right experiences, prepare all organic food, get the right training, and provide the best friends, my children will turn out well." It is true that parenting is hard work. But when we try to help God by exerting great amounts of our energy "helping Him," we eventually come up against our own limitations and want to throw our hands into the air and give up.

Which of these three hindrances is most tempting to you?
How might you take a step toward walking in faith today?

Fear not, for you will not be put to shame;
and do not feel humiliated, for you will not be disgraced.

ISAIAH 54:4

GOD BROUGHT ME TO THE END of myself by giving me interesting situations: three children who were clinically asthmatic, various mental health issues, many moves, church splits, fire and flood in our home, car accidents, etc. There was no way I could do it all or be perfect!

Instead, God wanted me to walk by faith in Him. Every day I learned to give to Him my fish and loaves: "Lord, I know I am not perfect. I cannot provide all my children need. But I am giving you my best, my heart. Here's what I have; please make it enough." God, our devoted and ever-present Father, wants us to come to Him, to ask Him to work, to ask His grace to fill our homes, to ask Him who has access to the brains of our children to draw them to Himself.

And so, miracles happen when God is the One we depend on to work. We acknowledge we are not adequate, but He is. We release our problems and sadness, our limitations and fears into His hands, leave them there, and move to an attitude of worship. We do what He leads us to do and live within our own limitations every day. Whatever we do not get done, we put back into His file and know we can have a go again tomorrow. He is the source of supernatural life, and He wants us to walk this parenting path as we walk all the other paths of our life: by faith.

He is the ultimate source and answer and strength.

Take some time today to put your own concerns into
the file drawer of heaven. Trust God to work.

AUGUST 9

Greater love has no one than this,
that one lay down his life for his friends.

JOHN 15:13

WE WANT SO MUCH TO GIVE our lives to the "bigger" cause. We want to invest our lives for what is important. And yet, is there anything more important than the building of a righteous soul?

The laying down of our lives is not just about moving to the most impoverished country or preaching to thousands, but loving the one right in front of us: the child who would long to have our comforting touch and gentle voice speaking lifegiving words, that he may imagine the voice and touch of God.

The child who needs one more song to be comforted before sleeping, so that he might be able to believe in a God who is patient and willing to answer prayer.

The child who is lonely, confused, and hormonal who will feel the sacrifice of God as we give up the rights to our personal time and comfort to listen and show compassion and sympathy for what is on her heart.

Love is given through lighting a candle and serving a special breakfast one more time on Sunday before church as we open the gospel together, giving up what we wanted to do or the job we hoped to have in order to build a soul, looking into a child's eyes with true interest and compassion instead of looking at a screen while only half-listening. These are the sacrifices of our love, the moment-by-moment giving up of ourselves, the constant, year-in, year-out practice of worship as we serve those in our home in order to please His heart.

It is for Him, for His Kingdom that we serve with willing, generous, lifegiving hearts, building His Kingdom one heart and one sacrifice at a time.

Thank you for loving your children well today.
It is the very best way to show the world true love.

AUGUST 10

When the Son of Man comes, will He find faith on the earth?

LUKE 18:8

THERE ARE SO MANY THROUGHOUT history who would say, "It can't be done" or "You'll never make it" or "At this time in our culture, you just can't expect anyone to live a holy life." And of course, a million other negative outlooks on every situation can be expressed.

These are some of the things naysayers have said to me:

- "You just may not be the type to get married." Clay and I were married when I was twenty-eight.
- "You may not be able to have children." We have four.
- "If you start your own ministry or business, you will most likely fail financially as others do and go under. It just isn't the wisest thing to do." We went four and a half years without a salary, shopped at Goodwill for many things, and by God's grace we got WholeHeart and WholeHeart Press up and running—as it has been for over two decades now.
- "Homeschooling is too hard. You will never be able to do it, especially not the high school years." We made it all the way through with each one.
- "You will never teach this one to read." That child now reads constantly.
- "He will lose his faith for sure. Look at the people he is running around with." No, he didn't. He actually loves God so very much and has a heart for those who are lost.

Satan would just love for us to give up on our ideals, on our marriages, on our families, on our kids, on our churches, on ourselves. Now, I did have my days of doubt, and pathways of darkness, but God kept reminding me of faith and hard work and trusting Him. We are so very glad we did not listen to the voices.

Don't listen.

What naysayers have been talking to you? Spend some time in the Word, pray, write down your commitments, hold fast, and determine to live like what you are—a person of faith!

AUGUST 11

Who is among you that fears the LORD, that obeys the voice of His servant, that walks in darkness and has no light? Let him trust in the name of the LORD and rely on his God.

ISAIAH 50:10

THERE ARE TIMES FOR EACH OF us when it appears that all light, all hope, all strength, all answers are seeping out of our lives and we can do nothing to stop the darkness from coming. It is a wilderness of the soul when we feel that we are at an impasse and do not know what to do or where to go. We are tempted to think that we cannot go one step more. We may even think that the Lord has abandoned us.

God led Abraham into the wilderness, where he was asked to sacrifice his only, beloved son—the one for whom he had waited years and years.

Joseph was brought unjustly into prison where he remained for years after being falsely accused of immorality by a devious woman.

Moses kept sheep and wandered the wilderness for forty years before he became the one who would lead the nation of Israel out of slavery.

Even Jesus was led into the wilderness to be tempted.

There is a mysterious value from heaven's point of view to being in the darkness of life and still choosing to believe in a God who seems to have forgotten us. Darkness is part of the school for the soul, an opportunity to delve into what really matters. It causes us to put away all that is frivolous or vain and to sift through our lives to find the treasures. When we are desperate, we are serious, focused on what life is all about, and what He is all about. Even in this darkness, God tells us what to do—trust in the name of the Lord our God and rely on Him.

Are you in a time of darkness right now? Can I encourage you to be still, to submit, to listen, and to allow God to do whatever work He is after within your heart?

AUGUST 12

*Behold, God is my salvation, I will trust and not
be afraid; for the LORD GOD is my strength and
song, and He has become my salvation.*

ISAIAH 12:2

WHEN WE FIND OURSELVES IN difficult circumstances, especially in seasons where trouble seems to come in waves, we see ourselves for what we really are. Our souls are laid bare. Our limitations, vulnerability, and weaknesses are exposed, as well as our inability to do anything to save ourselves.

The situation for each one might be different: a broken marriage, a prodigal or otherwise seemingly impossible child, financial issues, loneliness, failure, deep soul wounds and rejection at the hands of those who should have loved us, broken dreams. Whatever the situation, we feel alone, unnoticed, helpless.

Of course, this is just the place where God can teach us to rely on Him completely. He so desires to be the One who fulfills our greatest longings. He wants us to know His voice of guidance, purpose, love, and mercy.

It seems those who are wisest, most true, and deepest in humility and gentleness have had to walk through many such times of doubt and testing. Because they have lived through those times, they are deeper, more aware of their need for God, more thankful for His mercy, more focused on eternity, more compassionate toward those who are lost, and more humble in their demeanor.

Sometimes, in all of our efforts to control life and to accomplish our works, we subtly think our success depends on ourselves. Our happiness can be found by striving enough. A loving Father must bring us to the edge of our own limitations, so that we can live above our mere worldly focus and become more familiar with His strength and mercy and love and ways.

*Today would it help to just admit your inability to provide for your
own needs, come up with your own answers, or change yourself without
His strength, wisdom, and love? He's waiting to respond to your cry.*

AUGUST 13

These things I have spoken to you, so that in Me you
may have peace. In the world you have tribulation,
but take courage; I have overcome the world.

JOHN 16:33

PERHAPS I AM JUST MORE OF a wimp than most moms and was less prepared and had a weaker character, but I have struggled so many times in life! My days have been made up of thousands of little moments, insignificant to the public eye: changing one more diaper, listening to the heart's cry of one more teenager, encouraging Clay through one more year of financial difficulty, living through one more season of faith when it all has felt overwhelming.

Isolation and loneliness have been aching companions at different times—feeling that I don't fit in with many people. I have felt lost in the storms of life.

Other times, I have felt like I would drown from feeling the weight of my children's lives and trying to keep them afloat—struggling with differing personalities, meeting their needs, answering their spiritual demands, bearing with them through very difficult seasons like the sleepless nights of babyhood and the mysterious years of toddlerhood, all the trials and joys of elementary school, teenage storms, and young adult decisions and pressures.

Yet somewhere, deep inside, God gave me a tenaciousness to keep going through the storms, to keep trusting Him, to keep believing Him, to have faith that He is good, even when I don't feel His presence.

Integrity in these seemingly insignificant moments will become the measure of integrity over a lifetime and build a picture of faithfulness for others to recall when they go through their own hard times. "Oh, I remember—Mom kept going. She kept loving. She kept believing. I guess I can too. Her story is my foundation for encouragement."

Ask the Lord today to strengthen your own resolve to keep
moving forward. Be the person you needed as a child, and
give your children a picture of faithful steadfastness.

AUGUST 14

A word fitly spoken is like apples of gold in pictures of silver.

PROVERBS 25:11, KJV

TWO DAYS AGO, I talked to one of my children who was feeling quite discouraged by months and months of an uphill climb in this challenging life. I intentionally poured Scripture, love, affirmation, exhortation, and faith into the hungry heart of this child. Today, another phone call came to let me know my words had set him to pondering God's dreams and plans for him, and consequently, he was dreaming world-changing dreams once again.

Words can give great hope to the discouraged. Especially words like

- "I believe in you."
- "You are such a dear friend to me."
- "Your integrity has been such a model for me to follow."
- "I love you for going to work every day and serving me and the kids so diligently. You are a wonderful provider."
- "I love who God has made you."
- "I appreciate your faithful heart and your ability to keep going even in hard times."
- "I love you for knowing me and still loving me!"

Our children need a treasure chest full of our good words to draw from in challenging times. Our words literally build the garden of their souls.

Words are created to be a spring of life by the Word of Life, Jesus, who uses people with real bodies to give His own encouragement through our hearts.

Who needs you to write them a note full of lifegiving words today?
Who needs to hear your words of love and encouragement in person
or on the phone? Who are the five people that God could use you with
today to give them just what they didn't even know they needed?

AUGUST 15

If that is how God clothes the grass of the field,
which is here today and tomorrow is thrown into the fire,
will he not much more clothe you—you of little faith?

MATTHEW 6:30, NIV

WOMEN CAN BE SO UPTIGHT and prone to worry, can't we? I wish I had just learned at a much earlier age to chill more, to dance more, to stop and smell more roses. Each of us has been given a different puzzle—different circumstances, gifts, personalities, families, children, husbands (or lack thereof). I wish I had not been such a people pleaser, trying to live up to the expectations of others—my family, my critics, my peers. My family puzzle just did not fit into the pattern of others' expectations, so trying to live up to those standards was impossible. I wish I had accepted that at the very first instead of fretting about things I could not change.

Some of the cards we have been dealt are pleasing, and some just drive us crazy. But I think the reason we often struggle with His will is because we find ourselves and our circumstances unacceptable, embarrassing, and/or less than perfect.

We can't truly find peace until we relinquish a tight grasp on our rights and learn to rest in the places in which we find ourselves.

To have peace and rest, we must die to ourselves, our failures, and our expectations and hold our hands up to our Father just as a toddler would and say, "I need You. I need Your love, grace, joy, peace today. Without You, I am not able to experience rest in my heart. Help me to see Your presence in this place, this time, these circumstances, within my own limitations. Open my eyes to beauty, to Your fingerprints all around me today."

Hold your arms up to Him, even now. Know He bends low
to pick you up and He will never leave you alone.

Hope does not disappoint, because the love of God has been poured out within our hearts through the Holy Spirit who was given to us.

ROMANS 5:5

AN ACHING LONGING PULSES beneath every person's confident exterior. As the body requires food to live, so a child hungers for love in order to stay alive. Each of us longs for love that embraces, validates, affirms, and whispers to us, "Just as you are, I adore you. You delight me. I think about you. I cherish the day you were born. You are my beloved and always will be, no matter what."

Each of us was crafted with a space deep within our souls that was meant to be filled with love. No one can see from the outside whether ours is completely empty, containing just a bit, or full to overflowing. Yet each person also has the capacity to fill up another's deep cavern with words, touch, and affection. When our soul's space is full, we are most likely to understand and worship God.

Without that filling, we will search for it all of our lives, even in the wrong places—places that promise to give love and fill our hearts, but steal and destroy instead.

A mother's love is the most constant resource of God's love, able to sustain, strengthen, heal, and restore a child.

Hundreds of times in Scripture, He speaks to us of love: "Beloved, let us love one another, for love is from God; and everyone who loves is born of God and knows God" (1 John 4:7). "All men will know that you are My disciples, if you have love for one another" (John 13:35). "Beloved, if God so loved us, we also ought to love one another" (1 John 4:11). "Love covers a multitude of sins" (1 Peter 4:8).

And so we see the necessity of focusing our own lives on love—for God is love.

Is your own soul empty or full today? Spend some time meditating on the truths above, that you may be filled as you remind your soul of God's deep love for you.

AUGUST 17

Make it your ambition to lead a quiet life and
attend to your own business and work with your hands.

1 THESSALONIANS 4:11

THE WORLD IS NOISY, busy, active, loud, relentless.

The Bible says, "Make it your ambition to lead a quiet life" (1 Thessalonians 4:11). The world promotes power, money, things.

The Bible says, "Store up for yourselves treasures in heaven" (Matthew 6:20). The world says, "Beauty is on the outside."

The Bible says, "Man looks at the outward appearance, but the LORD looks at the heart" (1 Samuel 16:7). The world says leadership is found in position and power.

The Bible says, "Whoever wishes to save his life will lose it; but whoever loses his life for My sake will find it" (Matthew 16:25). The world says, "Do something great you can be proud of."

Jesus built deep relationships for three years with a dozen men and a few others in a community of friends. His ministry was small and personal, meeting needs, eating meals, living life with a focused few, serving them. He never traveled more than a hundred miles from Galilee. He never wrote a book, spoke on television, wrote a blog, or lived prominently.

Yet more words and books have been written about Him than any other. Lives have been changed, centuries of history rendered totally different because of the power of truth lived out and spoken from the quiet, gentle, humble life Christ lived during His time on the earth.

Could Jesus still live through me, faithfully, quietly, personally, powerfully, right where I am, so the impact of my life of integrity would reach the far corners of the earth if I lived according to His ways and not the world's?

How should this apply to you and help determine your priorities
and values as you seek to live for God's glory? How can you live a
servant-oriented, children-valuing, eternity-focused life, centered
on listening to Him and closing out the voices of the world?

AUGUST 18

Be strong and let your heart take courage; yes, wait for the LORD.

PSALM 27:14

AFTER-WEEKEND DUTIES CRY OUT EACH Monday morning as I slip down the stairs, still sleepy and in need of my morning cuppa. After all these years, last night's dishes still accost me as if they're a surprise—coffee cups, plates of now-dried-on snacks, all sorts of evidence that we spent hours together on Sunday relaxing, eating, laughing, and making messes—and now it must be dealt with, again.

Of course, there are all the worries of life still there to greet me too: money issues, problems with children, pressures of family and marriage. They are still there, piled high when Monday morning comes with yet another week of challenges ahead. In the midst of all the daily chores, there are always these bigger ones also hovering over us!

Waiting, working, fretting, wondering—what is going to be the end to all of this, the end points for all these wonderful people in my home with various strengths, weaknesses, hopes, and dreams?

Waiting on the Lord for answers and for life to change and for help to come has been my most common challenge throughout life—waiting to get married, waiting to get pregnant, waiting to have the baby, waiting for the baby to sleep through the night, waiting for myself to be mature someday . . .

Waiting with a gentle spirit is difficult and miraculous, an acquired habit that comes with much practice and experience. One of the most important ways my children learn about faith is to watch me wait, in grace, through all the trials of my life. Putting a flower in the vase, lighting a candle, and filling our home with music communicates my belief to them that God will show up. He is with us. He hears us and will answer, and I am going to prepare for the day by celebrating life, looking to the time we will see and know His presence and faithfulness.

How can you wait in faith today in a way that
is visible to you and your children?

AUGUST 19

If there is any encouragement in Christ, any comfort from love,
any participation in the Spirit, any affection and sympathy,
complete my joy by being of the same mind, having the
same love, being in full accord and of one mind.

PHILIPPIANS 2:1-2, ESV

J. R. R. Tolkien's Lord of the Rings series is a favorite of our family. We all want to be part of a greater story, to feel that our lives are meaningful, that we are not invisible, but that our personality, our faith, and our work will produce something of eternal value in our lifetime.

The fellowship of the men who went in force together to return the ring to the fires of Mordor is a picture of the strength, valor, and encouragement necessary for all of us to complete the journey of our own great callings. The church, too, was called to be that: a community of like-minded believers who would be there for one another in all seasons of life. We were to have the voice of God coming to us through friends, family, and those who surrounded us, our own "fellowship of the ring."

Yet Satan has crafted and promoted the ideal of fierce independence and a lone ranger mentality. We have come to admire those who strike out on their own, handle their own problems, and seemingly rely on no one. We go to large churches where we are not held accountable and do not know our neighbors. This has never been God's plan.

We need people to rally us to our best, to hold us accountable, to talk us out of compromise, to pray with us for miracles.

Today, make it a point to call your friends, write or call your children,
send a card to a friend, make a memorable meal, plan a coffee date with
your husband. Develop your own fellowship of the ring, that you might have
foundations of strength, support, and love in all the seasons of your life.

AUGUST 20

*Make me know Your ways, O LORD; teach me Your paths.
Lead me in Your truth and teach me, for You are the
God of my salvation; for You I wait all the day.*

PSALM 25:4-5

THIS MORNING, when it was still dark, I crept out of bed so as not to awaken anyone in the house. I have always had a child's delight in being alone in the early morning, like I was playing hide-and-seek with those asleep in my home. I made a big mug of coffee with a dash of vanilla and drove away from my home at 5:45, just as the sun was peeking out from behind the clouds.

I was in need of time with Him. Sometimes with all the bodies and voices swirling about in my home, I lose track of Him. And so, I have learned to get away sometimes and to always invest my morning hours in Him who is always waiting to talk to me.

I read Psalm 25 many times this morning, and the words became my prayers. God reminded me of how David waited for Him, trusting Him for deliverance. He refused to forcibly take the throne from Saul, but humbly waited on God to make His move. For years and years He waited, writing and praising all along. Is this why David was called a man after God's heart?

And so, this morning, my soul is once again filled with joy, peace, worship, and rest—I do not know the future, but I rest in the One who does. It all comes from a habit, a rhythm of making time to be with Him, to hear His voice, to follow His ways.

---

*May He guide you to His presence today. Do you need to
find a place where you can get away to be with Jesus?*

AUGUST 21

They tie up heavy burdens and lay them on men's shoulders, but they themselves are unwilling to move them with so much as a finger.

MATTHEW 23:4

SUPPOSE MY HUSBAND CAME TO me one day and said, "Now, Sally, these are my standards for what I expect in our home. I want a clean house and a homemade dinner each night. Our children should behave, memorize Scripture, learn to play a musical instrument, be mannerly, and have godly character. I expect you to read a chapter of both the Old and New Testament every day, and I want the kids to have three books of the Bible memorized by the time they are ten. I will be checking with you every day to correct anything you have done that is not up to my standards. If we keep these ideals, our children will turn out to be moral, spiritual, hardworking adults. Agreed?"

What if, then, my husband would come to me every day and say, "I noticed that someone left a sock on the den floor, so you have not succeeded in training our children well. And I also did not appreciate that fast-food dinner last night. You are becoming a bit lazy, since you did not make me a homemade meal. I noticed that two of the kids misspelled a word on their thank-you notes to the grandparents. You need to work harder, get up earlier, and make a better schedule, as we are falling behind on our goals."

Of course, goals given to me as a list by a husband who dictated what my behavior should be, without consideration of a relationship, would produce death, not life, in my relationship to him.

Why do we expect a different result if we treat our children this way?

In looking at this imaginary situation humorously, is anything coming to mind that may have caused a pang in your heart? Ask the Lord to show you any areas where you are putting expectations onto the dear ones in your family that are arbitrary and without a basis of kindness, invitation, and relationship.

AUGUST 22

*I am the good shepherd, and I know My own and My
own know Me, even as the Father knows Me and I know
the Father; and I lay down My life for the sheep.*

JOHN 10:14-15

GOD IS SUCH A WONDERFUL PROVIDER FOR US. Take a moment to look at nature and all the flowers and color and creatures that He crafted for our pleasure. When sin separated us from Him, He came among us, giving up the comfort, glory, and honor He held in heaven to serve, feed, live with, and encourage His own precious disciples.

Our life with God is not just made up of a list of rules He has given us. He comes as the servant King, the One who lays down His life, the One who is humble and meek. As a good parent, God gives us wisdom and guidance so that our lives will be healthy, strong, and protected.

This becomes our pattern for parenting. He served and loved and sacrificed and gave of Himself so that we would long to be holy out of our gratitude and reverence and love for Him. He called His disciples to serve, to love, and to be holy. He gave them true life and beauty that filled their deepest needs, as well as fulfilling their longings to live a purposeful life.

Getting the rules right or defining all of the rules and theology correctly will not make our children want to serve God. It is laying down our lives for them—serving them, listening to them, loving who God made them to be, that will secure in them a desire to love God with all of their hearts. By experiencing our love for them, they will more easily understand and receive God's love, as it will already be familiar to their hearts and minds.

---

*Do you realize how precious you are, that Jesus would lay down
His life for you? Let it soak in today. You are dearly loved.*

AUGUST 23

The wise woman builds her house, but
the foolish tears it down with her own hands.

PROVERBS 14:1

A NUMBER OF YEARS AGO, our family had the opportunity to build our dream house in the mountains of Colorado. We selected a site especially for its views, chose a floor plan that would be just right for us, and thought through how we would furnish it to suit our family. And of course, first we had to dig a foundation! A beautiful, sturdy home doesn't just sprout from the ground; a plan must be put in place.

As we raised our children, making a plan for how we would train them was paramount. In a nutshell, training a child means constant instruction, interference with immature and inappropriate behavior, consequences of some sort, then modeling or requiring a correction of the behavior, with constant attention to the relationship.

We said, "No, not that way—this way" over and over again, gently, lovingly, firmly, and consistently. We were also ready to praise for good choices and say, "You are growing so strong inside, and I see you making such wise choices."

We did not want to control our children because we were bigger and louder and could create havoc in their souls with our anger, but we wanted to train and motivate them so they would understand early on that they had the capacity to decide how to behave. If they responded to our wills and desires by following our instruction, they would be blessed. If they did not respond correctly, they were choosing to be disciplined in some way—the choice was theirs.

"I cannot make you strong—only you can decide how strong and excellent you want to become. But I believe God has created you to be wise and strong and valiant. So, I am hoping that you will choose to obey Mommy, so that you can be blessed and happy."

When you think about training in your home, which areas
might need to be strengthened? How can you encourage
your children to make right choices today?

[Jesus said,] "How often I wanted to gather your children together, just as a hen gathers her brood under her wings, and you would not have it!"

LUKE 13:34

I GET GIDDY JUST THINKING about the last week in August. Family Day is a time each year that we gather with all of our children and their families to celebrate the Clarksons. My mother heart longs to have all of us together, close, touching each other, enjoying each other. My children are my beloved ones, the ones to whom I am related—they came from my body, I have nursed them and loved them. They are my brood. We eat our family's favorite foods and have feasts together. We spend all of our time, just us, talking, giggling, celebrating life, sharing our dreams and thoughts, cuddling together on the couches watching favorite movies, going hiking together, and taking intentional time to remember together all the ways we have seen God answer prayer and provide for us as a family.

It is a time I am blessed to gather my brood under my wings. As a mother, I delight in sharing the company of my precious children and loving and ministering to them and sharing hearts one more time, before they all go back into the world.

And so in today's verse Jesus shared with us the same mothering example—He longed to gather His brood under His wings, so to speak. Jesus wants a relationship with us. But we, too, must be intentional.

In what ways are you intentional in gathering your family to remember who you are and what you love? In what ways are you intentional about your relationship with Jesus?

AUGUST 25

Rejoice in the Lord always; again I will say, rejoice!

PHILIPPIANS 4:4

ON JOY'S FIFTH BIRTHDAY, I planned a party I thought would please her. I spent the morning Martha-ing about, putting out cake and balloons, making finger sandwiches, preparing what I thought she would like.

The children finally came, and for the next two hours, they fought over toys, spilled red punch on their clothes and the floor, and one little boy threw a toy across the room, hitting another little girl in the head and making her cry. It was a memory of messes, crying, friction, and stress, and Joy was unhappy the whole time, trying to please me by staying at the party even though she wasn't enjoying it.

When the guests finally left, I heard the sound of little feet running across our deck. I walked out the kitchen door and glanced into the afternoon shadows, and there was sweet Joy.

Dressed in her favorite, lightly stained and torn ballet outfit, she was running across the deck with a bubble wand lifted high, bubbles flying out behind her. I stopped and sat on our picnic bench and watched her as the sun went down. For an hour she played and ran and delighted in the beauty of her own bubble parade. I took it in, cherishing the picture in my mind, and chastised myself for missing the glory of her beauty and youth in my striving to fulfill the expectations of the party I thought would make her happy.

"Oh, Mommy!" she exclaimed, "This is my favorite time of the whole day! I am having so much fun. Thank you for giving me such a wonderful present!"

She climbed into my lap and snuggled up with a happy sigh. So I melted into her little body, breathing in her purehearted, innocent love. Finally, I was able to cherish the moment and took the time to take a soul photograph, the imprint of which will be with me forever.

How can you let go of expectations and
throw your own bubble parade today?

Therefore there is now no condemnation for those who are in Christ Jesus.

ROMANS 8:1

WHEN I DRESS UP AND LOOK LIKE a real adult at conferences, speaking passionately about all my ideals and commitments, it would be easy for me to give the illusion that I am a perfect person who has finally reached maturity. However, when I return home, I still have to live with myself! And myself is still sinful and selfish at heart. Even in the midst of grand ideals, I can still stumble and trip over the most menial issues like traffic, or a crowded seat on the plane, or a night without sleep.

We all live in this broken place, this place separated from perfect love and grace. It is not wrong to feel anger or depression or discouragement or deep fear or even hate. You are not an unattractive personality or person if you feel these things. Do not listen to the lie that it is all your fault and you stand condemned, as that only leads to despair and hopelessness.

The question is, what do we do with all of these feelings? You are not a bad person for being immature or even for feeling anger at the stress another sinful person brings to you. But how you live by faith in the next moments, how you speak to your own brain, will determine if you will become more free, more loving, more filled with grace and compassion, or if you will become a victim of the darkness caused by living in a sinful world.

It is best to not allow the "bad" people in your life to define you. You cannot make immature people mature. You cannot control how they behave. But you can control your own actions: what you think, practice, and cherish inside your heart. This is the foundation of your whole being.

---

*Remember who you are: you are forgiven. You are royalty
in the eyes of God. You are not your past; the old things
have passed away, and all things have become new.*

AUGUST 27

He was saying to them all, "If anyone wishes to come after Me,
he must deny himself, and take up his cross daily and follow Me."
LUKE 9:23

I AM SOMEWHAT OF A POLLYANNA at heart and would love for everyone to be happy and living in harmony with each other. However, God has not allowed that to be my story. I have many conflicts that it seems will never resolve, challenges, issues, and the typical and atypical stresses that come from being in a fallen world. Many of these anguishing difficulties I have had to bear for years, waiting for God's answer to my prayers.

But in this moment, with only Him and me talking, I realized that these "crosses" are just what my heavenly Father wants me to take up. These spots of pain in my heart are just the places in which He wishes me to trust, to worship, to accept limitations as part of the story of my life that can glorify Him if I am willing to bear it all joyfully, right where I am.

My Christian life cannot consist of one round after another of, "I am Yours, but I know You will let me whine and complain about this particular issue or person because it is hard for me." If these crosses are what He wants me to pick up and carry, they are part of my purpose in this world, and somehow, when I carry them as a gift, I can better reflect His glory.

So what cross is He asking you to bear by faith and as a point of worship to Him? Is it a trying child? A difficult marriage? Irrational or angry or passive family members? An illness? A death? A disappointment? It is only as we pick up our crosses and carry them to the place of dying to ourselves and living for Him, in every circumstance, that we will live in freedom, grace, love, and worship.

What cross will you carry, for His glory, today?

I press on toward the goal for the prize
of the upward call of God in Christ Jesus.

PHILIPPIANS 3:14

MANY YEARS AGO, Joy and I were at one of my conferences and at the end of one long day, we were lying under the stars on some lounge chairs having a lovely conversation about the need to cultivate our souls. I was sharing what I would plant in my own soul garden, and what I needed to pluck out (sin, bad attitudes) in order to be sure that my heart was always growing more into the person I want to be, when I grow up into His likeness.

So each of us came up with five attributes describing the person we wanted to grow into. Here are mine:

1. I want to be a person who is characterized by biblical, generous love—to all people, in all situations, as much as possible.

2. I want to always lean in the direction of faith at every curve in my path— to believe in Him, always, and honor Him with a heart of faith.

3. I want to leave a legacy of truth, wisdom, and righteousness through teaching and writing and speaking, that others may know and love Him more because I was intentional in their lives.

4. I want to be humble, gentle, and gracious—redeeming the lost, healing the brokenhearted—and bring this spirit into my relationships.

5. I want to take initiative to serve and reach out to others and be a faithful servant leader—to be as Jesus was. While we were yet sinners, Christ died for us—He sought us.

So what do you want to be when you grow up? Whatever grid you establish in your mind is how you will live and how you will invest. I am praying that you will be inspired to live in the excellencies of His Spirit, who is stirring inside of you.

What five attributes do you want to characterize your life?

AUGUST 29

Her sins, which are many, have been forgiven, for she loved much; but he who is forgiven little, loves little.

LUKE 7:47

WE ARE ALL BROKEN, and this world we live in is a broken place, where death of heart, of relationships, of love is prevalent. Often we mask deep, dark feelings of regret over various failures.

Moral failure before marriage, failure to create an intimate marriage, or fostering anger and resentment in marriage and then feeling like a failure for never being able to become close or get rid of our pettiness . . .

Failure with our children, having shown anger or neglect to them, not really liking them, or doing everything we could to reach their hearts but ending up with a prodigal who breaks our heart . . .

Failure with friends, petty quarrels, difficulty forgiving and forgetting . . .

Living with habits such as eating disorders, overspending, cherishing idols we know consume our souls, reading dark novels, or more darkness with sexual habits than we can admit . . .

We are all broken people. Yet, we must understand that He does not define us by our failures. He is "mindful that we are but dust" (Psalm 103:14). It is an illusion that anyone you know is perfect or can become perfect through lots of effort. No one can. All we like sheep have gone astray. We simply cannot hold to our ideals by striving toward them, and we are all in total need of His mercy and grace every day.

We want to serve Him. We want to be holy. We intend to be gracious, loving, and patient. But we all fail and fall short, again and again and again.

So, do not judge others—or yourself!—but love outrageously, deeply, compassionately, just as He, gentle in spirit, has loved you. And in consequence, we will see love—deep, grateful, healing love—abounding, flowing out all over, because of Him.

Knowing you've received forgiveness from God is the first step to offering it to ourselves. Do you need to forgive yourself for something today?

AUGUST 30

I am confident of this very thing, that He who began a good work in you will perfect it until the day of Christ Jesus.

PHILIPPIANS 1:6

THE LEAVES ARE STARTING TO turn from various shades of green to vibrant oranges, golds, and reds. Crisp morning air greets us as we close the bedroom windows before heading downstairs to brew a hot cup of tea. A fresh, new season is just around the corner! As many families prepare to go "back to school," our hearts wonder what God has in store for us next. What classes has He enrolled us in? Is it "Patience 101" again?! Will I learn more about His love? Grace? Discipline?

Fall has always felt to me like the real new year, and I have great anticipation to begin with a clean slate, with (as Anne of Green Gables said) no mistakes in it yet, just all new possibilities. So it is exciting to see how the schedule will come together and what we will pursue in the way of commitments and activities.

It is also a strategic time to reflect on our children's character and our own. One filter that helps me determine which commitments to make is ensuring that my calendar is not so crammed with activities and lessons that the only time I have with Joy is in the car.

Fall is a reflective season in which to take some time to pray over each of my children, asking the Lord for wisdom in how to help each child grow in their faith—those who are in my house and those who are far away. I ask God to show me their potential, their gifts, their temptations, the areas in which they need to grow. Wisdom comes from the Holy Spirit, who has access to my children's hearts, minds, and souls.

What's on your agenda this fall? Ask God what's on His agenda for your family before you make many plans!

AUGUST 31

We are God's masterpiece. He has created us anew in Christ Jesus,
so we can do the good things he planned for us long ago.

EPHESIANS 2:10, NLT

IT IS SIMPLE TO SEE ALL THE FLAWS in my children and myself. And it would be easy for me to take the blame for my children's failures, since I am their mother and responsible for training them! However, rather than focusing on the bad, it's more beneficial to focus on faith and the potential someday to be realized after years of praying and seeing God work. It's better to have faith that God can take my honest offering of steadfastness and hope.

He will make up for my deficits. Though I don't understand why bad things happen, He is stronger and bigger than all the "bad," and in His time, He will redeem it all. Faith must be in His power and not my own. Rather than focusing on my own lack of strength, I trust His ability to reach my children. Giving Him my best, I leave the results in His hands, waiting for His timing. This relinquishing happens one minute at a time—one detail of my life at a time.

When the enemy convinces us that our concentration should be placed on what is lacking in our lives, our personality flaws, our family's difficult places, we become unable to affect the world in a positive way. And that is a terrible loss, indeed.

Do you know that you, too, are a beautiful masterpiece crafted by
a talented Artist? (Read the verse again!) How does that knowledge
affect the way you see yourself? Now look at what you were
created anew for—so you can do good things planned long ago.
Take some time to consider yourself in light of the needs around
you—and the possibility that you've been created to meet them.

SEPTEMBER 1

The Lord is not slow about His promise, as some count slowness, but is patient toward you, not wishing for any to perish but for all to come to repentance.

2 PETER 3:9

SOMETIMES I THINK IT IS BECAUSE most families are smaller these days that we micromanage little children. When a mom has numerous children who are constantly in need of food, clothing, and being trained to do chores and accomplish their responsibilities, she is much more gradual about the training of her little babies, and each just lives and grows naturally in the warp and woof of family life.

My children tended to learn together what the Clarkson values, manners, and expectations were. With asthmatic and ear-infected siblings, they often had to wait their turn. Life itself gave them ways to learn to be unselfish and to learn to serve, because I needed their help!

And eventually, they all grew up. None of them now need a pacifier, wear a diaper, or want to sleep with me every night! God has put maturity into children's very DNA and brain cells. It is ours to be patient with the process, to enjoy it and to learn from it.

If we learn to walk with our children patiently and look to God for guidance while training them little by little, the mysterious life of God begins to work in and through their hearts and lives. We must remember to lean into the maturing process patiently and not fight it, and to cultivate joy along the way.

Do you realize that God is patient toward you and wants you to come to repentance—that He is not in heaven just waiting for a chance to whack you over the head, but longing to see you come to Him and be changed? He is not in a hurry or frustrated with your immaturity. Ask Him to reveal His heart and help you pass that grace along to your children.

SEPTEMBER 2

If I go and prepare a place for you, I will come again and receive you to Myself, that where I am, there you may be also.

JOHN 14:3

At 5 o'clock on a Friday morning several years ago, Sarah crept into our darkened bedroom and said, "There was a call on your cell phone in the living room a few minutes ago."

My brother was on the other end of the line. "Mom just passed away, and I wanted you to know."

We had anticipated this moment for a long time, as she had been ill. Now, it was final. There would be no more opportunities for words of life between us, no sweet caresses against warm cheeks, no putting to rest any unsettled issues, no more moments to bless or take away curses. Her opportunity to live a story was now over.

I wondered then if the One who said He was going to "prepare a place" for me in heaven had prepared a welcome committee that morning for my mom. Perhaps my dad would be there, my oldest brother, my mom's parents, and maybe even her grand-parents. It made me smile, to imagine her feeling well again, laughing, hugging those who had shared in her life.

Memories began to flood my heart: birthday celebrations, candles lit and music playing as she put on bright red lipstick each evening to welcome my dad home after work, the ways she served me as an asthmatic child, singing songs in the dark nights of difficult breathing, the way she gently played finger games with me in church to pass away the long minutes of the sermons, her willingness to listen to me for many hours throughout the passages of childhood, the little welcome signs that greeted me every time I came home from college or for holidays. I will always be grateful for the gracious ways she mothered.

What beautiful, lifegiving memories will you make with your own children today?

SEPTEMBER 3

When you pass through the waters, I will be with you; and through the rivers, they will not overflow you. When you walk through the fire, you will not be scorched, nor will the flame burn you.

ISAIAH 43:2

STORMS OF CULTURE AND LIFE ARE COMMON, and they wreak havoc with us as we are tossed about from without and within. As we look at the wild waves threatening to overcome us, panic is a natural response. Fear paralyzes.

There are three things I am learning to do in the midst of my own storms, which I encourage you to try:

1. **Remember and list all of the ways you have seen God's faithfulness and answers to prayer.** This is why our family celebrates family day. Even in the most difficult years, we could look back and see His handprints in our lives— He was always there, He was always providing.

2. **Find a promise, and hold fast to His Word.** Have you ever been in the car with your children and all of them start speaking to you at once, as though you can hear their voices above the roar? The voices of the world, fear of what-ifs, all speaking at once, drown out His voice. We must still our lives and sit quietly, that He may speak to us.

3. **Determine to hold fast and to be a courageous warrior in your battles.** Your children are looking to your story to give them courage in the stories they will yet live. Hold fast, find a friend to pray with, and stand strong. You only have the promise of this moment to proclaim His faithfulness in your own life for all generations to see.

Find a way to stay strong in your own storms. Pray every day with a friend. Fill your mind with beauty, songs that bring courage, stories of those who have gone before. Rest deep and watch for evidence of His love for you.

SEPTEMBER 4

In the beginning God created the heavens and the earth.

GENESIS 1:1

I LOVE FALL THE BEST, I think. Chilly air begins to fill the nights so we must close our windows and snuggle under covers. Warm, simmering, pungent soups bubble on the stove while scents of herb-crusted bread waft from the oven. Fireplaces and candles dance with flames, and music floats into our subconscious to please and soothe the rough places of our souls.

The spirit of home stands at the doorway, to compel those outside to enter into a place of life, comfort, rest, beauty. As women made in God's image, we are designed to create—to cultivate, to subdue, and to take all of the raw materials of our lives and craft them into something beautiful.

When God laid the foundations of the earth, the splendor and magnificence of vibrant color, eye-captivating beauty, and melodious sounds, the spontaneous response of the sparkling morning stars was to celebrate with heavenly choruses, singing His praises and worth, while the sons of God shouted and celebrated wildly with joy (Job 38:4-7). What an overwhelming display of vibrant, heart-filling celebration of His glory it must have been!

If we want to display just a small bit of the divine through the beauty of our home, we must rule over our domains with order, rhythms, traditions, and anchors in our schedule that work together to reflect the divine.

You may say, "My life is already so busy, I don't have time to add one more ideal." The dilemma, then, is how to weave beauty, color, celebration into an already busy life. Where is the space in your schedule for such effort? If you can find none, consider what may need to be removed in order to make room.

He summoned the crowd with His disciples, and said to them,
"If anyone wishes to come after Me, he must deny himself, and take up
his cross and follow Me. For whoever wishes to save his life will lose it,
but whoever loses his life for My sake and the gospel's will save it."

MARK 8:34-35

ROUSING TALES OF HEROES SAVING damsels in distress, romantic accounts of valor and sacrifice in history, or heartwarming tales of family, home, children—I just love a good story. All of my life, I have been able to lose myself in captivating tales.

Scripture is full of dramatic stories of bravery (David and Goliath), romance (Ruth and Boaz), courage (Moses stepping into the Red Sea with a couple of million children, animals, and adults screaming behind him, being chased by the strongest army ever known), and so many more. And of course, each of us is also living a story.

Maybe yours doesn't feel exciting at this moment or strategic in light of history. But most people who are considered heroes of the faith were normal people amid normal life circumstances who trusted God even when the others surrounding them were naysayers and could not see Him.

The story told about you in the future depends on the story you are living today.

In other words, the situation you find yourself in today, whether it requires excellence in morality, courageous endurance, faithful belief, or overcoming love, is the basis of your integrity or lack of integrity tomorrow. You cannot leave a story of faithfulness in the minds and hearts of your children, grandchildren, and others unless you actually live your story with faith, courage, moral excellence, self-discipline, and sacrificial love today.

All of us love to hear great stories, and your children long
to see you as their hero. How might the way you want to
be remembered affect the way you live this day?

SEPTEMBER 6

I do not ask You to take them out of the world,
but to keep them from the evil one.

JOHN 17:15

MANY EYEBROWS WERE RAISED when we announced Nathan's move to Hollywood, with people questioning our morality because it is such a difficult place. I did not ask God to send my children into morally challenging arenas, but I did ask Him to help Clay and me build them into godly leaders who would take His light to a dark world. Since they are adults and we have released them into God's hands to follow the roads He has put on their hearts, I spend a lot of time on my knees every day and ask for God to guide, intervene when necessary, and protect my children.

At some point in the Christian life, regardless of peers, our church's stand, our friends' opinions, blogs, or other loud voices pontificating, we must decide who we truly think Jesus is, and how His life and words should influence the way we live and the choices we make. He calls us to live radically, whether that means staying at home with our children or serving Him in the world in some unusual place. We must follow Him, not anyone else.

Jesus, the exact image of God, spoke kindly to prostitutes, offered them a clean slate of forgiveness, and allowed them to touch Him and wash His feet.

Jesus touched the infirm and contaminated—the lepers, the woman who was unclean, the blind, the sick. He looked out on the multitudes not with condemnation but with compassion and told us to pray that God would send laborers into the harvest.

I wanted an Anne of Green Gables life for me and my children that was safe, protected, and always G-rated. But that is not the world God has placed us in.

Have you been tempted to despair or want to hide your
children away from the ugliness of the world? How does
remembering Jesus' ways with people and His prayer that
we be protected from the evil one inform your thoughts?

SEPTEMBER 7

*Praise be to the LORD my Rock, who trains my hands
for war, my fingers for battle. He is my loving God and
my fortress, my stronghold and my deliverer, my shield,
in whom I take refuge, who subdues peoples under me.*

PSALM 144:1-2, NIV

OFTEN I SEE PARENTS WHO RAISE their children to run away from cultural battles and stay far off from those who are lost and broken and who have scars and difficulties. They find it easy to criticize those who are engaged in bringing the light of Christ into the arena of darkness.

I will admit that the world can be a very fearful place to be. But God has asked me, as a mom, to live by faith, not to look to the limitations of my own life and this wicked world we live in, but to the God who tells us to overcome evil with good.

So I had to ask, "Would He have me do anything less than send my own children, as God sent His own Son, into the world to redeem dark places?"

Preparing children to run away from the battle will require a very different parenting philosophy from preparing them to engage in it.

As for the Clarksons, we will seek to engage in the battle and rub shoulders with the lost, because we cannot do other than what our Lord and Savior showed us to do—to go into the world to make disciples, to see the multitudes with compassion, and become workers in the harvest field of the world.

*Pray with me, for your own children: "Lord, these are Your
children, created by You with a personality and purpose.
Train them for the spiritual warfare in which they will engage.
Prepare them for the battles they will confront. Be their fortress,
their stronghold, their deliverer and shield. They are not ours to
hold on to, but to prepare for Your Kingdom purposes. Amen."*

SEPTEMBER 8

I am writing to you, little children, because your sins have been forgiven you for His name's sake. I am writing to you, fathers, because you know Him who has been from the beginning. I am writing to you, young men, because you have overcome the evil one. I have written to you, children, because you know the Father.

I JOHN 2:12-13

PEDALING AS FAST AS THEIR SHORT pudgy legs would pump, two ruddy-faced, puffing, and deeply intent little boys came racing up beside me on red bikes. I was out for a late Sunday afternoon walk on a glorious Colorado day with my golden retriever, Kelcey.

"Hey, ma'am, what is the name of your dog? Can we pet it?"

Chattering, laughing, and petting ensued. "How old is this dog? She's big!" and "Where do you live? We found an amazing hill to race our bikes on, but we won't run over you," they burst out, words running one on top of another in their excitement. The glory of young manhood was at its best.

Oh, how I love childhood years. Each day is a miracle.

According to my sweet, learned husband, the Bible seems to divide the life of people into three phases: childhood, young adulthood, and adulthood. In our home, we treated our children differently at each phase. Each new level of life came with new training and responsibility in order to give them a heart for our King and for His Kingdom.

Helping our children understand that they are quite influential and crucial in extending the influence of the Kingdom of God in their lifetime is foundational. They must learn and embrace this theme in their inner being as part of the self-image, from the point of view of God's design and purpose for them. The home is God's perfect place for passing on these eternal values, and crafting such a home is an art and one of the greatest callings a mother can fulfill.

Which phase are your children in today? How might you adjust your expectations as well as training to embrace that reality?

Everyone who hears these words of Mine and acts on them, may be compared to a wise man who built his house on the rock. and the rain fell, and the floods came, and the winds blew and slammed against that house; and yet it did not fall, for it had been founded on the rock.

MATTHEW 7:24-25

BEING ABLE TO CUDDLE AND play with my sweet granddaughter, Lilian, is one of my greatest joys. I wish all of my children would get married, have lots of children, and move in next door. How I would love for our lives to reflect the fairy tale of family I have always dreamed.

But the reality is, God has chosen different paths for my children. It is important to spend the time our children are with us training them for the world they will inherit. The beginning point for our children is to build strong, firm foundations, emotionally, mentally, physically, and spiritually, on the Rock of Christ, so that they will be able to stand firm and strong.

There is a necessary sacrifice of the mom's life to build these ideals. They do not just happen from reading a ten- to fifteen-minute devotional a day. The principles must be a part of the mom's life, part of her regular instruction to her children, and then the air of the truth must be breathed in and out, morning, noon, and night, so that the child's very soul will be shaped on the principles of wisdom, godly choices, and convictions, which take years and years to build.

The soundness of all great structures rests on the foundation. We must build the foundation of our children's souls on solid truths that are timeless. We must be students of the Word, ingesting it deep in our own souls, as a teacher cannot pass on that which is not first hers.

Make a list of the foundations you believe are most important to share with your children. Start with one, and spend some time thinking about how best you could share that truth today.

SEPTEMBER 10

By wisdom a house is built, and by understanding it is established; and by knowledge the rooms are filled with all precious and pleasant riches.

PROVERBS 24:3-4

WHETHER A TWELFTH-FLOOR APARTMENT in Hong Kong, a weather-beaten farmhouse in England, or a suburban two-story in America, home is the place where souls are shaped and nurtured. Each of us, as mothers, has the ability to picture and embody the life of God in our own homes. We can cultivate samples of His creativity by filling our homes with art—pictures on the walls, books in baskets, arrangements of flowers strewn through our rooms, pianos or flutes or violins or whatever we like readily available so we can all practice music, paints and crayons for drawing pictures of things real or imagined—there is an endless amount of ways to pass on the reality of our living and vibrant God through our home life.

The starting point is to see our home domain as a kingdom. We are the queens, ruling those domains. As sovereigns, we have the responsibility to rule over them with excellence and intentionality, shaping the outcome of the lives lived there. A good queen always leads in the way that will provide best for those under her dominion, and so we may lead well, as we have observed many in history have done, or we may lead poorly, with devastating results for those under our charge.

Learning to embrace this vision is the beginning point of understanding the influence and capacity we have been given by God to lead, build, inspire, and train a generation of Kingdom workers who will bring His light to bear in their generation.

*What might you do today to add reminders of all
the beauty of God inside your own home?*

SEPTEMBER 11

In the world you have tribulation, but take courage;
I have overcome the world.

JOHN 16:33

RIGHT IN THE MIDDLE OF JESUS' LOVING, teaching, encouraging, and training His disciples, they embark on crossing the familiar lake where they have lived all their lives, and suddenly a life-threatening storm overtakes them.

How could this happen? Does Jesus want to lose all of His disciples at once? Is He trying to discourage them by letting this storm rage? After all, they had given up their whole lives to follow Him. Their hearts were dedicated to worshiping Him. They were busy serving other people day after day. And now this? I imagine they thought, *Is this any way to treat those who are following You?*

Just so, sometimes the "whaps" on our lives feel personal, invasive, and too much.

Have you ever felt that way? *I have cooked. I have washed dishes. I have lost years of sleep. I have loved and served and given—does anyone notice? Does it matter? And now this? Another storm? Another problem? The relentlessness of life is about to drown me, Lord.*

And so they wake Jesus up and ask, "Do you not care that we are perishing, Lord?" That is the question that we, too, have on our hearts when the storms come.

When He rises, He rebukes the storm's wind and the ship settles on calm seas. Then he asks, "Where is your faith?" (Mark 4:35-41). I suppose the men looked at one another, garments soaked and askew, hair going every which way, eyes a bit wild from the excitement and fear of those moments when it seemed He was unaware or unconcerned about their dilemma.

Yet, He was there all along, waiting for them to call on Him.

Are you feeling like the storms of life are too much for you today,
especially in light of all you've done to serve God? Remind yourself that
He is with you, and storms are common to us all. Hold tight to Him,
your Anchor in the storm, and know He has overcome the world.

SEPTEMBER 12

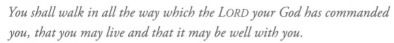
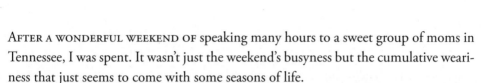

You shall walk in all the way which the LORD your God has commanded you, that you may live and that it may be well with you.

DEUTERONOMY 5:33

AFTER A WONDERFUL WEEKEND OF speaking many hours to a sweet group of moms in Tennessee, I was spent. It wasn't just the weekend's busyness but the cumulative weariness that just seems to come with some seasons of life.

My heart, though, was full of excitement, because my borrowed car was headed to the home of my forever sister-friend, Gwen, where I knew that God lived.

After sleeping for nine hours (unheard of for me!), I awoke and crept through the rooms to find Gwen in her quiet time chair—candle lit, Bible in hand, cup of coffee steaming. "Curl up in my bed, and I will pour you a cup of tea, and we will be friends," she whispered, gently wrapping her blankets around my shoulders and fluffing up the pillows.

A beautiful little candlelit tray came to rest near the bed, and life and beauty took place as we talked.

"Why are we so blessed? What shaped our lives so we have been able to live purposefully, seeing dramatic answers to prayer and God's Spirit swirling amongst the events of our lives? Why, in spite of the battles, do we see God's favor?"

She showed me a poem by an unknown author that she had copied into her Bible many years ago,

I heard Him call, "Come follow."
  That was all.
My gold grew dim, my soul went after Him.
  Who would not follow IF they heard Him call.

That was it. The secret. At an early age, we were both challenged to follow Him, to listen for His voice, simply to follow Him. And so we bowed our hearts before Him that morning, thanking Him for the miracle of the lives He has allowed us to live.

God has such good plans to be with you through all the seasons of your life.
Today, commit yourself again to His hands, as well as His plan.

SEPTEMBER 13

*No one has seen God at any time; if we love one another,
God abides in us, and His love is perfected in us.*

I JOHN 4:12

FOR THE PAST TWO DAYS, I have slept, eaten, been served by and talked with my sweet, kindred-spirit friend, Gwen. In between, as I sipped tea in her living room, she would help her ninety-six-year-old mom out of bed, bathe her, cook for her, dress her, undress her, feed her medicine, and do all the other things her mom needs to do but cannot manage on her own.

Throughout, I have heard a gentle, loving voice: "Hi, Mama. You are dearly loved." "Sweet, precious Mama, are you hungry? You sure look pretty today."

Gwen has been kind and tenderhearted in this way for the past ten years, as her sweet mom's brain has escaped into regions beyond her grasp, at least most of the time.

Last night as we both put her to bed, her mama had a smile from ear to ear. "I love you," she said. Her blue eyes sparkled, and we realized she was happy with us lying with her and kissing her soft cheek.

Later, I said, "Gwennie, you are so amazingly patient and kind and content, even though you have to stay here twenty-four hours a day, every day. How do you stay so joyful and content?"

And she responded, "My mama has lost everything dear to her over the years. She saw my brothers die too early, she lost all of her relatives and friends one by one. She has seen tragedy. But through it all, she resisted bitterness and chose to be joyful and give love. And so, even the model of my ninety-six-year-old mom has spoken to my own heart. If she can do it, I have learned how. Every day she greets me with a smile and gentle soul. It is what she practiced, and so it was easy for me to copy."

If your children copy your example, what will their own later years look like?

SEPTEMBER 14

My God will supply all your needs according to
His riches in glory in Christ Jesus.

PHILIPPIANS 4:19

TONIGHT, I feel small in the grand scheme of things. The world seems so caught up in what's overtly impressive—who has the most followers, who is the smartest, the most beautiful, the most successful. Whose voice is loudest? Who is most organized and on top of things and has everything together?

Unfortunately, comparing myself to anyone else always brings me up short. I must live happily in my own skin.

A wise friend said, "Never compare yourself to others, because you will either come up short and feel inadequate or you will think yourself greater and be filled with pride."

But when I look to His ways and observe what He has made, I see that He has made even a small, vibrant red leaf a thing of glory, heavenly art that amazes my heart and soul. In His hands, the small becomes significant. And so I take hope.

Those who humble themselves will be exalted. The little boy's two fish and five loaves fed five thousand. The idealistic youth defeated the giant. The poor widow with meager drops of oil fed the famous prophet, Elijah.

And so, my comfort is not in who I am, or how well I am doing, or in what I accomplish. My strength is in the One who is strong. My miracles are dependent on the God who threw the stars and galaxies into place.

Always, this has been my success—He is adequate, and I am dependent on Him. I am weak, but He is strong.

And so in my smallness, I find rest, quiet, comfort. Trusting in His provision, not my striving, will accomplish His will.

Do you find yourself exhausted, comparing yourself to
others and always falling short? Today, take a deep breath
and rest in God's love for you and His adequacy and
willingness to come alongside you in every area of need.

You will go out with joy and be led forth with peace; the mountains and the hills will break forth into shouts of joy before you, and all the trees of the field will clap their hands.

ISAIAH 55:12

YESTERDAY, the Lord prepared a party for me. I almost didn't go, because I had planned busyness and duties for the hours of my day. But something deep inside spoke to me of His invitation, so I put everything else aside and drove to the party where He was graciously waiting for me. I am so glad I showed up, as He had prepared so very much for me to enjoy. I would have missed out on so much had I ignored the invitation. His decor was exquisite, His design breathtaking. I sat at His table and looked out over what He had crafted for me to enjoy.

The gentle music of wind whispered among the aspen trees, ruffling their glorious gold across the mountainside. Leaves rustling, birds singing, and nature crying out filled my ears with delight and my soul with rest, comfort, assurance, and awe at such beautiful music.

I played amongst the trees, and drank in the sun. Pleasure abounded in my day as I picnicked with Him on the side of a cliff, gloried in my honeycrisp apples, roasted pecans, and strong organic English cheddar—the tastes beyond compare. What a feast, deep therapy to my thirsty soul. An unforgettable memory made with my Father who had prepared so much.

My heart was joyful, and I was hesitant to leave the party. But as I left, I realized, I felt His love so much more deeply than when I had awakened to face my responsibilities earlier that morning. Being at His party had changed everything.

Have you RSVP'd to your invitation yet? You will not regret it!

SEPTEMBER 16

Even the stork in the sky knows her seasons; and the turtledove and the swift and the thrush observe the time of their migration.

JEREMIAH 8:7

EVEN AS THERE ARE SEASONS of various types of weather, so there are many seasons to a mother's life. One day she loves her children and thinks they are the greatest gift God has given. Another day, she isn't sure she even likes them, but she is obedient and makes decisions moment by moment just to keep going.

Recently, a young mom I know confessed that she sometimes has a hard time feeling close to her young children and being available to them emotionally because she is tired. Most women feel this fairly often! There were many times throughout the years that I did not feel like giving of myself or doing housework, and I didn't always feel close to my children. So I would just put one foot in front of the other anyway, seeking to be loving and gracious and patient, even though I did not feel like it. Eventually, more joyful feelings would return.

Mine was a whirlwind of seasons: some when I felt lots of love for my children and they seemed to be growing and I enjoyed them, and others filled with darkness and struggle and seemingly no real life or growth in our home.

The truth is, motherhood has its seasons. A mama's faithfulness through all the seasons of home life profoundly affects the story the family will tell.

What does your season look like today? Keep in mind that just as the pages of the calendar turn, so the seasons of motherhood change. How will you prepare?

*He who overcomes, I will grant to him to sit down
with Me on My throne, as I also overcame and
sat down with My Father on His throne.*

REVELATION 3:21

STORIES TOLD BY THE PRECIOUS MOMS who are part of my Bible study reveal a multitude of challenges and difficulties: autistic children, single parenthood, cancer, financial problems, marriage problems, exhaustion, anger, depression—the list goes on.

We must understand that this is the fallen place, the place of spiritual battle. Heroes are made in times of battle, and our lives will tell a story. Each of us has been granted a portion from God—our own circumstances, obstacles, and challenges, in which we are the only ones who can choose to be faithful and courageous.

There are brave, courageous women in my midst who, against formidable odds, have held fast to Jesus, and their stories are breathtaking and encouraging and cause me to want to trust Jesus more for my own problems.

However, there are also whiners, women who nurture the idea that they are being "picked on" by God, that somehow He has given them more than they can take, and that they are victims of life. I see and hear from sweet women who have become victims because they have not had the heart to accept life as God has given it, but have practiced complaining and shaking their fists at heaven so long it has become a habit and robbed them of the ability to have joy or to see God at work.

The eyes of our heart and the obedient choices we make when we are squeezed by life will determine the kind of women we become.

---

*May God give you strength, in whatever you are facing. May you tell
stories of His miracles and provisions in heaven as you celebrate
what He was willing to accomplish through you in your lifetime.*

SEPTEMBER 18

Train up a child in the way he should go,
even when he is old he will not depart from it.

PROVERBS 22:6

AWAKENING TO THE DARKNESS OF an early morning, I sleepily sauntered into the kitchen to make my first cuppa. Joy had thought ahead and placed this napkin message at the place she knew I would be making her breakfast.

> *Hey Sweet Mama, You're tons of fun and a great cook. Joy*

Taking an early cup of tea upstairs to awaken her, then preparing a hot breakfast of some kind before sending her off to her college classes with a prayer and a verse is how our mornings go these days. It is my way of filling her heart cup just a little before she forays off into the world of clashing values, a variety of challenges, and interesting people.

Her gratefulness and willingness to give back to me is what warmed me when I found her sweet note. Gratefulness is not a natural character trait, but it must be modeled and cultivated.

I picture my children's souls as gardens and realize that greatness of character must be planted, cultivated, fertilized, watered, and protected while I consistently watch for and remove weeds and bugs and all that would kill what's struggling to grow there. I understand that discipleship must be very intentional. It must be a daily, moment by moment endeavor. It is a way of life. Excellence of character does not develop by accident, but it is an intentional goal that must be set and worked toward.

Think of a specific character trait you would like to see grow
in your children's lives this year. Take some time to ponder
what obstacles might be in the way, what weeds or bugs may
need to be removed in order for that growth to occur.

SEPTEMBER 19

Do not be conformed to this world, but be transformed by the renewing of your mind, so that you may prove what the will of God is, that which is good and acceptable and perfect.

ROMANS 12:2

WHICH PERSONALITY TYPES ARE THE most acceptable? Quiet or loud? Intellectual or artistic? Driven or gentle? Humorous or serious?

Early one morning, my little chatterbox boy ran into the room, jumped on the couch next to me, snuggled, and said, "Come on, admit it, Mama! You must love me the best, because I am the most fun of all your kids."

Followed by, "Nuh-uh! She loves me best because I help her the most and you just get into trouble!"

And so the conversation escalated. My answer: "I love you the Nathan-est! I love you the Joy-est! You each have a place in my heart that only you can fit."

We live in a world that values conformity. We want to use our force, our power, our authority to make people, and our children, fit into the box. Be good. Be tame. Be moral. Don't bring attention to yourself. Don't contend or question the norm.

All the personalities in our house have pushed my buttons through the years, but they have humbled me, too, in a good way. I know for sure that I cannot control my children—they are free agents with wills and desires and dreams, all unique to the call on their lives and the personalities God gave them.

No matter what personality each has, I am called to shepherd them to love God, to teach and train them to have the character they will need to complete the tasks God gives them to do in their lifetimes. Most importantly, I am called not to control but to release them into His hands to live out their uniqueness in a world that needs them to sparkle as God made them.

Do you have many personalities in your house too? Today, thank God for all the opportunities He gives you to learn humility and patience!

SEPTEMBER 20

*Which one of you, when he wants to build a tower, does not first sit
down and calculate the cost to see if he has enough to complete it?*

LUKE 14:28

THE PROBLEM WITH KNOWING we as mothers are called to build a heritage of godly
leaders right in our own homes is that most of us have had no training, preparation, or
education to prepare us for what it would take or how much it would cost! Most of us
just got married with the hope that someone would love and take care of us, providing security and affirmation . . . and then babies came and overwhelmed us. We had
never been trained for this job, had perhaps not seen it modeled well as we grew up,
and were never given a vision for how powerful a family that stood for God could be,
or how much work it would take to build.

So, overwhelmed women who have never had the opportunity to build a plan for
this vision may find themselves up to their eyeballs in details and duties and caring
for babies without sufficient support, input, accountability, or help from experienced
women who have built godly legacies. This is the greatest job in the world, one that
will indeed influence what our nation becomes. It's worth investing time and effort to
help prepare these precious and significant moms for how to do it.

Satan would love nothing more than for us to continue minimizing the importance
of deeply investing our time and lives into the minds, hearts, souls, and training of
our children, because he knows they are essential to bringing the Kingdom of God to
bear in their generation.

*Today, step aside from life for a bit and check what you are building.
Simplify your plan, and focus on the essentials: the rhythms that
need to be established to get the work done. Cut out expenditures
of time and energy and money that are not necessary to the overall
building, and be sure to plan for rest every week along the way.*

He took them in His arms and began blessing them,
laying His hands on them.

MARK 10:16

ONE WEEKEND AT A CONFERENCE, someone asked Joy how to best reach the heart of a child or teenager. She replied, "Every night, no matter what, I knew that my mom would come to my bed to spend time and talk and pray with me before I went to sleep. It was our time, where I could pour out my fears, secrets, confessions, and dreams. If you want to win your teen, you need to give them time to talk to you, and bedtime is a great time to do that."

It was true, no matter what a day held—fussing, conflict, excitement, drudgery, joy, celebration, hard work—ending it well was important to us. The idea was to tie all loose ends together with unconditional love by blessing my children each night, putting to rest the burdens of the day, and giving them into the hands of God.

"I love you no matter what. Forgive me for my impatience today, please?" Or "I forgive you for your disobedience today. You are very precious to me. I am blessed to have you. I love you, and God loves you, and He will be with you. Sleep in peace, my precious."

Bedtime gives our children one last impression of their whole day, and it is a redeeming time of offering and restoring peace.

Though it did require a commitment of heart and time on my part, as often Clay and I were ready to put the day away for our "own" time, I see now that this giving and ending with love meant so much to all of our children. It has become special to me that my twentysomething kids still want our affirmation, still seek our blessing.

What does bedtime in your home look like? Are bedtime
blessings a habit you've dropped due to the busyness of
life? Do you need to pick it up once again?

SEPTEMBER 22

It is the living who give thanks to You, as I do today;
a father tells his sons about Your faithfulness.

ISAIAH 38:19

WHEN EACH CHILD WAS OLD ENOUGH to be able to understand the meaning of their own history, I had them create their own memory box. We bought simple, lidded cardboard boxes at an office-supply store. They painted whatever they wanted to mark their box, and we named them after each child—for instance, "The Wonderful History of Sarah."

Into this box went things to help them remember who they are, what they stand for, and how special their lives have been.

- Birthday and Christmas cards from all the family who love them
- "I love you" or "I appreciate you" notes I had hidden under their pillows or placed on bathroom mirrors over the years
- Awards and prizes—Awana certificates, piano recital awards, group pictures of dramas participated in, sports, summer programs, history group, etc.
- Birth certificates, baby footprints, baby pictures, and any memorabilia that was important to them
- Samples of their writing, poems they had written, pictures they had drawn when they were little that were very special

We stored these memory boxes in their closets. On sick days or down days or snowy days, I would take down the box and let them put it on their bed. Each child loved having a box of memories about themselves—what love had gone into their souls, what our family stood for, how they were prayed into the world. It seemed to give them a deep sense of self-worth and a history stored in their souls.

Our children have roots, love, and a heritage, and know they will always have a place to belong, where they are safe and will be loved. The memory boxes are just one small way we documented that love and history.

In what way do you keep memories for your children so they
are reminded of who they are? If you haven't already, perhaps
start a similar memory-box tradition in your own home!

The unfolding of Your words gives light;
it gives understanding to the simple.

PSALM 119:130

ONE OF THE GREATEST WAYS we can love our children is by cultivating in them a love for learning, growing their intellect and giving them a broad base of education. Research widely indicates that a child who is read to will have a larger capacity for solving problems, possess a greater vocabulary, be more socially adjusted, test better, be more likely to become a leader, and the list goes on and on.

There is nothing more helpful for building the soul or drawing children to your ideas of faith than investing long hours reading together. A child does not just turn into a reader by chance; it is a cultivated habit, a discipline of life.

If you really want to give your children this profound gift of love, you must stop the other things you are doing and read every day. If you wait until you have time, it will never happen.

Delight in great stories, and teach the written word passionately. Treasure words and ideas and history in front of your children so that they will fall in love with language.

Plan a great list of wonderful books to cozy up and read with your children. Make it a daily ritual. Cuddle up on the couch. Use great voices. Get excited!

If we lose the gift of reading in this generation, we will lose the ability to reason, to understand God's greatness, to think well, to have convictions. We must keep literacy up! It is one of the most important works of our lives. If children do not learn to love to read, they will not become readers of the Bible—the best words. They will love reading if you read out loud to them and cherish them and celebrate great stories together with them in peace and joy.

How is the habit of reading being cultivated in your own life?
Filling your own soul is an important place to begin.

SEPTEMBER 24

You shall follow the LORD your God and fear Him;
and you shall keep His commandments, listen to His voice,
serve Him, and cling to Him.

DEUTERONOMY 13:4

NEW YORK CITY IS AWHIRL WITH OPPORTUNITIES: the lights of Broadway, international cafés, and the excitement of business and trade. It is also a place of drug dealers, bars, and a host of temptations. Yet this is where my nineteen-year-old son, Nathan, had received a scholarship to attend New York Film Academy.

As a mother, I hoped I had trained him to make good decisions, to walk with God in the midst of temptation, to be safe from the dangers of a big city; yet I knew at my core that I had no control over my son's life. I would have to leave him in God's hands.

Early one morning, after he had been bedazzled by the city, Nathan was jogging in a park near his apartment. As he ran, he said it was as though God spoke to him:

What kind of story are you going to write with your life? You are the one who will determine your reputation. People are only victims if they let their circumstances determine how they behave.

There are so many ways your life can go now that you are on your own in a big city with lots of pathways—those that could destroy your life and those that will create a life of godliness. Which life will you pursue? Will you chase after the world, or will you chase after Me?

My son said that at that point, he realized he would have to decide to chase after God and His ways if he wanted to grow in godliness and write a great story with his life.

How will you chase after God today?

Beloved, if God so loved us, we also ought to love one another.

I JOHN 4:11

ATTENDING A SECULAR LEADERSHIP conference by myself with over eight hundred people had made me quite shy. Yet the first night I attended this conference in a large hotel ballroom, a sweet woman called out to me, "I have an empty seat next to me. Do you want to join me?"

And so we began talking, and from that night on, we sat together. Over the course of the four days, we had talked and shared with one another and were becoming real pals.

One morning I said to her, "Tell me all about yourself! I would love to know your life story!"

"There is something I have not told you," she whispered, "and when you know, you will be ashamed of me, and ashamed to be my friend.

"I have been married and divorced three times, and I didn't want you to know."

I took her lovely face into my hands and said, "You have befriended me. You bubble over when you talk. You reach out to everyone you know. You are interesting, intelligent, attractive, loving, and that is what I know about you, my sweet friend. I would never define you by your past. I love who you are right now, just as you are, and I am so very thankful for you!"

Her eyes widened as though she couldn't believe what I was saying. We gave each other a warm embrace. She said, "No one has ever loved me like that before. Even my mother had a hard time accepting my loud, extroverted personality, and I have been looking for love my whole life. That is why I kept leaving my marriages—because they didn't fill my need for love."

And then, during the last day of the conference, she opened her heart to the love of Jesus.

What does it mean to you, to show love to your family,
friends, neighbors, and coworkers in a tangible way?

SEPTEMBER 26

Fervently love one another from the heart.

I PETER 1:22

OUR FEELINGS ARE A GIFT FROM GOD. Our feelings of love, compassion, mercy, sympathy, and tenderness are a part of our glory as women. When we exercise our feelings of love toward those whom God has brought into our lives—our friends, children, husbands, acquaintances—we bring great encouragement and strength to them.

But as deeply emotional beings, we are also very susceptible to feelings of guilt, inadequacy, fear, and insecurity. These negative feelings can grip us and build a stronghold in our hearts. They can keep us captive to the dark voices we often hear, either from others who have wrongly influenced our lives or from our own feelings of failure.

Loving generously and deeply is a beautiful mantle for a woman to wear. Jesus said that Christians would be truly known in the world by our love—unconditional, redeeming love for one another.

We must understand that Satan, the archenemy of God, knows how very powerful the love of Christ through us can be. He would do almost anything to keep us from understanding our great value to God. Satan just hates for us to know that we are anointed with favor from a God who delights in using normal people to accomplish great things. He whispers to us that we are not worthy in hopes that he can keep us from living a story worth telling through the days of our lives!

We cannot be free to love as long as we are dwelling on ourselves—our own inadequacies, bitterness, or lack of forgiveness for ourselves or for others.

Do you understand that loving yourself is a part of your spiritual worship of God? What do you need to address in your life so that you will love yourself as you are?

SEPTEMBER 27

The LORD your God is in your midst, a victorious warrior.
He will exult over you with joy, He will be quiet in His love,
He will rejoice over you with shouts of joy.

ZEPHANIAH 3:17

JOY MOVED FROM A CRIB TO A REAL BED when she was about two and a half years old. Often, at the crack of dawn, she would climb next to me in my bed, squeezing and snuggling tightly against my body. After settling in, she would fall back asleep for a while longer.

Her feather-soft hair would tickle my cheek, and her warm, pudgy body, soft to my skin, was a delight to me as I wrapped my arms around this tiny gift and held her tight.

"Mama," she said thoughtfully early one morning, "I want to be as close as I can get to you. I can feel your love better when I am closer."

Then a smile crept across her little face as she breathed out a sigh and settled into a few more minutes of "love."

Because Joy was my beloved, prayed-for little girl, I loved having her next to me. I cherished the times I still had a little girl who wanted to be so near me, one who would trust me utterly. As her parent, I was so thankful she wanted to be near her mama. When she crawled into my bed and cuddled next to me, I was filled with happiness and appreciation for the gift she was to me. I loved it that she loved me! It didn't matter what she had done the day before:

cried a lot
broken a mug full of juice
fought with her brother
disobeyed me

She did not have to promise to be more mature, or confess her faults, or stay away because of having a bad day the day before.

At any time, she could just snuggle up next to me, because as my daughter, she belonged there!

Do you know that God feels this way about you, too—that you are
His beloved child? How can you live out this identity today?

SEPTEMBER 28

I discipline my body and make it my slave, so that,
after I have preached to others, I myself will not be disqualified.

I CORINTHIANS 9:27

OUR FAMILY WAS ONCE AT a party when the sweet hostess offered each of the children a soda. Sarah and Joel turned to me with big eyes, shocked. "Mom, can we really have this all by ourselves?" When out to dinner as a family, we had often told them since drinks were expensive, we would just order one drink to share, or have everyone drink water. I think having to share helped them to be more thankful. Individual sodas made this a true celebration in their books!

But we weren't only focusing on frugality in those situations; we were also trying to make them understand the idea of self-denial just a bit more. Children can easily become the focus of well-intentioned mothers. Wanting to meet their needs, win their hearts, give affection, speak words of life, and give the best instruction can sometimes mean that before the family knows it, the children have become the center of life. Of course, I do believe moms need to turn their hearts toward home. But Christ and His Kingdom work must always be the center of those homes.

Our children are not big enough to be the goal of our lives! Only serving God can fill that position. If we make our children and their wants the center of everything, they will wind up stunted by the selfishness that has been allowed to remain in their hearts.

To really love a child means to consider what is best for the long-term character of that child. Because all of us are sinful and oriented to ourselves, a loving mom will train her children not to be selfish and will lead them and help them learn to give up their lives in service of others.

Do you tend to make your children the center of your home life?
What adjustment might be helpful or necessary?

SEPTEMBER 29

In everything give thanks; for this is God's will for you in Christ Jesus.

I THESSALONIANS 5:18

ONE BLUSTERY FALL DAY, I stood in the kitchen with thirteen-year-old Nathan. Outside, crimson oak leaves shook on limbs and wafted in the wind as the first storm of autumn blew in with dark clouds threatening rain. Inside, all was coziness and candlelight as the other kids prepared the living room for a morning of reading aloud. Nathan and I had the important task, at least in our family, of making coffee. As we waited for the water to boil, we looked out the window.

"Look at the colors, Mom," he said, as he leaned closer to the glass. "It's amazing out there."

I nodded as the kettle shrilled and Nathan turned to help me select the mugs, measure ground coffee into the filters, and pour just the right amount of boiling water. As I began to tend to the mugs of steaming coffee, Nathan took his aside and, with the air of a master chef, began to craft his own perfect mug of coffee—first the requisite sugar and cream, then whipped cream artfully squirted into a pointy mound, and finally a dusting of cocoa powder sprinkled sparingly on top.

"Look, Mom," he grinned. "It's a masterpiece."

Taking a first sip to sample his work, he rolled his eyes at the delightful deliciousness of it as he licked the whipped cream mustache from his lips. He held the mug out to me for a toast, and then suddenly spread his arms wide.

"God is absolutely the best, Mom! He made coffee, and cream, and chocolate, and," pointing to the window, "fall leaves and storms and everything! He didn't have to make us with taste buds, but He did, and life is amazing!"

I smiled. "Nathan," I said, "you are absolutely right. I hope you always remember that."

I often need the reminder that life is awesome, myself! What beauty might you find right around you to be thankful for today?

SEPTEMBER 30

The eyes of the LORD are toward the righteous and
His ears are open to their cry.

PSALM 34:15

I HAVE THE PRIVILEGE OF HOSTING several Bible studies with precious young moms in my home. Each has a different story, a different puzzle of life to figure out. Some work outside the home. Some live alone while their husbands travel. Others are single. And all are trying to live in a lifegiving way with these little ones who want to eat and to wear reasonably clean clothes every day and to be tucked into bed one more time.

Over the last weeks, I have asked my sweet moms, "How many of you have a grandmother, aunt, or someone in your life who helps you take care of your children occasionally, or is personally taking responsibility to help nurture and disciple your children?"

The result was shocking. Almost no one raised their hand; there were very few out of over a hundred that are in my various groups. It broke my heart that so many women were without female support for whatever reason—not living near their mothers or not having strong relationships with them.

I, too, spent most of my years mothering without support systems, help, prayer, or babysitting backup. But I would pour out my heart to God, and He would take me through one more day. His Spirit kept me going and filled in the cracks. He saw me on my knees. He saw in secret, and in spite of my limitations as a mom and wife, He worked.

I have prayed for you, precious one, who feel as though your
life is invisible. You are seen. He hears the pleas of your
weary heart. He longs to sustain you and support you. He who
sees in secret will reward openly. I pray you will know peace,
rest, beauty in the midst of this very important journey.

OCTOBER 1

*Truly my soul finds rest in God; my salvation comes
from him. Truly he is my rock and my salvation;
he is my fortress, I will never be shaken.*

PSALM 62:1-2, NIV

IT SEEMS TO HAVE BECOME A CULTURAL VALUE to be busy and justify ourselves by our activities. We seem to forget that God is our Father and that a good Father would not expect His little child to carry the load. He would carry the load—as well as the child! Sometimes, I find I have so much on my plate, the only thing I can do is reassess and cut back, so I can focus only on the agenda He has set.

Christ needs to be at my center. I need to have peace and quiet in my soul. I can say *no*, no matter how many people there are who seem to need me, so I can live at peace.

I am a baby to God, His toddler. He is in control. He does not want to abuse me. He does not want me to be neurotic and angry. He wants me to be at peace—sleeping in the boat in the midst of the storm, because I am resting in His ability to take care of things.

There will always be opportunities, but now is a good time to pace myself, to still my soul, to seek to live more simply, to say yes to my God-given priorities and no to all that will take me away. I could do lots more, but then I would become crazy and grumpy and tight and hard to live with, living by my own flesh and striving and works—and I cannot hold His hand and behave in such a manner all at the same time.

---

*Are you priding yourself on your busyness, trying to prove your
competency or value? Do you find it hard to hold God's hand at
the same time? Consider which you might want to let go.*

OCTOBER 2

The Spirit of the Sovereign LORD is on me, because
the LORD has anointed me to proclaim good news to the
poor. He has sent me . . . to proclaim freedom for the
captives and release from darkness for the prisoners.

ISAIAH 61:1, NIV

LAST NIGHT, after a dinner of homemade soup and a great movie, most of our family were sitting around in the den looking at our computers and phones, checking to see if anyone had loved or noticed us in the last two hours. Then we all started commenting on statuses of friends old and new on social media, offering our opinions on a few pictures and choices and commenting on various things that had happened to people recently.

Suddenly one of my kids said, "Look at us! We are all sitting around being petty. We need to stop being gossips, get off Facebook, and just keep enjoying this great night."

He was right.

Sometimes I feel discouraged, because I can have a wonderful quiet time first thing in the morning, then walk out the door of my room and immediately be impatient with someone in my family whom I love!

Jesus said he came to set the captives free (Luke 4:18). I am captive to my own human frailty, my own limitations, my own small-minded self. But Jesus saw me in my need and decided to have compassion. He gave me grace. He came and loved and lived so I would not have to live in this captivity to the limitations of my human, sinful self.

Today I am so very grateful that He came, He forgave, He sees me as though I am not little in spirit, but He sees me with the eyes of His love that covers my fragile state of being.

Do you know how great His grace is toward you?
Sit for a moment and ask Him to show you.
Remember, too, that everyone around you needs this grace.

*You desire truth in the innermost being, and
in the hidden part You will make me know wisdom.*

PSALM 51:6

IF SOMEONE COULD SEE THE INSIDE of your soul—the pathways of your thoughts, the flow of your worship, the landscape of your attitudes—what would it look like? Would it hold beauty or ugliness?

A beautiful soul is cultivated and crafted over time by the elements that surround it and pour into its inner chamber. If someone fills a pitcher with lemonade, lemonade pours forth. We must be careful to fill our souls with what is beautiful, true, and lovely if that's what we want to bring to others.

When my children were living at home, I sought to fill the moments of our days with all that was beautiful, inspiring, noble, lovely, good, and excellent, exercising vigilance to pick out stories and books that would inspire, seeking to protect my children from insipid, empty, dark, sarcastic, or shallow books, media, and people. I knew I was laying a foundation for life. I wanted them to have such a vast amount of truth, beauty, love, and goodness stored up in the deep vestiges of their souls, that they could draw from the wealth of that beauty for the rest of their lives.

My concern today is that many moms, exposed to contemporary culture, don't even have a model or understanding of what is good. Too often, our faith is mediocre and weak and insipid because our souls are as empty, shallow, and contaminated as the fallen culture that surrounds us. One cannot watch garbage and violence and adultery and not be affected. One cannot feed on what is shallow and not become shallow.

*How can you protect your own soul and the souls around you from
contaminants and instead fill them with truth, beauty, and goodness?*

OCTOBER 4

Hope does not disappoint, because the love of God has been poured out within our hearts through the Holy Spirit who was given to us.

ROMANS 5:5

LONG AGO, I realized righteousness is something each person must reach for personally and in private. Only I knew how I cultivated faithfulness in my heart when no one else could see. Only I could choose to believe God every day. Only I could choose to be thankful and to observe the tangible beauty that He had placed in my life for my own pleasure through creation.

Since that commitment was made, decades of my life have been invested in faith and hope. As a consequence, I have seen repeatedly how the Holy Spirit, as a spring of living water, fills my soul at the least expected times, giving me the ability to go on one more day, one more hour. My perspective has changed and deepened as I have learned little by little to let go of the things my hands grasped for in this world and to open my heart to eternal priorities.

The Holy Spirit springs up through living waters in my heart, enabling me to find peace and freedom from the bondage of pleasing others, more joy at small gifts—a sunset, a hug, a friend's kind words, a Sunday morning breakfast with all six of us laughing, discussing Scripture, sharing in our close fellowship and belonging as a family. My life is more centered in Him and less in my preoccupation with myself. This didn't happen overnight, though; it has come through many years of building little by little in this direction, amid a lot of stumbling and getting back up.

Are you carrying many burdens? Write down the things that concern you, using the written page as an offering to the Lord. Ask Him to show you where you can offer thanks for good things you might not see on the surface. Dedicate the things that concern you to Him, and ask for His love to be poured out within your heart!

While being reviled, He did not revile in return . . . but
kept entrusting Himself to Him who judges righteously.

1 PETER 2:23

SEEMS THERE IS CONFLICT EVERYWHERE. In my family, with my children's friends, in church, with coworkers—you name any place or group of people, and conflict is just lurking somewhere around the corner.

If there is anything that makes me want to quit, it is conflict or misunderstanding. And yet, if I am honest, I know it is in the times of conflict or difficulty He has worked most deeply in my soul.

It was in falling or being accused of falling that I learned more about the need to give people the grace I wanted. It was in being unjustly accused that I became more humble and in need of Him. It was in struggling through the conflict that has evolved over years in our family circle that I learned to have compassion on other women who struggle with their own backgrounds.

The older I become, the more I fall in love with Jesus. He could have screamed and yelled and become frustrated and accused others so many times! And yet, He has offered love over and over again. He is gentle and patient, loving abundantly and generously, even though none of us deserves it.

So, when there is conflict, I know running away is not an option. Bringing love and gentleness and courage into darkness heals and brings light.

If I want my soul to be made into the likeness of Jesus, I must seek to attain His gentle ways, His sacrificial love, His peacemaking heart. More and more, I humbly seek Him, asking Him to help me be filled with His Spirit, so that I may not offend Him, but may over the years become a true lover of people, as He is.

Determine to stay in the midst of the difficulties and conflicts
of your own life, that He may teach you to love well.

OCTOBER 6

Do not be overcome by evil, but overcome evil with good.

ROMANS 12:21

RAISING MY FAMILY WAS fraught with weariness, frustration, darkness, hurt feelings, criticism, difficult children, stress in marriage—you name it, I experienced it. Mamas are my wonderful heroes, you who would take on this enormous task of subduing and civilizing your home, your family, and your lives in a culture and time in which families are being torn apart and children's souls are being filled with darkness and despair. No easy task.

God wants us to understand that when we prevail over darkness in the power of His Spirit, through faith and obedience, we live out the reality of His power and presence in the same way that Jesus did when He was alive on earth.

There is no rational reason why someone would give up her life, her body, her time, her rights, for the well-being and building up of someone else. Servant mothers throughout history have portrayed Christ by living sacrificially and giving up their lives for others.

So today I wish you courage as you overcome. May you have a sense of victory and affirmation that you are among those who are modeling the reality of His great heart and soul by each tiny act of faith, as you choose to love the little ones in your home, when you choose to serve by making your home a lighthouse of righteousness, and when you bring the grace of forgiveness and peace to those who have fallen short.

Is there an area in which you've lately been tempted to give up?
How might considering yourself as a model of Christ's love and righteousness,
grace and peace, strengthen your resolve to stay in the battle and overcome?

This is the day which the LORD has made;
let us rejoice and be glad in it.

PSALM 118:24

I AM A FAN OF THE GRAND GESTURE and am pretty sure I could sacrifice my life for a cause—rescuing someone from some dire circumstances or being martyred for my faith. That seems grand and noble! It is the long-haul, day-after-day faithfulness, the years and months and days of mundane service, that test my spirit. I am not naturally a sit-still-and-work-hard type.

And so, to survive the mundane with some grace, I have learned to place small pleasures in my day. Every morning when I awaken and sneak down the stairs, I light a fire in my fireplace and candles around the room and put on some music, just for me. It pleases my heart to sit in a dark room, early in the morning, with candlelight and music and a fire shimmering.

This is why I also enjoy a one-woman teatime every afternoon, always taking some time to do something that I enjoy, whether reading a favorite magazine or book or watching a quick clip from a movie while munching dark chocolate sea salt almonds.

When my children were driving me crazy from being inside for too long, I would sometimes stop what we were doing and load them into the car and take them all to a bookstore, a park, a garden store, an ice cream shop, or somewhere else they could run and explore, just so I could breathe.

God showed me over many years that I am responsible for crafting a life in which I can last long-term with joy, so I can maintain the ideals I have established for myself.

It is not a luxury; it is a necessity. After all, God is the One who made color, beauty, music, stories, and food for our pleasure. It is in incarnating His fullness that my life can be lived well.

Today, do at least one thing that brings a little
pleasure to your soul to celebrate life.

OCTOBER 8

The kingdom of heaven is like a treasure hidden in the field,
which a man found and hid again; and from joy over it
he goes and sells all that he has and buys that field.

MATTHEW 13:44

IF I HEARD THAT HIDDEN SOMEWHERE in my home or yard there was a chest full of enough silver and gold to last my family for a lifetime, I think I would spend much time and great effort figuring out where it might be, looking and digging for it. I would go to great lengths trying to find and secure this treasure.

Is this the energy with which I seek God?

He has promised blessing and favor and help and rest and guidance and compassion and mercy in our lives. In many places in Scripture, we are reminded that God Himself is more important than silver or gold. But do our actions reflect our belief in that truth?

With all my heart, I know I cannot become the kind of person who is so full of God that people notice Him when they are around me, unless I have been spending time in His presence. I need to make Him my focus, spend time daily in His Word, and seek Him in every situation.

I so want to be faithful until I close my eyes on this place and awaken to His face—to have loved Him well, and to have shown Him my love through my trust and faithfulness. And so, if I am determined not to manipulate circumstances, not to try to figure out a formula or system to provide for our family's needs, if I want to trust Him for answers, I need to be sure I am not depending on myself or on idols to provide.

Instead, I have to seek Him as a treasure, waiting for Him, following Him, and being still enough to listen to Him.

Do you see God Himself as your greatest treasure? In what
ways are you particularly tempted to make your own way, or
seek something else as your source of joy and satisfaction?

OCTOBER 9

By You I can run upon a troop;
and by my God I can leap over a wall.

PSALM 18:29

ALL OF US HAVE WALLS IN OUR LIVES—circumstances that seem to stop our forward motion. If only we had more money, help, friends; if only we weren't plagued by this illness or difficult marriage, or, or, or . . .

The glory of a woman who has Christ in her life is to mount those walls. If we believe in Him, we have no other choice than to live by what we know to be true, regardless of our feelings, the circumstances, our friends' thoughts, or the world's opinion of our circumstances. It is to God's glory for us to live supernaturally.

When I accept the limitations of my own story, God opens channels of ministry that could never otherwise have been opened. My heart is unable to speak into other people's lives powerfully unless I have personal experience in mounting some of the same walls they're being faced with. Overcoming gives me a greater capacity for faith, compassion, and understanding of others in this battle of life.

I have loved David over the years because he faced so many incredibly difficult, seemingly insurmountable walls yet embraced God and believed that He was good. Because of this God-focused heart, he was chosen by God to have an inheritance forever and was called a man after God's heart.

And so, it is to the honor of a godly woman, in the presence of her family and friends, to mount the walls in her life with joy that comes from obedience; with strength that comes from trusting God; and with beauty that comes from choosing to believe in God's goodness and light in the midst of darkness.

What walls do you face today that will require determination?
Which walls ask for your acceptance? Which walls must be
struggled against even though there appears to be no possible way
of victory? By your God, you can leap over the walls you face.

OCTOBER 10

I do not ask You to take them out of the world,
but to keep them from the evil one.

JOHN 17:15

WHETHER I LIKE IT OR NOT, this world is a fallen place, broken by man's sin. I had to train my children with this in mind: someday, they would each have to take their place in the battle.

How is this training accomplished? Clay and I gave our young children a strong foundation of innocence, along with an understanding of goodness, righteousness, and moral strength. We taught them our values and the Scriptures to which those values are tied. We developed their soul appetites by giving them what was good, true, and beautiful.

Our home was a haven of rest as well as fun, with dress-up clothes and lots of pretending. They grew up on hundreds of books that filled their souls with captivating tales of bravery, heroism, faith, and friendship.

As they became older, we gave them freedom to make some of their own decisions, exposing them little by little to the world with us at their sides. We invited people from all sorts of backgrounds over to our home and brought our children with us as we interacted with others in places of politics, the arts, and scholarly studies. We made time for them, mentored them, and took them out singly so they could have their own time of talking with us about all that was going on in their minds and hearts.

Next, we looked for places to send them for training and exposure with others: a worldview and apologetics camp, a discipleship group at church, Bible studies with godly friends, even a worldview class in the evening with their peers in our home.

All of these prepared our children to be ready to take their place in the world. They perceived themselves as warriors, not as refugees who should hide and sequester themselves.

How can you encourage your children to engage in the battle?
Plan one thing to do this week that will move you toward that goal.

OCTOBER 11

Where can I go from Your Spirit? Or where can I flee
from Your presence? . . . Even the darkness is not dark
to You, and the night is as bright as the day.

PSALM 139:7, 12

EYES WIDE AND ATTEMPTING A SMILE, my dear friend was making a noble attempt to greet me with a cheerful heart. Time with friends usually far away is a gift, and she didn't want to waste any of it through sadness.

Embracing her, I whispered, "You are so very dear to me and to the Lord. He loves you more than you will ever know. He sees you, He is with you, and He will hold you and guide you."

Tears filled her eyes and burst over her dark eyelashes as she whispered, "I feel so lost. I can't find my old self anymore. I don't know how to come back to the light."

"You feel lost, but God is not lost, and He has not lost you. Just wait and be still, and in time the light will come gently pouring into your heart once again," I whispered with as much love as I could pour into her darkness.

God's ways are always best and bring joy, beauty, and life when they come to completion. He enters into our grief and frustrations, and He grieves with us when we are brokenhearted in the meantime. As a loving Father, He must interfere with our expectations that we can find true joy and happiness in this world if we are just able to control it enough.

We are all so shortsighted and limited, being held fast by this earth, that God has to pry our hands free from our strong clutches on this world, to force us to look more astutely toward eternity, where we will finally live forever and ever in His true light.

Do you need the reminder today that God is not lost, and neither are you?
Take a moment to breathe in deeply and ask Him to show you the way.

OCTOBER 12

Who laid [earth's] cornerstone, when the morning stars sang together and all the sons of God shouted for joy?

JOB 38:4, 7

SOME YEARS AGO, our family was sharing delectable hamburgers and steaks on the mountainside deck of close friends. They had borrowed a high-powered telescope to give all of us an opportunity to celebrate the sky on a clear summer night. Having never had this experience, I had no idea how deeply beguiled my soul would become from viewing the intricate artistry of God in the constellations, cast out seemingly infinitely among the heavens above.

After each child had taken his or her turn at the amazing telescope and gasped and danced in delight, they all insisted, "Mom, you have to see this—this is your star! It is bright blue!" They all knew blue is my favorite color.

After my eyes adjusted to the enlarged picture as I peered into the scope, I was suddenly confronted by an astonishingly bright, blue, dancing star, seemingly sparkling and turning in beauty and celebration of life. I was mesmerized, as I had heard all my life of "twinkling" stars but had never seen something so beautiful with my own eyes. The telescope had revealed to me what had always been there but was imperceptible to my own limited vision.

I was deeply and unexpectedly changed that night, confronted once again with the true greatness of God, the divine beauty and power beyond my understanding.

Serving God requires seemingly endless waiting on His timing and His ways. Gazing in wonder at the universe He made can remind us that there are things going on that are truer and greater than the present issues and circumstances we perceive. God is shaping our souls, building our characters, stretching our spiritual and mental and emotional muscles to become holy. If we obediently trust Him, wait for Him, and rest in the knowledge that He is good, we will live to see His goodness and His abundant blessings in His time.

How might you put yourself in a place to be confronted with the true greatness of God this week?

OCTOBER 13

It is vain for you to rise up early, to retire late, to eat the bread of painful labors; for He gives to His beloved even in his sleep.

PSALM 127:2

A CUP OF COFFEE AT THE NEARBY CAFÉ was a favorite treat when we lived in Austria. It was served on a table with flowers, in a china cup with a little spoon to stir with and a little glass of water to chase it down. I wish there was such a café down the street now!

Do you ever feel as if everyone wants something of you and more is demanded of you than you can possibly give? Motherhood has a gazillion days like that. Today is another one for me.

There are issues within, issues without, people wanting me to return calls, people I know I should call—and so, today, I am easing into my schedule. Taking a deep breath and figuring out how to manage this life so I can last. I must plan strategically about what I can reasonably hope to accomplish in the next few months and still be alive!

To add a few little pleasures into my day, I am going to

- have a white chocolate cappuccino—just because I want one;
- walk on the trails near our home to expel some adrenaline;
- sneak into my bedroom, close the doors, light candles, put on some music, and just gaze out the window and sort out what is in my heart.

Of course, I will spend most of my day getting things done; there are lots of piles to deal with. I will take it all at a casual pace instead of breakneck speed, as whatever is unfinished will be waiting for me tomorrow.

I think some days are days for grace. Be kind to yourself. Put beauty into your day. Turn on some music. Kiss a few people and hug them. Dance to music as you wash the dishes. Get a cup of coffee with an extra shot. Eat at least one square of dark chocolate. Peace be yours today—the Lord is near.

OCTOBER 14

The ways of a man are before the eyes of the LORD,
and He watches all his paths.

PROVERBS 5:21

MOST OF MAMA LIFE IS INVISIBLE. This noble cause we embrace is often fraught with relentless repetition, exhaustion, draining of our emotions, and spiritual challenges. Yet it is also the very place we are called to worship. This is the place faith is being forged and character is being modeled and love is going deep into the hearts and minds of our children. This is why I champion the cause of motherhood. What you are doing matters so much. And Jesus, who sacrificed His time, His emotions, and ultimately His very body, sees you and is so very pleased, cheering you on from the heavenly realm.

No one said to me, "Yay, Sally! You chose to be patient with one more ear infection and sleepless night!" "Congratulations! You are the queen of children with mental-health challenges, asthma, and learning issues! Of course, all four are sinful and fuss and make messes and want three meals and relatively clean clothes every day." "Congratulations! You are so very patient with those hormonal teenagers." "You just waited for your toddler to get over his tantrum, and you handled it patiently. You are a hero!"

My home and all the little choices of each day became my sanctuary of worship, my sacrifice of praise. Bringing light into the potentially dark corners of our lives together, singing and dancing and celebrating God's reality in the mundaneness of dishes, late nights of Winnie-the-Pooh and ear infections and steamy showers to alleviate croup—these are the places my children felt the comfort and grace of His touch through me.

It is indeed the glory of a woman when she chooses to love and
embrace her precious child as a gift from the hands of God.
How might you express this to your children today?

OCTOBER 15

I have chosen him, so that he may command his children
and his household after him to keep the way of the LORD
by doing righteousness and justice, so that the LORD may
bring upon Abraham what He has spoken about him.

GENESIS 18:19

WHILE VISITING VIENNA THE past few weeks, I was struck by the beauty and quality of design in almost all of the buildings downtown. Each building was constructed with an elaborate plan, not only considering structural strength, but also beauty and detailed design evidencing the skill and craftsmanship of the architect.

Our modern-day homes lack the craftsmanship and artistic skill of historical buildings that were built to last for centuries. The pragmatic and commonplace have swallowed up the art and strength of dwellings crafted for beauty and visual design as well as structural strength and longevity.

When God created the heavens and the earth, He created them with minute and detailed intricacy and order. There was color and form and beauty woven into every aspect of His creation as an expression of His own life art. The pinnacle of creation, though, was the crafting of man and woman in His image. He then created order and beauty within the structure of the relationships He designed: family—meaning father, mother, and children—and generations of family connections.

God's purpose in giving order and structure to these relationships was to provide a community of security, comfort, pleasure, inspiration, purpose, and belonging. When children are born into families where the structure is intact, there is beauty, health, and moral and educational strength. Family was the perfect design before the Fall, before there was any sin in the world.

Even in less than ideal circumstances, we can be encouraged to pursue God's beautiful, original, meaningful design for motherhood and family.

*While no family is perfect, whatever situation you find yourself
in, ask God to renew your vision for motherhood.*

OCTOBER 16

Rejoice, young man, during your childhood, and let your heart be pleasant during the days of young manhood.

ECCLESIASTES 11:9

My children are naturally given to enjoying life, giggling, doing loud or outlandish things, and usually making messes along the way. As a mom who is busy and has an agenda, I am usually in a purposeful, intentional, "get my list done" sort of mode.

I remember one time when I came into the living room where my children were all lounging and talking and munching on snacks and giggling together after we had just returned home from a trip. It was really a lovely moment—and now going back to that memory, when they were all small enough to gather on one couch and laugh together, I would give a zillion dollars just to have them here doing such a thing again. But the house was all awry, and as I walked into the room, I was taking on my General Mom persona and putting aside Easygoing Mom and my sense of humor.

I ignored their contented togetherness and took on my best authoritative voice, listing all that would need to be accomplished—bags unpacked, clothes washed, house straightened, mail sorted, rooms cleaned, groceries bought . . . and that was just the beginning.

My oldest son looked up and said, "Mom, don't worry. We will get it all done, and then it will just get messy again and we will get it all done again, but please lighten up a little and enjoy a few minutes of downtime. We just got home, and we are having fun for a few minutes! When you are happy, we are all happy, but when you get upset, we all start feeling guilty. So lighten up, and we promise we will help you get it all done."

I took his advice. How I wish I had fretted less and laughed more!

Could you embrace this day's messes, knowing that your happiness is key to your children's happiness?

In Him was life, and the life was the Light of men.

JOHN 1:4

WHEN THE LIFE OF JESUS IS IN our midst, there is a palpable crackle in the air, a sparkle to the lights and shadows of His dance among us. Imagine the Creator of the universe, the One who played games with galaxies and atoms, who gave us romantic love and sunsets.

Yet most people I know, including me so much of the time, live as though their feet are tied to the ground by heavy loads of duty, works, guilt, worry, comparison, inadequacy, boredom . . . etc., etc., etc. He did not create us to live in such a way. He came to give life, and life more abundant. The joy of the Lord is to be our strength. What have the voices of this world done to our joy?

Who in your life points you passionately, irresistibly into the arms of a loving God, a gentle Shepherd, a compassionate Father, an interesting Artist? He is the God who longs for us to celebrate life, to exist above the mundane present to perceive the invisible life of the Kingdom He is shaping through us for eternity.

Knowing Him should create in us a powerful sense of life, excellence, and expectancy from a heart filled with faith, love, and anticipation.

Jesus "was the true Light which, coming into the world, enlightens every man" (John 1:9). In leaving everything behind and pursuing Him—not rules or laws or formula or morality, but the Person who has so much more to offer—we find light and life. His Kingdom is the pearl of great price, worth selling all that we have in order to grasp it and hold it fast.

So, I ask today: Are you finding deep fulfillment and a bubbling up of life from deep within? A feeling of heaven meeting earth in your home right where you are?

OCTOBER 18

We have this treasure in jars of clay, to show that the surpassing power belongs to God and not to us.

2 CORINTHIANS 4:7, ESV

JESUS IS IN THE WORLD TODAY, at this moment.

He is present and alive, His Spirit blowing through the moments of our days. He is seeking someone to heal, someone to save, someone to whom He can extend redeeming love—and it will all happen through mere humans, those whose feet are made of clay. He is alive, and He lives through us.

All of us, with different skills, shapes, personalities, liabilities, and stories, are here for a short few years to faithfully live out a miracle. His presence invades the things of the earth. His love permeates the places of the lonely, His joy fills the air—but how? Through *us*. He is in us and wants to bring the miracle of Himself to this world, through limited, earthly jars of clay.

How will we honor this vast miracle of His life in us?

Today, who needs us to give something He wants to provide?

What do we have in us today that His Spirit would give to those present in our lives?

Someone needs His words of encouragement and hope—who is the person He would love through us?

Someone needs a cup of cold water, a sandwich, a cup of tea, an eye-to-eye encounter that says, "You are of great value—you are not condemned. I love you. He loves you." Who will that be?

Being wrapped up in ourselves, being consumed with our own needs, inhibits His ability to work through us.

Will your children, your husband, your friends, see the reality of Jesus today, because you allowed Him to be alive through you in all the moments of your day?

Let not a wise man boast of his wisdom, and let not the mighty man boast of his might, let not a rich man boast of his riches; but let him who boasts boast of this, that he understands and knows Me.

JEREMIAH 9:23-24

WE LIVE IN A WORLD THAT VALUES THE opinions of others very highly. Seeking to keep up with the Joneses is an age-old pursuit. But Scripture is clear: God wants our focus to be on Him.

Surrounded by a world that gives us permission to be self-centered, we constantly look at ourselves and our pictures on social media, listening for the notification that says someone has "liked" us. We become our own idols, striving for recognition and affirmation. It is not wrong to desire to be loved and to belong, but Jesus meant for us to find our meaning first in Him, then in our family, our community of believers, and those we serve in our own day-to-day lives.

In the story of the Good Samaritan, Jesus tells of those who could publicly pontificate and argue the law and posture on their supposed righteousness, yet these men neglected those who really needed redemption and help, embodied by the man caught by robbers and left for dead beside the road. Who has time to give to such a person even today? We have our appointments and to-do lists to keep so we can appear to be productive.

As I read the words of Jesus over and over again, I understand anew that it matters little what others think of me if God is not at the center of my life.

When I live in true integrity, following hard after Him, my children can find the real Jesus living in my home. Not someone who wants to keep up appearances, but the real Christ who lays down His life and shepherds the sheep of His fold, the servant King who cares about the unseen people.

True personal integrity comes from following hard after Him and loving those He has called me to love and doing what He has called me to do.

What does integrity look like to you?

OCTOBER 20

Blessed are the peacemakers, for they shall be called sons of God.

MATTHEW 5:9

HE ALWAYS . . .

gets his way, takes my toy, gets the biggest piece, makes my room messy.
She never . . .

cleans up, does her share of the work, says nice things to me, helps me.
No one understands me.
Everyone criticizes me.
I hate you—oooooooohhhhhh!

Sin means we fall short of God's holy standards. It means to be separated from His perfection because of our imperfection and self-centered disposition. And yet, Scripture says that those who are peacemakers will be called sons of God. They will be most like Him.

It cost everything for Him to make peace with us, as laying down His life made a bridge between us and Him. And so those who lay down their lives, humbling themselves and becoming servant leaders, will also bridge the gap.

I have a close friend who designated a peacemaking couch in her home. When her children were arguing or fussing, she would read them Scripture about peace and forgiveness. Then she would sit them on the couch and say, "Neither of you may get up from the couch until you have made peace with one another, prayed, forgiven each other, and can say that there is peace between you." So, her children learned that they were responsible to make peace with those with whom they were angry. They learned a pattern for marriage, for work, for friendship.

All of us are petty and selfish and angry from time to time, but if we all had a peacemaking couch and couldn't leave until we made up, we would have such sweet, grace-filled relationships and, indeed, such a close resemblance to God that we, too, would be called sons of God.

*Is there anyone you need to bring to the peacemaking couch? Perhaps
your husband, a child, a friend, or a fellow church member?
Maybe today, pursuing peace, you could draw on His grace to
heal, reflect His glory, and make this day a new beginning.*

No one can serve two masters; for either he will hate the one and love the other, or he will be devoted to one and despise the other.

MATTHEW 6:24

WE LIVE IN A TIME IN HISTORY when culture tries to convince us that we can do it all. However, each of us only has one life to invest in what matters. Each of us is limited in the amount of time we can use to invest in the priorities of our lives. We have to choose what we will focus on, and our choices will have lasting consequences.

Pouring into the souls of our children, developing sharp minds, protecting them from the draw of culture, passing on faith—these do not come about by chance. God will hold us responsible for the ways we use our lives to cultivate the spiritual lives of our children.

I do not think there is one formula in regard to accomplishing these things, and all of us have different pressures, issues, and puzzles to figure out in regard to motherhood. But we cannot foster a divided heart and be able to truly pass on a legacy of righteousness. Our hearts must be devoted to the stewardship of the young lives that have been entrusted into our hands. We cannot serve the world and God's purposes.

He allows us free rein, the ability to ignore and go against biblical logic and wisdom, but we will usually be left to live with the consequences of unwise choices.

After all these years of mothering my own children and observing many families, I know that if children do not find stability, love, training, spiritual reality, purpose, and comfort in their own homes, they will look for them wherever they can find them. They will become like the places where they spend the most time and like the people they spend the most time with, because they are shaped by the culture in which they invest their hearts.

Is your heart divided? How can you make your home a haven for your children?

OCTOBER 22

As each one has received a special gift, employ it in serving one another as good stewards of the manifold grace of God. Whoever speaks, is to do so as one who is speaking the utterances of God; whoever serves is to do so as one who is serving by the strength which God supplies.

I PETER 4:10-11

M<small>Y CHILDREN ARE VASTLY DIFFERENT</small> from one other—in personality, looks, body type, preferences, growth and development, intelligence, and skills. To compare them or discipline them the same way or expect them all to behave the same would place undue pressure on them—and me, as the mom!

When Sarah was a little girl, if I just glanced the least bit disapprovingly in her direction, she would immediately repent of whatever she was doing. Joel, my abstract child, would often be in his own thoughts and totally oblivious to the fact I had been talking to him. Nathan was my confident, strong-willed child, and his extroversion and active little mind and body required a different focus. Joy, self-sufficient and calm, was very intuitive about our expectations as well as being full of her own.

I was praying about an issue with my children one day, and the Lord made it very clear to me that they would be used by Him in different ways to reach different people. Sarah leans more to the introverted-intellectual side of things; Joel is an artist and musician; Nathan is quite gregarious and people oriented, and is a performer, actor, and musician; Joy loves speaking, being involved in ministry, and influencing people. Each child has had their own Achilles' heel, of course, but as long as each is progressing in his or her heart, I validate their unique personalities and design.

Take a moment today to write down and rejoice in some of the ways each member of your family is unique!

OCTOBER 23

The faith which you have, have as your own conviction before God.
Happy is he who does not condemn himself in what he approves.

ROMANS 14:22

DO YOU HAVE ANY FAVORITE FAMILY RECIPES? On Saturday nights, my family loves to make whole-wheat pizza with hamburger, onions, and green peppers. Beloved recipes can reflect our heritages, experiences, stories, traditions, backgrounds—so many different attributes that encompass the personality of a family.

I believe God offers us great freedom in exercising authority over our children and home. There are "many ways to skin a cat," as the saying goes. There are also many ways to love and discipline and instruct children. Yet many women live under a phantom overseer all the time that says there is only one way to get it right.

So how do I find my own "family recipe"? I must establish my standards on Scriptural principles. For example, as our standard for the kinds of things we should allow into our minds and hearts, we have always used the guidelines from Philippians 4:8: "Finally, brethren, whatever is true, whatever is honorable, whatever is right, whatever is pure, whatever is lovely, whatever is of good repute, if there is any excellence and if anything worthy of praise, dwell on these things." Yet when Clay and I decide what meets those standards for our family, those items may not match up with the standards you have for your family. Some of the movies my children are allowed to watch may be offensive to you. Some of our standards may seem too strict to you. Our choice of clothing style might fit well with your values but compromise the values of others. The same applies to choices about books, food, schooling, college, screen time, and so on.

What does your family recipe look like? What voices create insecurity or condemnation in your life? What pressures make you feel like you need to conform to others? How do you make decisions regarding your family's standards? Determine to make God's Word your primary adviser!

OCTOBER 24

I have no greater joy than this,
to hear of my children walking in the truth.

3 JOHN 1:4

AFTER FRYING A WHOLE PACKAGE of bacon, toasting a loaf of homemade bread and coating it in melted butter, scrambling cheese eggs, and pouring countless cups of tea and coffee, I gather my four now-grown children into the living room together for one more moment to point them to Him—the One who is my life and strength.

I do what we did every day for years and years, taking them with me before the throne of God to look into His heart and His Word. I ask them, "What is the verse that serves as the foundational focus of your life right now? What is giving you strength to hold fast to the ideals we have always cherished in our home?"

All four pour out their hearts honestly, and the comfort and miracle for me is that each one is holding fast to the Word of God. They share their verses . . .

Nate—"Greater love has no one than this, that one lay down his life for his friends" (John 15:13).

Joel—"Be strong and courageous. Do not be afraid; do not be discouraged, for the LORD your God will be with you wherever you go" (Joshua 1:9, NIV).

Sarah—"I pray that the eyes of your heart may be enlightened, so that you will know what is the hope of His calling" (Ephesians 1:18).

Joy—"Without faith it is impossible to please God" (Hebrews 11:6, NIV).

In my living room, this weekend, amid all the messes of our lives, I saw eternity in their hearts, faith that informs and leads and gives strength, and the God who is leading them all. There was a miracle in this quiet moment, unobserved by the world, but celebrated in heaven.

Amid jammies and tousled hair, I saw the hand of God.

Take some time today to ask your children what their favorite verse might be.
If they don't have one, maybe go on a Bible hunt together!

The righteous choose their friends carefully,
but the way of the wicked leads them astray.

PROVERBS 12:26, NIV

IF YOU'VE READ MANY THINGS I'VE WRITTEN, you know this: I don't believe in formulas! However, in thinking about what has worked in terms of building relationships with my children over the years, there are five things in particular I have found to be key components:

- **Time and Availability:** Whatever the age, children develop better when they know I will make our time together a priority. People grow close not through monitoring one another's behavior but by working together, playing together, talking together, celebrating together, weeping together.

- **Unconditional Love:** In building relationships with my children, I must learn to accept unconditionally the person God made each of them to be—even with personality traits that differ from mine or that make me uncomfortable. I have to love my children with a mature commitment that reaches past my feelings, which can change from circumstance to circumstance.

- **Affirmation and Encouragement:** I believe most children are acutely aware of their limitations and their failures. While they often need correction for their mistakes and even confrontation for their sinful selfishness, they also need recognition for their real efforts and accomplishments and positive reminders of who they can be with God's help.

- **Grace:** Our children need us to give them the grace to grow. If we make them think that we expect perfection, then eventually they may give up trying to please us, because they know they will always fail, or they may spend their whole lives feeling guilty for their failures.

- **Relationship Training:** We need to consciously train our children in the skills and attitudes that will enable them to sustain positive relationships. A person can only experience true intimacy when his or her heart has been deepened and exercised in real love and commitment.

Are you building your relationships with your children in these five
ways? How might you take a step closer to your children today?

OCTOBER 26

He who walks with wise men will be wise.

PROVERBS 13:20

ABOUT TEN YEARS AGO, Nathan and I went along to watch Joy perform in a national competition for actors, singers, and dancers. One of the perks was that the participants met with producers, agents, record companies, and directors from Hollywood and Broadway.

Soft blonde curls, large blue eyes, and sophisticated clothing left quite an impression on us as we met a lovely woman who was a Broadway producer. She wrote an evaluation for Joy's performances and later told her, "Joy, you are indeed quite naturally talented at acting and communicating. However, what you need most is to be surrounded by people who are more talented and more experienced than you are, who will challenge you to move further ahead in your skills. It is always wise to put yourself in the company of others who are more excellent than you."

What great advice! This is a principle I adopted in my own life many years ago. I began to look for friendships with women who challenged me to be "more" than I already was.

Cultural voices tell us that we deserve a break, that it is okay to compromise. These voices give us permission to rest on our laurels, to stay complacent, and even to learn to whine about our difficulties.

I believe that if we understand that we have an amazing capacity to be excellent, hardworking, bright, authoritative, and influential because we are crafted in the very image of God, we will always be striving, in a positive way, to become all that He created us to be, in order to fulfill our potential in life.

Intentionally placing ourselves in the company of other excellent people, reading inspiring and challenging books, studying Scripture in depth, practicing anything in which we would like to become more excellent, will expand our capacity to accomplish great works in our lifetime.

Who in your life is more excellent than you?
Who might you plan to spend more time with in order to grow?

David was dancing before the LORD with all his might.

2 SAMUEL 6:14

THIS HAS BEEN QUITE A SEASON.

Fires, floods, heat waves, and other storms have ravaged our country. It's amazing the perspective we gain when such gigantic, uncontrollable things happen, reminding us that our own problems are not quite as large as they perhaps looked. Others fight health battles that are never-ending and seem larger than even the natural disasters on TV.

So how do we respond to difficulties, whether individual battles or larger calamities?

With so much sadness and so many daily burdens to shoulder I wondered, *How does a Christian woman maneuver steadily through this journey of life with joy and peace intact? What does it look like to be a woman filled with joy every day, no matter what? How does she face each situation with peace in her heart, despite the things that would rob her of emotional and creative energy, such as chores, bills, arguments, and messes? How does she maintain joy in the center of more devastating troubles: a divorce, the tragic death of a loved one, a child who has a chronic illness or a disability, rejection by family members, alcoholism and drug-related scars, a job layoff?*

Then the Lord reminded me: we need to dance.

He wants us to dance inside our hearts, no matter what is going on outside in our circumstances. To dance is to celebrate life, to make merry, to physically live out the reality of internal joy. Those who walk closely with the Lord have a secret inner joy, a dancing energy just from knowing Him. It is in having Him as a partner, in letting Him take the lead, that we will be directed around the "dance floor" of life. He is the One who will show us the steps, how to listen to the music, how to engage our hearts with Him and to stay in sync with Him, the real Source of the music, the dance, and the everlasting joy.

Today, remember He is holding all, even you,
in His hands—and choose to dance.

OCTOBER 28

Rejoice always, pray continually, give thanks in all circumstances;
for this is God's will for you in Christ Jesus.

1 THESSALONIANS 5:16-18, NIV

THERE IS NO SCRIPTURE I KNOW of where God says it is okay to grumble, pout, or complain. I sure would like to find one, but so far, it's not there. (I'm still looking!) There are, however, plenty of verses where God says to be thankful.

When I pout instead of being joyful, grumble instead of praying, and complain instead of giving thanks, I am in effect telling God that He is mishandling my life and I don't like it. I am telling God and myself that only if my circumstances change can I be happy. And that, according to Paul, is when I step out of God's will.

Embracing the Lord's will for my life means accepting the exact set of circumstances He has handed me, one day at a time. Today, I have a choice to make. Will I grumble and complain? Will I stomp and lament and wonder why He isn't changing things?

(I do that, sometimes.)

It takes an act of my will and the grace of the Holy Spirit to pull myself back into line again.

Will I drink the cup He has placed before me? As Luke 22:42 tells us, Jesus prayed in the garden, "Father, if You are willing, remove this cup from Me; yet not My will, but Yours be done."

I think it's important to see here that Jesus did ask for the cup to be removed! We are not offending God when we ask Him to change our circumstances. But when we pray and He doesn't change them, when the fires rage or the waters rise, it's there we find that the question remains: Will I drink this cup? Will I do it with grace?

How about you? What cup is the Lord asking you to drink? Pray about it.

OCTOBER 29

TWENTY-FOUR HOURS OF FLYING and waiting and standing and carrying bags left me a bit weary and exhausted, but the feeling was a familiar one for me, and I knew that in a few days I would be over the jet lag. On my journey, I sat next to a young mother from Paris who had a nine-month-old baby to wrestle through all the wakings, feedings, and "play-ings" that would come with a long flight.

As I was watching her in constant motion—changing, cajoling, nursing, bouncing, and doing it all over again, I was reminded again how much being a mother has shaped, stretched, and enlarged my soul. I could almost literally see the soul and character of this young woman being stretched over our hours together.

Oftentimes, we consider the tasks we perform as being for the benefit of the children or babies we serve. God sees so much more! He gave us children so that we might become unselfish, love generously, work more heartily, understand forgiveness, learn perseverance, develop endurance, grow in graciousness, expand our creativity, and learn the skills of lifegiving parenting. He knew through this great work of motherhood, we would slowly be conformed into the image of Christ, and from this commitment we would come to better understand His fatherhood, His sacrifice, and His unmerited favor toward us.

His plan for motherhood became the long-term instrument through which He shaped and crafted my soul. To become a vessel where He is willing to dwell, to become a soul reflecting Him and His gentle love and powerful reality, we must submit to the building and crafting He has designed by making us mothers after His own heart.

Do you know that the work you're doing is important to God not only because of what He wants to accomplish in your children, but also because of what He's doing in you?

OCTOBER 30

In you and in your descendants shall all the families of the earth be blessed.

GENESIS 28:14

IN THE PAST FEW DAYS SINCE I've returned home from a ministry trip, I have had hours and hours to hear the heartbeats of my precious children. This week, I chose to carve out time to spend with my dear ones, leaving my suitcase packed, dishes on the counter, emails unanswered, texts unread. I have made my choice, because I know choices have consequences, and this is the best one I can make right now—focusing my heart, eyes, attention, and love on the precious treasures God entrusted into my hands.

Real moments of life have been shared deeply and will live on in my heart: one child in jammies next to me on the porch, with tea in hand and blankets folded up to our knees in the early morning chill of the mountains. Another, leaning against me on my small love seat, with a hand to hold and stroke, sharing lifetime dreams, wishes, secrets, and prayers.

Another coming to lie next to me one night just after I had climbed into bed, to talk deeply about life and all that is taking place. A long phone call, filled with antics, robust laughter, fears, stresses, and requests for affirmation. "Yes, I value you, your work, your efforts, your integrity. I am beyond blessed to be your mother."

This is my joy: being the best friend and most trusted counselor of my dear children.

It starts on the rocking chair when you sing lullabies to infants, cuddling and rocking and playing childish games with toddlers, reading sweet books, giving playful back rubs, and listening to all their little hearts will pour out at bedtime. The staying up way beyond midnight and allowing teens to question, pour out, vent, share insecurities without criticism or lectures. The sharing of life—pointing them to His truth, His ways, His love—this is the essence of discipleship.

This is the secret of a blessed motherhood.

---

*Your children are a blessing to the world, and to you,
too. Breathe deep today and enjoy them.*

*Jesus replied: "Love the Lord your God with all your heart
and with all your soul and with all your mind."*

MATTHEW 22:37, NIV

GATHERING MY CLOSEST LOCAL FRIENDS weekly over tea, coffee, and snacks to study the Word and discuss different issues has been one of the pleasures of my fall. They help me grow in truth and knowledge, practicing thinking clearly and well.

This week we discussed how Jesus said we are to love God with all our minds. Christianity is not just a list of rules of behavior, but the truth through which we may see all of life as it really is. When we are stewards of our brains, women who think well and clearly, we can teach and lead with truth and conviction.

Yet, I have talked to countless women who say the same thing: "I don't meet many women who know how to think biblically, or who walk in personal convictions regarding God's truth and wisdom being the foundation of their lives. Though I have looked, I haven't been able to find a mentor whose life seems worth following. That is why I love this group—we push each other to think well and to live by convictions developed in His light."

No matter what else you are doing, you cannot please God and become closer to Him and understand His ways, making them a light to your path, if you are not studying His Word, reading books by wise people, and thinking true thoughts.

So many women and men I see in this generation want to rely on someone else to tell them what to do. The thing is, if you look hard enough, you can find a book or authority figure who will give you permission to do just about anything you want to do. But what does God require of you? How does God want you to live your life? The answers to these questions can only be found in His Word.

How do you practice loving God with all your mind?

NOVEMBER 1

Walk in the Light as He Himself is in the Light.

1 JOHN 1:7

BEFORE CLAY AND I WERE MARRIED, he used to dabble in creating with stained glass. The image of a lighthouse is one that has always stood out to us as a picture of what we wanted our family to be: beautiful colors shimmering as the light comes through. Yet, if you walk by stained-glass windows in the middle of the night, they're not very pretty.

Similarly, a soul drained of life doesn't display much beauty. If the light isn't shining from within, life isn't shining without. If I light an oil lamp, it burns beautifully. But when the oil runs out, the flame disappears. In the same way, we are unable to burn and burn without replenishing the oil in our own lamps. And when we fail to shine, the world suffers. It lacks the beauty we are created to bring to it, the beauty intended to help us lead people to Him.

There are many things that drain life from us. Hurry, negativity, illness, natural disasters, and circumstances beyond our control often assault when we're not expecting them. And then there are the situations intrinsic to being a mom. A feverish baby will need cuddling and cool baths and doses of medicine, often in the middle of the night. A husband needs a listening ear and attention. The kitchen counters have to be wiped down at least once in a while.

There's nothing wrong with feeling weary, exhausted, and depleted. All of us feel that way sometimes; it is the nature of life in a fallen world. But Jesus has light for you. He wants you to walk with Him, in the light, that the Light of the world may shine through you.

Today, slow down long enough to make space to seek Him by reading
His Word and asking to be filled again with His Spirit. You will find
He is always willing and able to flood your soul again with light.

The LORD is my light and my salvation; whom shall I fear?
The LORD is the defense of my life; whom shall I dread? . . . Though
a host encamp against me, my heart will not fear; though war arise
against me, in spite of this I shall be confident. . . . For in the day
of trouble He will conceal me in His tabernacle; in the secret place
of His tent He will hide me; He will lift me up on a rock.

PSALM 27:1-5

WHEN JOY WAS LITTLE, we had a closet at the entrance of our bedroom. It was a small, angular room that was a bit awkward and not suited to hold much. But Joy found a use for it: her own little hiding place! We hung a battery-operated lantern on a little nail on the wall, and she would take all of her stuffed animals and her beloved blanket inside to hide, pretend, and play for hours. When I read this verse, it reminds me of Joy's wonderful hiding place—a place safe from the outside world, hidden in our room, away from all the visitors who came to our house.

It seems I am surrounded by women who are in the midst of difficult circumstances—hurting marriages, rebellious children, family members who are ill, economic crises, broken relationships, and hurtful misunderstandings in friendships. I so wish I could make all these difficulties go away, knowing the deep struggles many are experiencing during the dark times of life.

Over the course of many years, I've realized that I never really had a realistic picture of just what it means to live in a fallen world. This earth is the broken place. Heaven is the place where we will see justice being done, wrongs being righted, and hurts being healed. In heaven, we will enjoy deep, bubbling-over happiness and freedom from the burdens of life. Here . . . not so much.

Have you accepted that this world is a broken place? How can you
develop a place with the Lord where you, too, can hide away?

NOVEMBER 3

My people will live in a peaceful habitation, and
in secure dwellings and in undisturbed resting places.

ISAIAH 32:18

MANY YEARS AGO, the elves' city of Rivendell in the Lord of the Rings trilogy captivated my family's imagination. Cultivating our home as a place that celebrates all the great beauties of life from eras gone by has been one of our goals, giving us inspiration for hours of collecting and crafting over the years.

A library that holds all the great books of children's literature, classics, biographies, and beautifully presented information is a must. Our home library has turned into a tearoom of sorts now, with comfy chairs, its own tea set, paintings from places we've visited and lived, and always candlelight and music. And of course, there's a bookshelf in every room, with each child collecting his or her own library.

We must have a well-stocked kitchen with all sorts of recipes crafted over years of testing: traditional holiday food, meals for those who are ill, birthday fare, cold-winter-night soups and breads, and all sorts of healthy variety in between.

Cozy living rooms with fireplaces are where stories are told and ideas discussed and children cuddled. Bedrooms have comfy chairs and piles of books in baskets to encourage reading and quiet times. And, of course, there are candles galore.

Clusters of chairs encourage close conversations—rockers on the front porch; love seats and big chairs around a firepit on the back deck; chairs in twos all over the house.

This is what I have had in my heart to shape: a haven that breathes life and truth and love into all who would enter. I wanted to make sure my home, for my family and friends, is indeed a homely house and that all things excellent and worthwhile over the ages are celebrated in its walls, because everyone needs a place to belong and a home where a welcome is always available.

Today, find a spot in your home that you might rearrange or decorate in a
way to make people feel more welcome—including those who live there!

NOVEMBER 4

I glorified You on the earth, having accomplished the work which You have given Me to do.

JOHN 17:4

ONE THING I THINK MANY MOMS find difficult is the fact that every yes is by definition also a no. A yes to time watching somersaults in the backyard is a no to a phone call, a glance through a magazine, or a bit of alone time. A yes to asking friends over for a time of encouragement is a no to the free time you might have spent on yourself, rather than cleaning the bathroom, organizing your notes for the evening, or baking cookies to share. Yes to the car pool means no to sleeping in; yes to playing during bath time means no to your favorite television show . . . and on and on it goes.

As moms, what we really need is long-range vision! While the decision to draw your circle of direct influence a little smaller than many around you choose to draw theirs might appear to minimize who you are, the truth lies elsewhere. Think about a drop of food coloring splashed into a cup of water. The more water, the more diluted the color. And so it is with each one of us. When we spread ourselves thin, leaving no time for snuggles and back rubs, Bible study and reading deeply, family vacations and Saturday afternoons at the park, our influence becomes diluted.

So, may I suggest something, mama? Feel free to say lots of yeses to your littles, and lots of nos to others. Limit yourself in this season of mothering young ones, and watch your influence grow where it's most important.

I have never heard a woman say, "I wish I would have worked more hours while my children were young" or "I wish I would have read more magazines and watched fewer somersaults." Rather, the longing is for time long slipped away, somersaults tumbled and blown away like so many autumn leaves.

What might you need to say no to, in order to say some better yeses?

NOVEMBER 5

Jesus answered, "My kingdom is not of this world. . . .
My kingdom is not of this realm."

JOHN 18:36

OCCASIONALLY, responsibilities overwhelm me, and the free spirit in me longs for adventure, beauty, wildness, and the wind on my face. I long to escape from all that is mundane, maybe to sit on a beach in the dark of night listening to the waves crashing on the shore, or a spot on the side of a mountain somewhere watching the stars.

I am a restless sort, probably not responsible at heart. I'm committed and loving, and that takes me a long way in this world of duty and "shoulds," but I still find myself longing to be somewhere else sometimes.

Although I sincerely love and serve those in my life, I sometimes long for a place that is not this place, no matter how beautiful and lovely this place is. Is your life ever quiet enough for you to sense the longing for the place He is preparing, as you sense that this is not it?

God would not have us feel guilty for those places in our hearts where mystery swirls and sways with no defining lines, no neatly wrapped package with all the answers tied up. Faith is a willingness to sit in the tension of a place with no answers, while saying in our heart, "I will hold fast even when I don't see or know or understand."

Eternity was placed in our souls by Him, the Creator; we were made for another world. He never wanted us to love this world that will pass away, or to be so rooted here that we didn't want to leave, but to remember what He said: "My kingdom is not of this world."

Do you ever feel that longing and ache for what is not here yet but will be?

Whoever in the name of a disciple gives to one of these little ones even a cup of cold water to drink . . . shall not lose his reward.

MATTHEW 10:42

A CRISP FALL EVENING FOUND us taking a moment to admire the blazing sunset of reds, pinks, and corals from the back deck. As we sat there taking in the beauty, the front door opened and twenty-six-year-old Joel strode in with a weary face and an exhausted body.

"I just decided to come home rather than returning to my apartment after working all last night and today, because I need some rest and peace."

I quickly made a plate of savory cheese and whole grain crackers and poured a bubbly drink in a glass, offering, "Just a little something to hold you over 'til dinner is ready." Joel's furrowed brow softened as he gratefully sank into a chair.

Often when we think of having company over, we may dread the work of preparation. Yet when I ponder Jesus, I recall that before He gave His last, heartfelt words to His disciples, He chose a home with an upper room and sent a servant to prepare it as well as a meal for the evening, so that His words would fall in the atmosphere and beauty of a prepared place. I have to assume that the God who prepared a Garden of such beauty at the beginning of the world also put thought into preparing the place of the Last Supper with an eye toward comfort and beauty.

The giving of hospitality to our beloved children is an art that can truly reach their souls and give them a reason to believe in the God of love. When physical and emotional needs are met, and minds are filled with inspiration, souls are predisposed to want to follow the God who is revered in all of these rituals.

It is not the indoctrination of theology that crafts a soul that believes; it is the serving and loving that reaches souls.

Have you ever stopped to consider that Jesus is,
right now, preparing a place for you?

NOVEMBER 7

God is faithful, who will not allow you to be tempted beyond
what you are able, but with the temptation will provide the
way of escape also, so that you will be able to endure it.

1 CORINTHIANS 10:13

LIVING THROUGH MANY SEASONS of challenges and difficulties has taught me that I am capable of more than I sometimes feel I can handle. When a mom learns, by faith, to reach beyond what she thinks is possible, to search for joy and beauty in life, she glorifies God. When things go wrong, as they so often do, I might feel like having a spiritual tantrum—and sometimes, I do!—but I have learned that complaining and retreating into the darkness doesn't change anything. Slowly, I have learned to choose the higher road of searching for Him and His wisdom at every turn.

It has been the twists and curves that have humbled me, helped me understand others, stretched my capacity to believe, and caused me to see that God is much bigger than my problems.

In the same way that a child develops maturity and strength over days, months, and years, so, as God's children, we develop slowly over time. Each new challenge builds our spiritual muscles. Sometimes we feel that if we just did all the right things, our lives would be easier. Yet, that's not what God has invited us into. He doesn't want us to perform for Him or follow formulas. Instead, we are invited to a loving relationship with Him that will grow over time.

Lean into the process of life. Live beyond what you think is presently possible. Keep praying and believing and loving and disciplining. Do you sometimes think, *If I could only find the right book or formula, life would be perfect?* There is no silver bullet. As we live in this fallen world, God invites us to grasp the reality of our desperate need to trust Him.

Have you been tempted to give up in the midst of difficulty?
Please know God is with you and will provide all you need along the way.

*Do you think lightly of the riches of His kindness
and tolerance and patience, not knowing that the
kindness of God leads you to repentance?*

ROMANS 2:4

OLD BOOKS, WORN WITH TIME, are some of my dearest companions. I often find that classic writers carry the feelings of empathy and grace toward children better than contemporary ones seem to, and this understanding seems more like the grace of God I actually experience. How very grateful I am for the patience of God as He leads me, His child. He is committed to my holiness and sanctification, but is so wise and patient with me as I make slow progress.

Thank goodness, He has never shown me all of my sin at once! God gently works on one of my sin areas at a time, rather than bowling me over all at once by rebuking all of my immature attitudes. At sixty-five, I am still disappointed at my great ability to sin and to be imperfect when I am trying to learn and grow every day. Still, He loves and forgives me and shows me His path.

While I have tried to live in this same way, copying His example with my children, I also trained and corrected them, teaching the truth of God's Word and showing them consequences of their choices. However, the more mature I became, the more I understood God's parenting of me, and the more I had the desire to reach the hearts of my children with grace, just as God had won my heart that way.

Whether a baby, a toddler, a teen, or an adult, our hearts are open to those who develop a loving relationship with us and those whom we can trust to do us good and not evil—all the days of our lives.

*I pray that God will show you His love and mercy today, so your
heart will spill over to your children with love and mercy, and that
you will become their advocates for good, even as our heavenly
Father is our advocate and the gentle Shepherd of our souls.*

NOVEMBER 9

There was the true Light which,
coming into the world, enlightens every man.

JOHN 1:9

DARKNESS HAS INVADED ALL of our lives far more often than we would like or expect. When news of another tragedy explodes over social media or the news, we feel sorrowful and angry, and sometimes afraid and confused. Our children, of course, experience all of this too.

While we tend to our own spirits in such difficult times, we mamas must remember we are the ones who also tenderly hold the hearts of our own children. We need to be guardians of the flame of faith inside of them, until they are old enough to guard their hearts themselves. In a world of media and video games and TV and movies and cell phones that can carry the images of all sorts of evil, one of the best gifts we can give to our children is the gift of an innocent, protected heart.

Children are made to be innocent, to believe in mystery, to be good and pure of heart. The longer we can keep them in this place of storing up hope, believing in miracles and light and courage and redemption, the better. As parents, we are meant to be guardians, to protect our children as much as possible from all that is evil or wicked, so they have time to grow to be strong.

So, when a tragedy occurs, we must, as the strong ones, bear up the difficulty and tragedy inside our own hearts, pray, and walk with the Lord and in the comfort of other spiritually mature adults.

We must seek Him who is the light in the darkness and look more profoundly into Scripture, which reminds us that we, and our world, indeed need a Savior. He is with us, He is our hope, and He has never, ever left us alone.

How does picturing yourself as a guardian change
what influences you allow to affect your children?

God is not unjust so as to forget your work and the love
which you have shown toward His name, in having
ministered and in still ministering to the saints.

HEBREWS 6:10

ALL FAMILIES WILL TRAVEL INTO the eye of a life storm at some point. It is not evidence of a bad family, but the reality of a fallen world, with rebellion and brokenness evident in every dark cloud.

It is not the grand, noble accomplishments that are most profoundly valuable to God, but the unnoticed, invisible moments of being faithful and courageous when no one else is looking that become the jewels of our faith in the eyes of God.

Accepting a loud, boisterous child and seeking to be patient and gentle over and over again when feelings threaten to erupt into frustration and anger. Working beyond exhaustion and getting up in the middle of the night, again, for a sick child. Enduring the heavy burdens and tests of marriage. Cleaning up messes again and again and again. Making one more homemade meal and drawing the family circle together to celebrate life when a nap seemed more desirable. Having one more devotional in the midst of wiggly, distracted children, and believing that somehow eternity is entering their hearts . . .

These and more are the noble and valiant works of motherhood. I can see the results of this now in the lives of my children. While I worried the instability of our family life would ruin them or my flaws would harm them, the Holy Spirit was making them strong, showing them how to exercise muscles of faith in dark situations.

Somehow the life of God and the strength He gave in the face of powerful winds of temptation and fear became, in my children, a work of heart that gave foundations of faith, for it was those storms that prepared them to be strong.

Take courage today, sweet, tired mama. Your labor is not in vain,
but it is the very heart of your best work for all of eternity.

NOVEMBER 11

God is not unjust; he will not forget your work and the love you have shown him as you have helped his people and continue to help them. We want each of you to show this same diligence to the very end, so that what you hope for may be fully realized.

HEBREWS 6:10-11, NIV

THIS LABOR OF LOVE THAT WE mothers diligently pursue is not about *now*. It is about investing in the Kingdom of God, doing His work today, living out our conviction that people have eternal value and that we are willing to be shepherds for their souls. We are planting seeds for the future.

If there will be a resurrection, an accounting to God for our days and for our children—and there will be—then we must be ready. If He has entrusted us with this charge of raising our children for His glory—and He has—then we must complete our task with diligence. We will only do so if we understand that someday, this story we are living will be told and our lives of faithfulness will be a testimony of our worship and belief in Him.

Our hope is in Jesus. And because of Jesus, our labor is not in vain. We can have hope knowing that God sees us and has appointed us to steward the lives of little ones whose souls will have eternal impact.

If we connect to Him who is life and listen to His words and admonition, we have reason for hope. We know we are investing in eternity. We are shaping history. We are giving shelter and nurturing, working to create a place where children can be taught wisdom, truth, and love in the stormy moments of life. Truth and purpose give us a reason to live this life of giving, serving, exhausting ourselves for the sake of living a story we won't see the result of for a long time.

We can live *without* this vision, experiencing our days as filled with endless, pointless work. Or we can live *with* it, and while our days will still be full of work, we can be assured that our work will have divine purpose.

Do you find your life to be full of purpose? Ask the Lord to renew your vision and hope for the future as you work!

There is nothing better for a man than to eat and drink
and tell himself that his labor is good.

ECCLESIASTES 2:24

"Mothers of little boys work from son up to son down." This saying always made me giggle, and it certainly works that way for mothers of little girls, too!

The pressures of being a mom aren't small, and they don't come only when you are ready for them. Here are a few things that have helped me over the years to keep from exploding under the pressures of being a mom.

1. **A bit of variety.** When my children were young, I found that if life got too stale, I would go under. When things felt boring, we would take a trip to the park or the zoo, meet with friends for a picnic, or get in the car and drive just to shake things up a bit.

2. **A bit of quiet for me.** If I am around people all the time for days and months on end, I will indeed explode! Clay and I figured out that I could go to a coffee shop early a couple of days a week to have coffee and a quiet time, write in my journal, and then come home a couple of hours later, before he left for work—and I would feel like a different person.

3. **A bit of quiet for them . . . okay, all of us.** Every afternoon in my children's early years, I would put books and fun magazines in a basket for them along with a cup of something to drink. Then, everyone had to stay in their own areas for an hour. It helped my kids to become readers and to learn to enjoy time alone. Perhaps more importantly, it gave me a bit of time to look forward to every day, where I could have my own cup of tea that no one else could drink and a little time to regroup or rest or make a phone call.

How can you add these "bits" to your day?

NOVEMBER 13

Two are better than one because they have a good return for their labor.
For if either of them falls, the one will lift up his companion. But woe
to the one who falls when there is not another to lift him up.

ECCLESIASTES 4:9-10

DEEP, DARK LONELINESS WAS a constant companion for many years. I ached inside for a friend, someone who cared for me. As a relationship-oriented person, I had known deep friendship before I had children, but it seemed that once I became a mother, no one had time.

Besides the verse above, there were the Titus 2 verses about older women teaching the younger about motherhood, marriage, and all the rest. However, I did not know any older women who wanted to spend time with me, and let's be honest—there were very few women whom, when I observed their lives, I wanted to influence me.

I knew I desperately needed a friend with whom I could share my burdens, doubts, insecurities, fears, and struggles, and I realized that if I wanted godly friends in my life, I needed to look for them, cultivate them, love them, and encourage them as I would want to be encouraged. So, I began inviting people to my home, singly and in groups. Often, it was in reaching out to others and building small groups that I found my best friends. We sewed the threads of our lives together by serving side by side in ministries we loved. Then, our children would also become friends, serving alongside us.

Friendship and mentoring relationships are an investment and require intentional giving and planning. Even as building a house requires a plan and effort, so friendships only grow out of intentional giving and cultivating.

And so it is true in life, "Two are better than one. . . . A cord of three strands is not quickly torn apart" (Ecclesiastes 4:9, 12). Working diligently to pursue godly friendships yields a treasure.

Do you need a true heart-friend? Take some time to pray today about this
and ask God to bring to mind a person to whom you can reach out.

In the day of prosperity be happy, but in the day of adversity consider—
God has made the one as well as the other.

ECCLESIASTES 7:14

BEING A MAMA IS A LONG-TERM COMMITMENT, isn't it? When I find myself depleted, I try to stop and take stock of what is going on in my life. I place the worries and anxieties in heaven. I simplify my schedule, plan a snack-style dinner of crackers and cheese or fruit and toast, and break out the paper plates. I take a day off from regular commitments and plan to be still. The next day, I again put away normal commitments, but this time in order to attack the demanding tasks that are increasing my burden. Planning other simple pleasures—making time for several cups of coffee or tea, having a nap, watching a show, or reading a magazine—helps too.

When my children were little, on burned-out days, I would do whatever would free me for just a time: let the kids blow bubbles, give them a long bath with new toys, let them watch a Winnie-the-Pooh cartoon, take them to the frozen yogurt café, or make a quick jaunt to the park or playground. I crafted a way I might have a break from the banter and demands of my day.

Refueling just a little, to find joy, create pleasure, and celebrate life in the midst of all the demands, helped fill my heart up just enough to begin seeing light at the end of my tunnel. Slowly but surely, I would begin to see the miracles bubbling up. My Father delights to provide when I take time to breathe, listen, and rest from the daily grind.

A woman with a Martha heart, frenetically busy, won't see the miracles of God, as she is so busy living in the whirlwind of her own making and subsisting in her own meek provisions that she loses all hope and becomes a wretched nag. Sitting at the feet of Jesus instead, and just having some respite, will do wonders to change the day.

How do you incorporate joy-breaks into your own stressful days?

NOVEMBER 15

O LORD, who may abide in Your tent? Who may dwell on Your holy hill? He who walks with integrity, and works righteousness, and speaks truth in his heart.

PSALM 15:1-2

OUR FAMILY HAS SPENT MANY HOURS around the piano and various instruments in our home, someone inevitably taking up music and another joining in. Lessons were just part of "being a Clarkson" for at least a year for each child as we felt knowing how to play something was important. Of course, merely having a piano in a home and allowing a child to bang on it will not produce a classical pianist! To become excellent in playing, the child must be instructed over a period of many years, and hours must be given to practice.

It also takes years of instruction to develop character. Because our culture is so given to crudity and a devaluation of human beings, as secular media dictates and shapes the values of children, many people reflect shallow character and lack wisdom and discretion. Couple this with a lack of intentional training on the part of parents, with moral compromise at every turn, and many children are at a disadvantage in their lives because they have never developed a strong moral character or seen one in the lives of the adults around them.

A child who is not trained and taught to exercise righteousness, a strong work ethic, and integrity will often be at a disadvantage his whole life, because instead of his character serving him, his lack of training and ignorance will detract from his ability to live in an excellent way.

I believe that many moms struggle with motherhood and the burden of raising children because they have never been stretched or trained in character. Character matters! Training excellent character into the very fiber of children takes intention, perseverance, commitment, wisdom—and honestly, it requires character from our *own* lives.

Do you feel your character was disciplined and trained during your own childhood? If not, how can you grow in that area now? If so, how will you pass it on?

NOVEMBER 16

*Applying all diligence, in your faith supply moral excellence,
and in your moral excellence, knowledge, and in your
knowledge, self-control, and in your self-control, perseverance,
and in your perseverance, godliness, and in your godliness,
brotherly kindness, and in your brotherly kindness, love.*

2 PETER 1:5-7

SCRIPTURE TELLS US TO "train up a child in the way he should go" (Proverbs 22:6). When one is given knowledge about how to act, behave, and implement certain skills, the natural consequences include having wisdom, confidence, and skills to employ in life. For this reason, training is essential to the well-being of a child, so he or she may live life in a strong and healthy way.

Training can be illustrated in many ways: an athlete must learn and train to become a champion. A pianist must be instructed and practice to become a concert performer. An artist must learn the skills and philosophy of drawing and painting and then practice to become masterful at his or her craft. And so it is with any craft or skill.

Shouldn't all true believers be able to call forth excellence and integrity as a reflection of Him in our lives? Yet excellence and integrity are personal issues. One can only grow in these areas through personal commitment and a decision that says, "Regardless of what is happening around me, I will be the best I can be, work the hardest I am able, and pursue the highest standards, especially for my personal life where no one but God sees. I have been bought with a price and have His Holy Spirit living in me. My worship of God requires that I pursue the standard of His holiness as an affirmation of His reality in my life."

This labor of excellence, personally and in the lives of our children, will take many long years. But if we are not committed to pursuing whatever it takes to build this excellence, then what hope do we have for our future, and how can we represent Him, who has given all?

*God longs to live a life of excellence through you. Today, commit
to becoming all He has enabled you to be.*

NOVEMBER 17

Just as a father has compassion on his children, so the LORD has compassion on those who fear Him.

PSALM 103:13

ONE AFTERNOON WHEN I WAS pregnant with Nathan, I poured bubble bath into our double sink with Sarah, four, on one side and Joel, just under two, on the other. I gave them small plastic cups to play with, thinking, *This will hold them for at least thirty minutes so I can get a break* as I waddled to a nearby chair to watch.

All of a sudden, little Joel stood straight up in the sink. With a huge smile, he screamed in delight and started scooping bubbles and water out of the sink and onto the floor as fast as he could, having a merry old time. He was just being an exuberant, happy little boy.

Something in me burst. I started screaming at him with vein-popping intensity. "What are you doing? You are making a mess all over my floor! Stop it. Don't you know you are making a mess?" The lecture had evidently been stored up for months.

My stunned, easygoing boy plopped down and looked at me with big, sad eyes and burst out crying, as though I had wounded him for life. Immediately, I felt awful. *What had happened to me?* Shame poured over me in waves. All afternoon, I shook my head over the incident. How could someone who called herself a mature believer lose it like that?

I prayed desperately that God would help me, and little by little, over the next hours and days and years, He started cultivating in me a philosophy of parenting, motherhood, and home building. I found grace and freedom as I slowly grew. This took years and was never easy. But my home became a place of deep happiness and fulfillment.

Knowing my limitations, God was compassionate towards me, and He still loved me. And so I learned to have compassion on my precious little ones and practiced loving them more each day.

How is the God of compassion inviting you to grow as a mom?

NOVEMBER 18

I am sure that neither death nor life, nor angels nor rulers,
nor things present nor things to come, nor powers, nor height
nor depth, nor anything else in all creation, will be able to
separate us from the love of God in Christ Jesus our Lord.

ROMANS 8:38-39, ESV

"MOM, IF THERE IS ONE PLACE in the world where I fit, it is in our family. It's not about the place; it is about belonging to each other, 'getting' each other, accepting each other, and celebrating life together. That is what I most miss about being at home," one child said to me over the phone, anticipating a return home for an upcoming holiday.

Every child longs for a place to belong, a sanctuary that gives life and love and protects from all the evils that lurk outside its walls. Love should be the very air that our children breathe, the foundation from which character is built and from which all instruction comes.

Love, first.

If we really studied, pondered, cherished, and applied the ways of Jesus' love as it is shown in Scripture, wouldn't the way we mother look different? Do we love our children the way God calls us to love everyone?

If love is the foundational need in the deep places of our hearts, then knowing that our children have this need should shape how we seek to influence them. Our children will measure and assess in their hearts the reality of God by how we display His love in our home. We are to love our children as much as we love ourselves, to lay down our lives for them, as He did for us.

God's love covered us when we were still failing, stumbling, wallowing in our self-ishness. God, as our Father, saved us while we were still in our sin. Children know they are imperfect and stumble and sin. Can we love them, as God has loved us?

Is there any attitude or action that can separate your child from your
love, or is it generous, consistent, forgiving, and long-suffering?

NOVEMBER 19

He said to him, "'You shall love the Lord your God with all your heart, and with all your soul, and with all your mind.' This is the great and foremost commandment."

MATTHEW 22:37-38

WHEN I READ BIBLICAL ACCOUNTS of people who saw the glory of God, they are often bowing down in reverence and hiding their eyes because it is so wonderful and great. Yet that response is far removed from our experience today. All that used to be considered sacred, whether people, places, even concepts like marriage and childhood, are regularly devalued and ridiculed in contemporary culture.

At this time in history, then, we must seek diligently to give our children not just knowledge of what the word *holy* means, but tangible practices where they can come to understand that some things are sacred and set apart, deserving of our reverence and worship.

Consequently, as we begin the training of our little children's hearts and souls, we must figure out how to convey to them that life is not about us. Our lives are about pleasing, serving, loving, worshiping, and living for the very One who is the Lord of the universe, the Creator of the world, the King forever, God the Father, the Holy Spirit, and the Lord Jesus Christ.

One of the ways we implemented a sense of reverence and holiness in the lives of our children was teaching them that there were places to use "quiet voices and respectful hearts"—like in church, at concerts, at funerals, at graduations, at recitals. Before we went into these places, we would talk to our children about our expectations ahead of time.

If this is not built into the warp and woof of your life, then when it comes to adulthood and worshiping and reverencing God, there will be no pattern, no practiced understanding of what it means to love and obey our Lord with wholehearted devotion.

How have you instilled reverence and devotion to our holy God in your family?

The fruit of the Spirit is love, joy, peace, patience, kindness,
goodness, faithfulness, gentleness, self-control.

GALATIANS 5:22-23

THIS MORNING, I was thinking about how to prepare myself for a wonderful holiday weekend. I love Thanksgiving and enjoy the feast, but sometimes with all the cooking and work and family and ideals flying about, we can find ourselves in the midst of a lot of extra stress. Children eat more sugar, sleep less, have to share more, are in unfamiliar places, and so . . . the potential for disaster is higher! Knowing this, the best way to arm ourselves is to walk by the Holy Spirit so we can give them the gift of a Spirit-filled mom.

I am going to yield to the Spirit's work of producing fruit in me:

Love—I want to love, affirm, and look at my sweet ones with eyes of gratefulness that they are my beloved.

Joy—I am so blessed. God is good. He is with us. I will choose to be joyful in what He has provided.

Peace—Peace will rule me, so no matter what happens, I will keep peace and give peace in every situation.

Patience—By choosing to exercise patience in every situation, I will bring the music of God's heart to the atmosphere of our holiday.

Kindness—Giving a kind word and graciousness to each person, seeing their heart needs, and serving them will bring a sense of His presence into our day.

Goodness—Because He is good, I will rejoice and be glad in the reality of His promises and in His willingness to provide.

Faithfulness—I will be faithful to serve all the people around me, to do the hard work of cooking, washing, and serving, that others might know the joy of celebration and beauty.

Gentleness—On a day heightened with emotion and expectations, I will bring Jesus' gentleness to each person in each moment.

Self-control—I will choose to control my spirit, tongue, and attitudes and give to God my worship through my Spirit-controlled attitudes and heart.

Ask God's Spirit to shine through you as you interact with others today.

NOVEMBER 21

Above all, keep fervent in your love for one another.

1 PETER 4:8

MOST MARRIAGES START OUT with at least some idealism and romantic expectation. Mine was no different. Clay won me with bouquets of yellow roses (I was his yellow rose of Texas), romantic cards, and lots of dinners out.

And then . . . there was life! Seventeen moves, six internationally; four children, three miscarriages; deaths of family members; car wrecks; financial challenges; illness; a fire and three floods in our house; church splits; ministry problems . . . and lots and lots of stress. Nothing quite prepared me, as a very immature, untrained young woman, to know how to bear all of the stresses we would face just being a family.

One evening, I was sitting on my bed in the darkness, venting at God about Clay and how he had hurt my feelings. I was rehearsing the injustices of our relationship because, from my point of view, he was much more the problem than I was!

Yet, as I sat there pondering these things, tears streaming down, it was as though God whispered, "What if the most profound work you ever did to please Me was to love Clay? If he never changes, can you worship Me in this place and release your expectations to Me?"

Early, I learned that my marriage was a place of worship into which I could bring God's love, healing, and grace every day, or I could just live as a hypocrite saying that I was committed to God and would serve Him, except in my marriage because that was just asking too much!

I think there is a point when a godly woman in a marriage must say, "This is the reality of the puzzle I have been given in my life and marriage, and this is the story I must stay in and live to the fullest with grace."

Are you working to keep fervent in your love for your spouse, even in spite of imperfections?

NOVEMBER 22

Love covers a multitude of sins.

I PETER 4:8

IN MARRIAGE, comparing oneself to others or wishing for a different reality is a waste of time. It only brings discontent and depression. I can either bring light, life, beauty, and redemption into this situation and to this husband, or I can live in disappointment and destroy hope, happiness, and joy. In a fallen world, there will always be stress and sin, but I do not have to let this determine my happiness or contentment.

The reality is that all marriages are filled with potential challenges and difficulty. I believe one of the glories of women is the opportunity to spread the gracious spirit of love and peace as a fragrance and evidence of life in her home.

It is all dependent on the way a woman sees her lot in life—as an opportunity to worship and bring light, or a place for complaining and discontent. A critical spirit wreaks havoc on children when they live with it on a constant basis.

All children long to see their moms and dads love each other and be partners in life. As Clay and I have cultivated this kind of grace-giving love, it has bloomed in the hearts of our children. They know we are not perfect, but they believe in the strong love that is the oxygen of commitment in our home.

But the foundations of strength and longevity start with a commitment in my heart. When I accept our limitations and lean into our story with grace and love, it becomes a love story worth telling generations to come. God joins our meager commitment and sprinkles His grace and goodness over it, working a miracle that our children will cherish their whole lives.

Are you willing to accept your story, your husband, your children?
Will you cultivate His story through your lives today, just as you are?

NOVEMBER 23

Do not fret; it leads only to evildoing.

PSALM 37:8

"WHAT WAS THE DRIVER IN THAT CAR THINKING? I can't believe anyone would drive that way!"

I have noticed when I am too busy and have taken responsibilities on my shoulders that only God can carry, I become harsh. Busyness and overcommitment lead to a loss of desire for the things that are normally important to me. I care less for the lost, have little patience for my children, and tend to see people as irritating. God is a distant thought that I glance toward with guilt, thinking He must be disappointed with me because I just haven't had time for Him, but I have just been so busy . . .

Fretting is also a hint. When I find myself going over and over issues about money, family, children, church, ministry, duties, holidays, housework, and other burdens, giving so much energy to fretting, when the Bible clearly tells me not to, I know I've gotten too busy.

Then, I tend to become cynical. "I do so much, and there is no one to help." And of course, "If I don't do it or take responsibility, no one else will."

It is so easy to begin to live a works-oriented life, and then to think that without me, things will fall apart. That is when I become weary. Then I say, "Lord, don't you care that I am drowning?!"

God is not biting His nails wondering if I am going to get it all done. He is not abusive, watching from heaven just waiting to give me more than I can handle. So slowly, I have had to learn if I am consistently feeling too much stress or too much weight on my shoulders, that means I am attempting to do things that He has never asked or expected me to do, or else doing my legitimate tasks in my own strength.

Are you feeling overwhelmed today? What are you carrying in your own strength? How can you release your concerns to God?

NOVEMBER 24

Finally, brethren, whatever is true, whatever is honorable,
whatever is right, whatever is pure, whatever is lovely,
whatever is of good repute, if there is any excellence and
if anything worthy of praise, dwell on these things.

PHILIPPIANS 4:8

A FEW WEEKS AGO, I had the privilege of attending a tea given in the home of one of my friends.

The fare was simple but elegant. Grapes, tangerines, and strawberries were served on a crystal dish with three kinds of cheese and multigrain crackers. A course of scones and jam followed. Then, delicious finger sandwiches were served—cucumber, egg salad, ham and onion cream cheese. To crown the lovely meal, we were presented chocolates with petits fours. Classical music wafted through the air as all the women present (including me and my two daughters) talked quietly.

Between each course, our hostess showed us various Pre–Raphaelite prints from England. These were beautiful prints of feminine women, knights, heroes, and saints as depicted by artists in the 1800s who set out to return elegance and beauty to art. Between the prints, she told Alfred, Lord Tennyson's life story, as many of the pictures had been painted to reflect his poetry.

I could see Joy sitting straighter as she was inspired, desiring to become more ideal. All because a woman, who is herself always learning and studying, wanted to pass on civility and beauty to her friends. It was a great amount of work, but her labor exalted our souls.

The wonderful thing about adding beauty is that you can start with just a few items that make a big difference! Candles can be gathered at the dollar store. Beautiful music can be found for free online. Flowers from your yard or inexpensive ones from the grocery store can help transform a room and make your family feel special.

How could you do something that would add to your home's
beauty and help you pursue Philippians 4:8 today?

NOVEMBER 25

He who walks with wise men will be wise,
but the companion of fools will suffer harm.

PROVERBS 13:20

WHEN YOUR CHILDREN WALK WITH YOU, are they walking with a wise person? Can they look at your seasoned responses, your insightful understanding of people, your fortitude in difficult times as they walk with you in the moments of your daily life? If you think about it, teaching our children to walk never really ends. They watch us, listen to us when we speak to others, hear us talking with our husband behind closed doors. Our lives are the walk that our children will imitate.

With confusing voices, compromised ideals, wavering morals, secular values, and so many opposing opinions, where will our children find clarity and strong, secure values to embrace? As mothers, we must be ready and equipped with steady feet and strong souls to lead the way for our children with integrity. We will give them confidence as we walk, staying close to them, holding their hands, and showing them sure footsteps to follow.

No matter how old your children become, you are the example for them. They will always be looking at you for a vision of integrity, ideals, and ways to interact with God. The longer you provide your children with wisdom based on truth, the more they will consider your advice as they walk their own adult journey.

Are you walking in wisdom today? Is your life one you want your children
to follow? Is your pathway in your life with God getting brighter and
brighter? May God lead us on His path with integrity in each step.

Remember the Sabbath day by keeping it holy.

EXODUS 20:8, NIV

How do we experience God's gracious heart? His grace flows from channels He created us to experience, but we must make time to experience His provision.

God intends for us to stop and rest. Contrary to all the commercials for this and that product made to help you keep going despite your cold, your exhaustion, or your depression, the truth is that God understands and wants us to sometimes take a break from all the activity happening around us. The Hebrews were given a law about setting aside one day a week for rest; they were forbidden to do work of any kind. Jesus taught that the law had been made for man, so that we might experience rest.

In our home, we decided to be very intentional about making every Sunday after church a special day of relaxation and fun: a breakfast feast, coffee, and community. We have a delectable treat for teatime. We enjoy board games, watching a mystery series, time with friends at a local café, glorious naps, and lively conversations where nothing serious or stressful is allowed! Resting from worry and strife and work helps us meet Mondays with renewed strength.

I think sometimes we stay busy because we are insecure. The voices in our heads tell us we are supposed to do all that our friends are doing, even if it leaves us in a frenzy. We have developed the idea that if we stop, if we don't meet the needs of everyone around us, every second of the day, if we don't answer the phone, if we don't take that position at church, and . . . and . . . and—the world will stop on its axis, and somehow, we will be disappointing God.

His Word tells us something different.

*How are you doing in the rest department? Make plans to have
an especially enjoyable, soul-renewing Sabbath this week!*

NOVEMBER 27

Behold, I will do something new, now it will spring forth;
will you not be aware of it?

ISAIAH 43:19

IT IS DIFFICULT TO CHANGE—SCARY, EVEN. Often, we are fearful of current culture and how it might corrupt our children. Really, though, the important issues are still the same as they've always been. There might be different wrappings on the outside of teenagers, but the heart is still the main thing: their need for love, affirmation, friends, and purpose, and their desperate need for God to guide them in truth and morality.

I have had to change with the times and learn through much thought and prayer what is of eternal value and what is only a "standard" I used to think was a spiritual code, but really had only a cultural, historical value.

God has never let me just rest or stay still in my life as a parent, marriage partner, or ministry speaker and leader. He always requires new things of me, giving me new lessons and raising new issues of faith. But in the end, as I hold to Him and not to my rules, I find He is faithful and true and good and still reaches hearts as I walk with Him in front of my children. So, I trust Him today, that He has access to each of my children's souls, and I seek to cultivate a spiritual life, not based on style or fashion or music, but on heart—the part that never changes in its needs or design.

God doesn't change . . . but everything else does, and so must we,
it seems! Is there an area in your life in which you're resisting change,
but sense the Lord might be urging you to move forward? Examine
your pet issues to make sure you're clinging to biblical values and
not simply cultural preferences that really don't matter!

Hear, O Israel! The LORD is our God, the LORD is one! You shall love the LORD your God with all your heart and with all your soul and with all your might. These words, which I am commanding you today, shall be on your heart. You shall teach them diligently to your sons and shall talk of them when you sit in your house and when you walk by the way and when you lie down and when you rise up.

DEUTERONOMY 6:4-7

GOD TELLS US TO TRAIN UP our children in the way they should go. According to these verses, a lot of training is just talking throughout the day according to what the issue of the moment is, and of course at night when they go to bed and are asking questions. We are to have His words on our own hearts. From there, we will teach them wisdom personalized every day according to the need of the moment.

Your family is your own particular puzzle. God has given you your children, your husband, your home, and your community in this time. And no one else can tell you exactly what you ought to do with them! But He is faithful, and He desires to help and instruct you as you walk with Him. A list of rules and regulations to follow—do things this way, every time, with every child, in every circumstance!—would only separate you from your need to communicate with God and obey His personal instructions to you.

We have great freedom in Christ. Don't give it up for a yoke of slavery to any thing, any person, or any set of rules! Being a great mom is not about rules or formulas; it is more like a dance—moving to the rhythms of life, listening and paying attention to the mood of the music in your children's lives, and choreographing wisdom as the words to the song.

What are some of the formulas you have followed that have led to legalism? How can you reprogram your thinking to embrace your freedom in Christ?

NOVEMBER 29

The LORD said to Eliphaz the Temanite, "My wrath is kindled against you and against your two friends, because you have not spoken of Me what is right as My servant Job has."

JOB 42:7

MOTHERHOOD IS A NEVER-ENDING sacrifice of your time, effort, body: yourself. You are working uphill against sinful little creatures who insist on making messes every day and aren't always grateful for all you do for their good. They do not like it when you push against their little selfish wills, so they have various ways of pushing back.

During the toddler years, they fall on the floor and throw a fit because you didn't let them eat the candy they wanted. In the teen years, they question your wisdom and integrity and know just where to put in the knife. After all, none of us have been perfect, and we all have flaws, and our children tend to discover most of them.

Then there are always Job's friends in the crowd—those people who are quite sure they know why your life is not going well and what you have done wrong to make your life such a mess. Yet Job's friends were quite wrong! Job was being persecuted by Satan because Satan thought if a person were persecuted, he could not remain loyal to God. God had actually chosen Job as a model of integrity and faith, and Job's friends could not have been more wrong in their statements about his demise.

So don't pay too much attention to the critics. Their voices, though sometimes strong, are just part of journeying through this pathway of parenting and life. But let us seek to accept our limitations, create joy to refuel and keep going, get perspective, and please the One who is always going to be on our team—our heavenly Father, whose voice is always there to encourage.

How can you accept your limitations and tune out the voices of your critics—even your own children?

*What I am doing, I do not understand; for I am not practicing what
I would like to do, but I am doing the very thing I hate.*

ROMANS 7:15

A NUMBER OF YEARS AGO, I was sitting in my bedroom having a wonderful quiet time. I felt spiritually set for my day. Then, I walked into our living room.

There, among all of my best, breakable "stuff," were my boys, having an exuberant pillow fight. They hit some button I didn't even know I had. I went ballistic, giving them the lecture of their lives. They didn't know what hit them!

When it was over, I was as shocked as they were. How could I have just had a quiet time and then, not sixty seconds later, acted out in such ugly, frustrated anger? Of course, guilt and remorse pointed their accusing fingers at me. *How dare you speak and write books on motherhood? You have probably scarred the boys for life!*

Women carry all sorts of guilt on their shoulders. Many feel they have failed so badly there is no return, but God is always the God of second chances.

Abraham lied about Sarah, claiming she was only his sister, putting her in a compromising position with a foreign king. Moses killed a man and later lost his temper right after being on a mountain in the presence of God. Peter denied Jesus after living with Him for three years. Paul persecuted Christians before he was confronted by Christ on the road to Damascus.

The more I see how prone I am to stumble, the more humble I have had to become. I love Him more and more because I know how fallen I am, and yet He still loves me and is patient with me as I grow up, little by little.

---

*If you're tempted to give up on yourself, remember God never will!
He is the God of second chances; He is mindful we are but dust.
Let Him pick you up and dust you off, then begin anew.*

DECEMBER 1

What then shall we say to these things?
If God is for us, who is against us?

ROMANS 8:31

HOW WILL YOUR LIFE TELL OF God's faithfulness? How will you bring beauty out of chaos, integrity and faith to difficulty and testing, love to a loveless situation, hope and light to darkness? Heroines are made by being brave in difficulty, when giving up or giving in to fear would have been the natural response. But to be brave requires a will—a will that says, *I refuse to be overcome. I will trust God, battle for His ways, and work to make my story one of meaning, nobility, and goodness.*

To find the strength to do such a supernatural thing, however, requires some very practical soul care. A soul that is empty from the constant draining of life will not find resources to stand against the darkness that tries to overwhelm. One thing that helps me greatly is reading. My favorite authors become my friends. Just reading their stories has fed my soul and shown me how to live my life.

I save a bit each year for travel by putting away ten or fifteen dollars a month, because for me to get away from home with its dishes and laundry, email and phone calls is always a great break and rest for my soul. Of course, I also keep chocolate hidden as a treat for a difficult day, and I always have tea in a real china cup every afternoon with candles lit and just a bit of civility—even if only for fifteen minutes.

Most of all, I remind myself over and over again that God, my precious Father, loves me and wants me to experience His joy. I have resolved to look for His love and receive it by faith, even when I don't feel it.

May your story be the arena in which you find and spread God's light,
and may your children and your children's children be inspired to
have faith in a great God who redeems and loves beyond reason.

*Just as we have many members in one body and all the members
do not have the same function, so we, who are many, are one
body in Christ, and individually members one of another.*

ROMANS 12:4-5

THERE ARE SO MANY POSSIBILITIES when it comes to the various personalities and tendencies we may encounter in our children. Extroverts need to talk more and have lots of activities and people in their lives; introverts need more time alone to ponder, create, and go into their inner sanctum to be refreshed.

Some children just really want affirmation and hugs and listening so they will *feel* loved. Others want you to do something with them—to be active alongside you. Others want sympathy, and to have you understand all that's on their hearts. Still others thrive on quality time.

We are to accept and cooperate with our children's God-given personalities because God has a work for them to do in this world that matches their personality and gifting. If we want to be God's instrument to open their hearts, we have to study who they are and reach each one according to the personal design of his or her heart.

Children and adults are not cookie-cutter copies of each other who can all be handled the same way. Human beings are complex and cannot be generalized into formulaic solutions; they long to be loved and valued as they are.

We must live in the tension between respecting the unique design that our artistic Creator crafted into the DNA of our children and building a bridge of love to their hearts so they will be more willing to listen to the messages we live and speak. We are invited into a relationship with the living God, which is a pattern for how we live with our children. He is wild and wise and loving and deeply desirous of our personal, passionate love.

---

*How can you reach out to the people in your life and
show them you appreciate their individuality today?*

DECEMBER 3

Sanctify Christ as Lord in your hearts, always being ready to make a defense to everyone who asks you to give an account for the hope that is in you, yet with gentleness and reverence.

1 PETER 3:15

MANY YEARS AGO, I took Sarah, Joel, Nathan, and Joy to a children's museum in Fort Worth. We were standing in line behind what appeared to be grandparents with a little boy of about five or six. As we stood waiting our turn to enter, the little boy suddenly lay down on the floor screaming, and when his grandpa tried to pick him up, the boy started slapping, hitting, and spitting on him.

Immediately all four of my children turned and looked at me, with eyes wide. When I asked why, Joel said, "Mama, don't you know? We always look at your eyes to see what we are supposed to do and how we are supposed to react!"

Children naturally look to their parents for an example and model of what is expected. I believe one of the reasons God requires children to honor and obey their parents is so they will have an opportunity to practice what it looks like to honor and obey God.

I corrected my children because of the attitude I could detect—when they were willful or prideful or selfish in response to a person or situation—much more than I corrected for behavior.

But for a child to learn honor, a parent must display honor. The way we speak to each other and to our children should be with pleasant, loving words and voices. If we expect them to learn civility and honor, we have to exhibit it ourselves in the way we treat other people. When we do lash out in anger or raise our voices, we should always apologize. We must exhibit the same behavior we are expecting of them.

How are you modeling honor and obedience to God in your home by your attitudes and actions, so that your children will have a true picture to follow?

Sow with a view to righteousness, reap in accordance with kindness.

HOSEA 10:12

I have always loved fields of wildflowers. Whenever I see their beauty, I believe it is evidence of the invisible hands of God planting flowers in His gardens, reminding us He is still creating and perpetuating life, even when we are not aware.

When looking at a tiny seed, it is impossible to see what will grow from such a minute speck of nothing—the color of its blooms, the type of fruit, the size of the plant. There is vast potential locked within, and under the right circumstances—if it is planted in good soil, is watered regularly, and gets plenty of sunshine—a miracle will happen. The seed transforms into something more than itself.

God calls us to sow broadly, generously, diligently into the lives of our children.

We are asked to believe in the potential we sow, the latent miracles inside small life-seeds.

We are to sow with a view to righteousness, not knowing the vast potential of what is in our hands. Our task is to be faithful to sow, by faith, the seeds of promise given to us; His is to do the miracle, to take all the seeds of faithfulness, love, and service and grow them into such a bounty of beauty. One day we will finally see that He was creating the miracle in our children; the seeds will sprout into a harvest of righteousness and redemption that will be beyond what we could have imagined.

But the harvest of such sowing is only for those who plant, water, cultivate, and wait by faith, believing in the promise of what lies ahead.

So, dear God, let us look at the flowers You have planted and see beyond them to the beautiful harvest of our lives and the lives of our children, and help us believe in the potential of the seeds we are planting right now, which by faith will become a harvest of righteousness beyond measure.

*Are you sowing faithfulness, love, and service to your children
with a view toward righteousness and a hope of harvest?*

DECEMBER 5

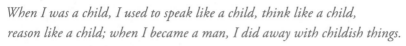

When I was a child, I used to speak like a child, think like a child,
reason like a child; when I became a man, I did away with childish things.

1 CORINTHIANS 13:11

THERE IS A BRIEF WINDOW OF time when children are dependent upon their parents, believing everything they say and wanting to please them. This season seems to go by quickly, and is the time to prepare their hearts as well as our own for the years when they will naturally begin to seek independence.

All teens must test what they have been taught and own what they really believe. Maneuvering through this transition with wisdom and faith is essential to coming through at the other end with a relationship still intact.

It is important to talk to your children about all kinds of subjects before they become teens and to develop a trusting relationship where they can confide their fears, thoughts, negative feelings, and even doubts about God. If they know that you will not react in fear or lay guilt on them, they will probably still want to talk to you about the mysterious issues of teenage life. They will know that you are their ally.

If they think you will get mad, make fun of them, yell, or not understand, often they will seek the input of others, who may or may not share your values.

Even though they may seem to be pushing you away, teens need you to walk beside them every step and to be involved in their lives, in order to protect them from unnecessary scars. They need your advice and guidance to help them make wise decisions.

Sometimes teen passages feel a little like the toddler years. You are supposed to be the mature one who doesn't yell and become emotional, but often when moms have teens, they are in the midst of their own hormones reversing and may have emotional and angry bouts themselves.

Grace, steadfastness, and love cover a multitude of sins!

Have you embraced the idea of your children
growing up and into independence? How can you walk
alongside them in an understanding way?

DECEMBER 6

Guard your heart, for everything you do flows from it.

PROVERBS 4:23, NIV

EVERY YEAR WHEN WE COME TO the busy season of Christmas, it seems we all feel the pressure to give perfect gifts to friends and family, becoming stressed trying to live up to expectations surrounding us. But long after each year's gifts have been forgotten, if we've given our loved ones the gift of a joyful heart, they will have something that will be with them their whole lives.

How can we do this? The first step is to have a heart that says to others, "I receive you into my life as a gift from God."

Then, a joyful heart seeks to encourage every day—to intentionally give words of life and encouragement to those who so need to hear that they are loved.

A joyful heart is one that plans surprises—lighting candles, putting on beautiful Christmas music, serving a cup of tea, hot chocolate, or coffee even in the midst of a busy day, maybe even with a little treat—and says, "Let's make a memory together right now—you are special to me." It might lead you to bring a single rose to a friend or leave a love note on a pillow or in an email to a weary husband, a struggling friend, someone you appreciate, or a far-off child.

Perhaps your joyful heart might cause you to take time to play a game, giggle at stories, lie in bed with a toddler or teen late at night even when you are weary and just want to go to sleep.

A joyful heart says, "Where can I leave a spirit of Christ's fragrance today? Where can I dance the dance of life in the midst of darkness?"

Where do your thoughts and beliefs about life, children, and your circumstances generally come from? We have to guard our hearts and everything that goes into them if we want to live wisely. What are some ways you may need to guard your heart so it might become a joyful one today?

DECEMBER 7

*See that you do not despise one of these little ones, for
I say to you that their angels in heaven continually
see the face of My Father who is in heaven.*

MATTHEW 18:10

ALBERT EINSTEIN WAS ONE OF the most brilliant thinkers of his time. His name is synonymous with the word *genius*. Yet, as a baby, his head was so large and misshapen, his mother thought he was deformed. As a child, he had a speech delay. He failed his college entrance exam. Yet despite all this, he became one of the most brilliant and world-changing scientists in history.

Each child is qualified differently for performing in life. How blessed is the child whose mother looks for his or her unique design and personality, who watches for the spark of interest her children show in different subjects, who asks the Holy Spirit to show her the place this child was crafted to invest his or her life for God's glory.

I once read an article that suggested every child had the capacity to become a genius in some area. Reading this one bit of information changed the way I looked at my children their whole lives. I did not focus on what they could not do, but sought to help them find out what they were made to do. Each child learned at his or her own pace and excelled in different areas, and each was validated for his or her own design.

God did not make any mistakes when He created our children. Each child is fearfully and wonderfully made. Consequently, we are wise when we accept them as gifts from God and love, pray for, and validate them as He made them. We learn wisdom in life by leaning into His will and ways—and part of that is in accepting the children He gave us as they are.

---

*Today, celebrate the differences, look for the genius,
and watch the life of God filling your home.*

DECEMBER 8

Do not neglect to show hospitality to strangers, for by this some have entertained angels without knowing it.

HEBREWS 13:2

OUR CHRISTMAS TEA WAS A SPECIAL event that had grown in importance over the years. It was a "high tea" with china, crystal, and silver. In addition to our old and dear friends, each year we would also invite two or three women or girls who didn't have family or friends in town, or who we thought might need some special encouragement.

Joy bedecked the table with delicate crystal glasses and serving pieces, Sarah made the cold raspberry soup we had learned to love on a visit to Hungary, and I whipped up the cold chicken salad. Chocolate mousse cake had become the traditional dessert.

This particular year, we invited a precious young woman who had grown up in such a broken home that she barely knew kindness and thoughtfulness existed. Her rough background had hardened her heart toward people and given her a defensive posture toward the world.

The tea went as usual that year until the end. After the meal, most of the women and girls chattered in the kitchen, washed dishes, straightened the table, and enjoyed the last few minutes of fellowship. In the midst of the relaxed gaggle, the young woman sheepishly walked over and tapped me on the shoulder.

"May I speak to you, please?" I nodded and said, "Of course," but before she could even begin speaking, she began to cry. I took her into another room for privacy, where we sat together as she told me her story.

"I am thirty-five years old, and I have never even had a cup of tea in a real teacup. I had read stories in magazines of friendships like this, but until today, I didn't even think they were possible. I just want you to know you have given me the best Christmas gift I have ever had—a sense of belonging."

Ask the Lord to bring to your mind someone who might need an invitation to grace this Christmas season.

DECEMBER 9

Not that we are competent in ourselves to claim anything for ourselves, but our competence comes from God. He has made us competent as ministers of a new covenant—not of the letter but of the Spirit; for the letter kills, but the Spirit gives life.

2 CORINTHIANS 3:5-6, NIV

THE DARK SHADOWS PLAYED UPON the window of my bedroom as the sun set over the mountains. The darkness seemed to match my mood. I remember this day clearly because I felt trapped and wondered if I would truly make it through the rest of the years of my children being at home. One more move, teens in the house, a sweet little girl who wanted someone to play Beanie Babies with her, and a hormonal middle-aged mama who was worn to the bone—it was bound to end in catastrophe.

There were many such days through the journey of motherhood when I felt fingers pointing at my heart, accusing me of the inadequacies and failures in my life. How about you? Do you feel guilty for yelling and becoming angry at your children too often? Are you regularly immature? In marriage, do you become easily frustrated, fighting with the spouse you know you should love?

Do you ever wonder if you can change? If you have been such a failure, do you worry that it will be impossible to redeem your situation or child or marriage? Does sadness fill your soul because you have a prodigal or rebellious, angry child and you think it is all your fault?

DON'T STAY THERE! MOVE ON!

There was some point in which I knew I could not live in a constant state of guilt or self-condemnation. The more I read Scripture, the more I understood that Jesus did not intend for me to live in that place because it is a place of destruction.

A mama who lives in a state of condemnation, guilt, and inadequacy is negative, depressed, and harsh so often that it also becomes a drag on her children. Today, determine to let guilt go.

DECEMBER 10

*He will feed his flock like a shepherd. He will carry
the lambs in his arms, holding them close to his heart.
He will gently lead the mother sheep with their young.*

ISAIAH 40:11, NLT

SOMEWHERE ALONG THE WAY, I decided to put the load of guilt from all the ways I had failed into the file drawers of heaven and mark *forgiven* over them. Now, when voices accuse me of once more blowing it, I just pray and again give my state of guilt to Jesus, seeking to stay alive in the freedom that He has provided.

You are still writing your story. That story cannot have a good ending unless you decide to celebrate life right where you are and lay your guilt, inadequacy, and condemnation at the foot of the cross and then move on to live in the freedom He wants you to have.

In the same way we would not expect a toddler to live a life without making messes, crying, and throwing a few fits, so God is not surprised at our incredible potential for messing up. In comparison to His holiness and perfection, we are mere toddlers—if that.

Do not accept the heavy burden of guilt—*choose* to live in your new freedom. *Choose* to put away the voices that condemn. Faith is a choice of your will. Believe that He is a Redeemer. He can draw back stray sheep because He loves them, and He especially wants to love and help you because you are a mama after His heart. He will redeem—buy back—all of those mistakes. Redeeming is what He does—He delights in doing what He was made to do. So don't waste your time worrying—leave your failings and regrets in His loving hands.

After all, I think mamas are close to His heart because, like Him, they make sacrifices for their sweet sheep.

---

*May you live in the resurrection power today and
each day until you see Him face to face.*

DECEMBER 11

I am continually with You; You have taken hold of my right hand.

PSALM 73:23

A SATIN DRESS BEDECKED WITH rhinestones and a swirly layer of ruffle at the bottom made the perfect swishing sound as the little girl danced around the room. "I want to be a *real* princess when I grow up and have a handsome man who loves me dearly all the time."

The mother heard the depth of longing in her six-year-old's voice and wondered at her intense interest in romance that had sprung out of nowhere over the past months.

"Why do you dream of this so much?" she asked her little one.

"I want to feel really loved and not be lonely anymore."

"What do you mean?" the mama asked, confused.

"You are never really with me, and I want someone to be with me," answered her daughter.

"I am with you all the time! I'm home all day with you and your brother. What do you mean I am never with you?"

"You are here in the house, but you are always busy with housework and the computer and we are always doing schoolwork. You don't play with me, or pretend, or sit next to me—really with me, doing nothing else. I wish you could really be my friend and like me, 'cause lots of times I feel lonely," came the innocent reply.

All children want to be loved and cherished and have close companionship. If it is not felt in the home, the child (or adult) will search for it wherever he or she can find it.

Often, without meaning to, we are busy straightening the pictures on the walls of a house that is burning down. If we are to win the hearts of our children or husbands or neighbors or friends with our messages, we must first woo their hearts with our focused time and attention, so they deeply feel our love.

God demonstrates love to us with His presence.
Are you truly with your children, so they feel your love?

DECEMBER 12

When a man's folly brings his way to ruin,
his heart rages against the LORD.

PROVERBS 19:3, ESV

IF A CHILD IS GIVEN AN ICE-CREAM CONE and starts running and wrestling with his brother, the likelihood that he is going to drop his cone in the confusion is high. The child is acting foolishly. Can the act be forgiven? Of course! The act can be forgiven, but the consequence will remain.

If a car is speeding down the road at ninety miles per hour in the snow and suddenly hits a patch of ice and skids out of control, it is likely the car will crash. The unwise, imprudent choice of driving too fast in the snow has consequences.

How often I see people shaking their fists at heaven, at God Himself, asking why they have been treated so unjustly. They are strapped financially, or unhappily married, or in the midst of relational turmoil. Often, these people have found themselves in a pickle of their own making—they used credit cards too much, or married an unbeliever against the advice of their parents, or have conflict with someone and are unwilling to extend forgiveness and leave bitterness behind.

How important it is for us as believers to understand that choices have consequences! If someone makes an unwise decision, havoc of some kind will probably result. One cannot expect to make a practice of acting foolishly and not have repercussions from his or her bad judgment.

God, our merciful Father, will indeed be with us and love us and guide us through the consequences of our choices. But He teaches us by letting the lessons remain, helping us learn to make wiser choices and obey Him the next time. We must learn to be humble, to repent and to ask for His wisdom, in order to benefit from His desire to bless us.

Are there areas in which you are suffering the consequences of unwise
choices? Repent, and ask the Lord to teach you what He wants
you to learn. Determine to seek His wisdom in the future.

DECEMBER 13

The beginning of wisdom is: Acquire wisdom; and
with all your acquiring, get understanding.

PROVERBS 4:7

IT IS ESSENTIAL THAT WE FILL OUR minds with biblical wisdom and not just man's advice. If you want to make wise decisions, you must adhere to the wisdom and insight of Scripture. Wisdom is at the core of living a righteous life and seeing God's favor unfold.

Don't be caught in confusion, looking for favor when you have lived unwisely. Choices have consequences. Seeking to become wise and humble, obediently listening to and following godly advice, is the only way to find a centered life with a foundation that will not be shaken.

Moral laws directing us toward purity were given to protect our lives. Staying married, caring for our children, and building a godly heritage by investing time in our children's lives require choices of obedience. Choosing love and service by modeling our lives after Christ is choosing to live wisely. We cannot compromise the truths and wisdom of God and expect to have the same consequences as if we had followed Him.

God is so very patient and gracious, and He will restore and heal us over time. However, God is not a Santa Claus who hands out answers to all requests just because we want something or have made a mess of something. He has made us in His image and given us the Spirit, so we are empowered to choose obedience, seek excellence of character, work hard, and keep our eyes on Him.

We are called to be stewards of the truth and wisdom He has provided. We must embrace responsibility for our lives. Our responsibility is to listen to His voice and follow His ways if we want to grow in order, strength, beauty, and soundness.

Christianity without godly character is a sham. May we be those who collect, acquire, and hold on to wisdom and obey His ways, so our lives may follow in the pathway of the Lord.

Do you seek wisdom in the voice of God through Scripture?

Rejoice always; pray without ceasing; in everything give thanks; for this is God's will for you in Christ Jesus.

1 THESSALONIANS 5:16-18

MANY YEARS AGO, as a young, idealistic mama, I wanted to give my children all the best experiences, opportunities, toys, and things we all feel pressured to provide for our families. When we started Whole Heart Ministries, though, we moved to a tiny town of 712 people, where we lived with my mother-in-law and got by on a negligible salary for several years.

Shopping at Goodwill was a necessity, and I couldn't give the children many things. But living in the country with lots of space to roam and lots of time together as a family is probably the best thing that could have happened to my children. Because we did not have lots of toys, they learned to pretend, create stories, make up games, read lots of books, play with animals, and generally keep themselves busy.

Because there was not even an option to have lots of things, they became content with what they had. I was the only one who had any idea that they might be missing out. There was no possibility to be constantly entertained because we did not have lots of electronic gadgets. There were few neighbors nearby to make them wish for toys they did not have.

Working, delaying gratification, sharing, patiently waiting for their turn . . . all of these were the ways God built thankfulness into my children's hearts. I was not smart enough to choose this purposefully for my family, but God in His wisdom knew just what my children needed to build character, and He gave us just the right circumstances to train them!

This week, every day, notice the things that God has provided.
Breathing thankfulness into your days creates a great pattern for life
and helps you become more satisfied with what He has given.

DECEMBER 15

As each one has received a special gift, employ it in serving one another as good stewards of the manifold grace of God.

I PETER 4:10

YESTERDAY, I spent an hour on the phone with a cherished friend. She is so alone in carrying heavy burdens of life that when an unsuspecting stranger asked how she was, the tears began to flow. She is beloved by so many, and yet no one knows her burdens, helps her, or reaches out to her.

But I have to ask myself, *How many people in my life have known the depth of my own soul battles?* Too often I don't want to burden my friends because they are all as busy and overwhelmed as I am.

We were made for friendship. Our hearts are prewired to be loved, to belong, to celebrate and share life together in community—to bear each other's burdens and so fulfill the law of Christ.

That feeling in the dark of night that your life is invisible—*Does anyone care? Does it matter that I keep dragging on day by day? Does anyone know the weariness of my soul? Do others swell with anger? Or wish for relief? Or feel a lack of worth? Or want to quit and don't even know what that means?*

So, at Christmastime, I call my friends together and we gather with food, drink, and a little reprieve from real life, to talk with and touch someone else who shares our world. We gather to listen to His words together. We gather to understand that our sacrifice is precious to the One who sacrificed all.

We gather to know we are not alone. We meet to find strength, love, laughter, understanding, and hope—the hope that keeps our feet on the path, our minds steadfast on our beliefs, our hearts willing to take another step of faith one more day, one more month, one more year, because once again, we know our life of giving and love poured out is changing the world.

Today, invite a friend, call a loved one, or take initiative to encourage someone else. Doing so will encourage you, too.

DECEMBER 16

Let us consider how to stimulate one another to love and
good deeds, not forsaking our own assembling together,
as is the habit of some, but encouraging one another;
and all the more as you see the day drawing near.

HEBREWS 10:24-25

WHEN MAMAS GATHER IN my home for our annual Christmas tea, we take time to ponder Mary, on her journey through countries, through years of questions, through people seeking the life of her Son. Because of her heart and willingness to believe, Mary found favor with God. He chose her to bring Jesus into the world through her own body, to nurture Him within her home, so the Son of God could find comfort, beauty, and love for the years He would live on earth, even as we provide comfort, beauty, and love so our children will experience God Himself in our homes.

Mary was a simple mother whose heart gave all, that He might have a safe haven and find rest for His baby soul.

The gift we give to our children and those around us when we take time to listen and share life with them is the gift of presence, the same gift Jesus gave when He came to be "God with us." It's easy to lose sight of the people in our lives during the busyness of the holidays. But our families and friends need to know they are seen and known and loved.

This holiday season, remember buying one more thing will not satisfy a human heart. Investing love and heart time, however, will restore, redeem, and bring life and hope.

Christmas is the perfect season to make time to love, to talk, to share hearts, to show compassion.

Who needs you today? How might you especially offer the gift of dedicated
listening and sharing time to a child or another family member this
week? Who do you need to celebrate life with in this season?

DECEMBER 17

Come, let us go up to the mountain of the LORD, to the
house of the God of Jacob; that He may teach us concerning
His ways and that we may walk in His paths.

ISAIAH 2:3

OVER AND OVER GOD BRINGS me back to my purpose: that through me, others may learn of Him, love Him, and know Him; that people who come into my home would sense immediately His welcome and His undivided Spirit's gentleness. I pray my home would be a repository of Him and His life in many dimensions, a place where people can enjoy and dwell in His love, see His beauty, know His approval, and experience His joy. A place where people can be inspired to live valiantly for His purposes—to live holy, excellent lives of beautiful moral character and sacrifice. I want people to come here to understand the vast truth and wisdom from His Word, to find healing, to know deep forgiveness.

I want the life of God to so fill my heart that people feel His presence when they come to my home.

God desires to pour out Himself through us to people who long for His reality. Yet, we must be filled up with God in order for our lives to be that channel. When we invest in Him, obey His will, and fill our souls with His truth, we will have godly substance others can draw from.

In my own life, I hear the sins of selfishness, guilt, anger, lust, idolatry, and lack of love call out, just as they call out to everyone through the voice of the world every day. These life-draining voices and pressures harden our hearts, creating indifference toward His priorities, which call us to bring His life into our worlds.

How can you go up to the mountain of the Lord today?
How will you share what you bring down?

Glory to God in the highest, and on earth peace among men with whom He is pleased.

LUKE 2:14

FLICKERING CANDLELIGHT; shimmering silvers, golds, reds, greens, and blues sparkling on a real tree inside the house; familiar songs that beg swaying and dancing; the smells of pine boughs, vanilla, spices, cookies, coffee, and breads filling the air with invitation each hour of the day; lots of friends and family and hugs and kisses and celebrations and presents; stories of babies, wise men, young mothers, and animals—all of these wrapped in one short period of just a few weeks—what's not to love about Christmas?!

Over the years, many women have asked if I thought it was pagan to celebrate Christmas and have trees and presents. Of course Clay and I studied the Word and pondered this many years ago, and we came to our own conclusions, as each family must. Looking back, we can see how the beauty and celebration of Christmas, the delights of our home and the filling of emotional cups, making of memories, and cherishing Christ every day, gave our children even more love for Him. Since our family is not pagan, the celebrations in our home are not pagan—nor the ways we choose to celebrate.

I think that sometimes people are afraid to have too much fun or to celebrate life! Yet, it is only when we do this fully from our hearts that we understand the joy of the Lord—the God who gave us the ability to be satisfied, to laugh and play games and eat merrily.

So, our family makes time to delight together. It is the organic life of Christ—the tastes, smells, fun, love, and theology—that gives the whole picture of this baby-become-King-and-Savior. And so in a spirit of love, we celebrate Christmas with joy!

Do you feel freedom in your celebration of the holiday?
Prayerfully consider what He would have you do,
remembering that He enjoys watching you enjoy life and beauty!

DECEMBER 19

Mary said: "My soul magnifies the Lord, and my spirit has rejoiced in God my Savior. For He has regarded the lowly state of His maidservant; for behold, henceforth all generations will call me blessed. For He who is mighty has done great things for me, and holy is His name."

LUKE 1:46-49, NKJV

MARY HAS BEEN ON MY MIND LATELY. Our pastor delivered an insightful sermon about her, and at the Christmas tea for my monthly Bible study, we talked about Mary's faith.

God chose Mary to be the mother of Jesus, the one who would daily mold memories in the life of her beloved child—who was also her Creator! She came from a common family, and yet she and Joseph were the ones entrusted to raise the Son of God.

What a statement the incarnation of Christ is—that a normal family could be the place true holiness would be lived out, a place competent to hold and protect and shape the human side of the Son of God. So the Incarnation speaks to us today in our own normal families, dedicated to His life and righteousness—these places, too, are adequate to be the home of God. But there is an attribute I've noticed recently about Mary that may offer a glimpse into just what might have qualified her for this task: she had invested her young life engaging in Scripture, pondering it, embracing it, and owning it for her own soul.

What was Mary's response when she met her cousin Elizabeth? Her words are recorded in Luke 1:46-55. She rejoiced! She called the Lord holy and talked about His strength, His provision, and His help. Mary knew the God who called her to mother His Son. She called herself "His maidservant" (Luke 1:48, NKJV).

This Christmas season, pray daily that He would make you His maidservant. Take time to read the Christmas story with your children, the precious ones God chose you to mother! End your reading time with a gentle kiss. May you be blessed as you minister to your sweet family.

If we have food and covering, with these we shall be content.

I TIMOTHY 6:8

OUR CULTURE PRAISES MATERIAL POSSESSIONS as a source of happiness. Those who have more are supposedly happier, and those who have less are somehow unjustly struggling. We believe a new house, a better car, or a larger salary will bring us happiness. Often, the longing for more things and money leads us to idolize wealth, work long hours to the detriment of our families, and seek a way to provide for ourselves instead of trusting God with our humble circumstances.

It is not sinful or wrong to have desires for something more in various areas of life. Our hearts can actually perceive a better world and more wonderful circumstances than we presently have because we were made for a better place. We were made for perfection, love, joy, and great blessing. It was in the heart of God to provide us a magnificent life.

The only way we will ever be able to be content, though, is to realize the nature of a fallen world. This earth is not heaven. We must cultivate a level of thanksgiving and contentment in the life we have been given, now. God calls us to find our contentment in Him, not in our circumstances or our material possessions. To choose to look beyond material possessions, to seek His fingerprints every day in our lives, to have an eternal perspective—this is the only way we will be able to be content.

Contentment is a heart issue. We cannot change our emotions and selfish desires by force. Our only hope is to look to God, to ask Him to teach our heart to be content, to want to trust Him and not live in ungratefulness or in looking to what others have.

As long as we covet what we do not have, we will never be at peace.

When you look into your heart, do you find covetousness there? Ask God to take it away and determine to rest in what He has provided for you.

DECEMBER 21

Do not let kindness and truth leave you; bind them around your neck, write them on the tablet of your heart. So you will find favor and good repute in the sight of God and man.

PROVERBS 3:3-4

CHARLES DICKENS WAS a master storyteller who described people in such a way that all of us readers feel we know his characters in real life. One of the most memorable characters, of course, is Ebenezer Scrooge. He looked at life through a lens of bitterness, criticism, and condescension, and he brought negativity everywhere he went. As the story of *A Christmas Carol* unfolds, we observe Scrooge seeing his life as if for the first time, shocked by just how dark his influence has been. Finally, he longs for redemption, and of course finds it, turning to become lifegiving, charitable, generous, and kind to all he comes in contact with.

Perhaps all of us have Scrooges in our lives. I wish mean-hearted, critical people would suddenly repent of hateful ways and become transformed on a more regular basis. Lately, I have realized that so many women I know have deep wounds of insecurity caused by others' criticism, hatefulness, and anger.

I have had to work through similar wounds in my own life. If I had chosen to hold on to destructive attitudes, like Scrooge did, I would leave a legacy like the one he left before his repentance: people being afraid to be in my presence, avoiding me, not trusting me, and talking about me behind my back.

But by accepting God's love and choosing not to live in bitterness or dwell in judgment myself, He turns things around, causing my own heart to heal. This allows me to be much more compassionate and sympathetic toward others who need to feel the same love and comfort in their own lives.

What's tied around your neck? Kindness and truth? Or bitterness, insecurities, and the residue of your own past hurts? Lay them down today, and ask the Lord to help you make as miraculous a turnaround as Scrooge.

DECEMBER 22

He gives strength to the weary,
and to him who lacks might He increases power.

ISAIAH 40:29

BALANCE IS OVERRATED.

One day a few years ago, I was zipping along in the car to Kohl's to look for jeans and a couple of things Joy needed, keeping in mind a meeting I had to drive her to in an hour. I also needed to pick up medication for the sinus infection I had developed, make it to an appointment we had to pray with friends at five, then pick up Joy from her meeting and head to Walmart for the things she would need while I was on a trip. Sarah and Joy and I had a cooking class at seven, we had plans to meet out-of-town friends at their hotel at nine, and then I would finish packing. Finally, I would leave for the airport with Clay and Sarah at 7:30 the next morning!

A friend said to me once, "The pendulum on a clock is only in balance at one point, as it constantly swings back and forth between the two sides." I think I would have been so much more content and joyful if I had known at the beginning that life for me would not be "balanced." It could still be meaningful if I would just accept the limitations of my day, my season, each of my children, my marriage, and my finances.

I don't think Scripture promises balance. Jesus' life did not always appear to be balanced. He had many days of people chasing after Him, and someone was always criticizing Him as He spent time feeding thousands and healing lepers and forgiving prostitutes and holding children and training His disciples. But we also know that Jesus frequently withdrew from the demands of life to rest and be in God's presence, which was essential for Him to be able to do God's will. If we, too, can see our busy days as part of the puzzle that brings about God's will, we can be content and joyful and enjoy moments of rest even on our busiest days.

When you are weary or in a particularly busy season that seems out
of balance, how can you find strength from God to keep going?

DECEMBER 23

She gave birth to her firstborn son; and she wrapped
Him in cloths, and laid Him in a manger, because
there was no room for them in the inn.

LUKE 2:7

ONE EVENING THIS WEEK, I was enjoying the sweet fellowship of friends at a Christmas gathering. I was captivated by a tiny, three-week-old baby girl, wrapped in red velvet and sleeping soundly in her mother's arms.

Musing on her delicate little hands and the tiny lips that opened slightly with each deep, sleepy breath, I was struck by her vulnerability. She was totally dependent on her mother for her very life. Cries of hunger would be satisfied by this mother's milk. This little baby was unaware of her need for protection, clothing, and the necessities of life, and her well-being would depend on the benevolence of loving parents. Her very intelligence, moral fiber, and vision for life would be shaped by the love bestowed, the integrity lived out, and the words treasured and spoken in the moments and experiences of her life with these two people looking lovingly at her.

What a wonder that the One who commands the myriads of stars and galaxies, earthquakes and storms, the One who numbers the hairs of each person born, subjected Himself to a fallen world by placing Himself in the hands of frail, fallible human beings. That God would condescend to become a dependent, vulnerable baby brought amazement to my heart.

What humility He portrayed for us, coming as a normal baby to live here on earth, entering the home of new parents who had the impossible job of raising the One who would become the Redeemer of mankind! How exalted a position we have that, like Mary and Joseph, we receive into our homes those dependent children whose lives have eternal consequence.

Pray this with me: "May Your humility give me confidence to
live humbly; may the integrity of Your heart shape my words and
actions; and may my family be that place of redemption from
which others may always find Your peace, power, and love."

DECEMBER 24

Greetings, favored one! The Lord is with you.

LUKE 1:28

OH, HOW I PRAY THAT THESE WORDS express how God feels about me! Does God see me as the kind of woman He could have chosen to mother the Most High God? By what means did she find favor?

Mary lived a humdrum life in a tiny, obscure village. Wheat was ground, bread dough kneaded on wooden tables, crumbs swept from the floor, siblings lovingly tended, the Shema recited every day over shared family meals. And yet, while she lived her life quietly, God noticed her. He saw her, and she found favor and pleased His heart.

God always sees, even when no one else is noticing.

Being the mother of Jesus would require a tenacious, steady, engaged faith. As His mother, her life would be in danger. Jesus would be pursued by a crazed king, and at every point people would cast doubt on her irregular, fantastic story. Satan wanted to prevent Jesus from becoming Savior, and Mary was to be His protector—a shelter from danger, a nurturer of His soul, a provider of truth, a teacher and trainer, a strength in storms. All this she would be asked to be for God's Son, the Baby entrusted into her hands.

Her life would be filled with stress, pressure, rejection, fear, loneliness, and questions. And yet, God called her favored. He looked for one who would serve Him willingly, readily, at the moment of His impossible request, one who would respond in utter submission.

Those who consider themselves servants live to accomplish the will of their master. Is that my heart—to obey, willingly, whatever He would ask?

Is obedience your response to God? Even if it means sacrificing
plans you hold dear? Even if it means being misunderstood?
Rejected? Inconvenienced? Even if it requires great courage?
Today, ask God to show you the responses of your heart.

DECEMBER 25

That night there were shepherds staying in the fields nearby, guarding their flocks of sheep. Suddenly, an angel of the Lord appeared among them, and the radiance of the Lord's glory surrounded them. They were terrified, but the angel reassured them. "Don't be afraid!" he said. "I bring you good news that will bring great joy to all people. The Savior—yes, the Messiah, the Lord—has been born today in Bethlehem, the city of David! and you will recognize him by this sign: You will find a baby wrapped snugly in strips of cloth, lying in a manger." Suddenly, the angel was joined by a vast host of others—the armies of heaven—praising God and saying, "Glory to God in highest heaven, and peace on earth to those with whom God is pleased."

LUKE 2:8-14, NLT

OUR HEAVENLY FATHER WAS the first to celebrate Christmas. He was the first one to document the birthday of Jesus—supernaturally, with music performed before humble shepherds. When I think about the wonders of the first Christmas—astonishing, bewildering, unimaginable beings appearing on the earth, extraterrestrial choirs filling the sky, a heretofore unknown star rising in the heavens, learned kings traveling from afar, a virgin birth in the midst of a love story, an old woman and an old man marveling and speaking of the Messiah as the baby is dedicated—I can't help but think they were part of God's plan to help us celebrate Jesus' arrival.

Christmas is a time when we bring friends and family into our home to be refreshed. It is a time of personal worship and a time of joy. It's a time of work and preparation, but all to say "I love you" and "God loves us and is worthy of our celebration of Him." In these traditions we understand that God wanted us to put aside special times for the passing down of His story and His love.

How will you celebrate on this day when we remember the birthday of Jesus?

DECEMBER 26

Now may the God who gives perseverance and encouragement grant you to be of the same mind with one another according to Christ Jesus.

ROMANS 15:5

ONE MORNING, I lay in bed mentally adding up all my responsibilities. Busyness with teenagers, a book deadline, and various serious health issues including Clay's excruciating ruptured disc had me bone weary. This fueled my frustration with Clay, lying next to me, oblivious to my burdens. I was sending mean thoughts his way when the Holy Spirit nudged my conscience. *Clay needs you to encourage him. He is so discouraged because of pain, mounting bills, and the insecurities of life all around him.*

Really, Lord?! I responded.

S-l-o-w-l-y, I willed my arm to reach out and scratch his back. "I just want you to know that I love you and respect how bravely you have borne this ruptured disc. I know you are in such pain every day, but I am praying for you," I whispered, in sheer obedience.

Almost imperceptibly, he responded, "I am so relieved. You have every right to be mad at me. I thought you were disappointed in me for not paying attention to you or taking care of you. But I have been so down and constantly in pain, and I have not meant to neglect you—there is just so much. Thank you for being patient with me. I really appreciate and love you."

I slipped out of bed, intending to head to the kitchen. As I approached the door of my bedroom, I saw my ten-year-old son lying on the floor, cuddled in a comforter. I had no idea he had been there!

"I was sleeping here because I had a bad dream, but I didn't want to wake you up. It made me feel happy to hear you comforting each other and saying, 'I love you.' I want a marriage like yours when I grow up. That would be so much fun, to live with your best friend!"

You never know who is listening.
What would your children hear?

DECEMBER 27

I have calmed and quieted my soul; like a weaned child with his mother.

PSALM 131:2, ESV

THE DAYS AFTER CHRISTMAS ARE always interesting. Moms everywhere have expended so much energy trying to make everyone happy, cooking, cleaning, loving, giving in every way until the adrenaline is all spent. What goes up must eventually come down, and after Christmas it seems that's you!

In my home this week, Boston-classical Joel was in the same room with Hollywood-contemporary Nathan; there were episodes of boys' humor versus girls' humor; introverted, used-to-quiet Daddy was adjusting to a once-again-loud-and-opinionated houseful of our own children; there was a lot of angst about jobs, school, money, futures, and present activities . . . It sometimes felt like riding the ups and downs of a roller coaster!

My personal place in all of this home reality is to be an immovable mountain amid the raging storms. I have taken on the role of peacemaker, soothing this one, encouraging that one, pushing the toe of one under the dinner table to gently encourage them to stop talking!

As I was pondering all of this in my quiet time this morning, I looked out the window and saw a beautiful, crimson sunrise. It was as though the gentle voice of the Lord called out to me: "I am here. Look for me today. Look for my presence in the midst of your messes and the life of your family. I am responsible for each of these precious ones—you are not. You walk with me, extend my love, and be my servant. All will be well."

My family is His responsibility. I am responsible to keep my heart and body as healthy as possible to be an anchor of His presence in the midst of it, but He is at work.

---

*How will you still and quiet your soul today,
remembering that God is with you?*

DECEMBER 28

The thief comes only to steal and kill and destroy;
I came that they may have life, and have it abundantly.

JOHN 10:10

MY ADULT CHILDREN AND I OFTEN work with teens and college-age groups. Last spring, I was speaking to a group of young women and asked them to tell me their impression of godly women. Their answers surprised me: *boring, legalistic, frumpy,* and *disengaged.* And most of these young women said they got this impression from their moms!

Motherhood is such a demanding call, and we have so many tasks to complete. But all of our work will be in vain if we do not seek to show the children in our home the reality of God's joy, love, creativity, and life.

Our view of God is reflected in how we live life in front of our children each day.

God is the author of all creation, including waterfalls, roses, puppy dogs, lightning storms, color, sound, food, and all delights. He designed and gave us the instinct to giggle and belly laugh; to sway and swirl with the sounds of vibrant music; to delight in the galaxies aglow on a summer's night; to touch, kiss, hug, and love; to work and bring color, beauty, and skill into the presentation of a garden; to write a story; to set a beautiful table; to cook a meal that delights the palate; to nurse the ill back to health; and so much more. Our lives should reflect this greatness of God, this joie de vivre, through the ways we face and celebrate life each day.

Instead of gluing our faces to a screen, instead of focusing on the drudgery of the everyday, let's look deeply into the eyes of these creatures of God living in our home, see inside their hearts, and affirm the beauty we find there.

Determine today to be a mother who will emulate His greatness, excellence,
civility, redemption, care, and truth so your children can see His life.

DECEMBER 29

How blessed is the man who does not walk in the counsel of the wicked, nor stand in the path of sinners, nor sit in the seat of scoffers! But his delight is in the law of the LORD, and in His law he meditates day and night.

PSALM 1:1-2

DISCIPLESHIP IS NEVER OVER. This past holiday, I made it a point to sequester each child to pour in vision and encouragement because I know how short my time with them is. I reminded them of the words of Psalm 1, and then over coffee and laughter, we shared our hearts, and I reminded them again to listen for the still, small voice and to seek the holy way above the distractions of life, to seek to see His fingerprints.

My family truly fills my cup, blesses me, and renews my own courage and faith because I want to be as strong as they believe that I am. Sometimes when I am exhausted, like now, and have lived through a looonnnngggggg year of trials, I am tempted to compromise my ideals—just a little here and there, in ways perhaps no one would notice.

But that is not His way, and I do not want to capitulate to the ways of weariness. As I served my children, I felt called to a higher standard just by hearing them talk and dream and idealize. Those I have served are now serving me and exhorting me to hold fast and stay the course!

And so, the next few days, I must follow the advice I gave to them for myself. I am about to put away the phone, go away by myself for two nights, and spend time before the Lord.

Here are the questions I'm asking. Maybe you want to use them too. "Lord, what work do You have for me this year? How can I serve Your purposes? What do I need to correct? How can I better serve You? Shine the light of Your life onto all the hidden places of my heart, and let me give all of them to You."

DECEMBER 30

Go to the ant, O sluggard, observe her ways and be wise, which, having no chief, officer or ruler, prepares her food in the summer and gathers her provision in the harvest.

PROVERBS 6:6-8

As young children, my little ones were fascinated with nature. Living on two hundred acres of wilderness in the middle of Texas provided many opportunities to catch and classify butterflies, catch bugs, put snakes into large jars to observe (I found one on the kitchen counter!), and see how God had built lessons of life into His world.

One evening, Nathan and Joel were running ahead as we sauntered on our traditional after-dinner walk. With the summer hours at night, we still had full light. Joel was captivated by a tiny ant carrying a leaf almost five times its size.

"Mama, if a tiny little bug like that can work so hard for his family of ants, maybe we could do a lot more than we think."

Three days later, we received a shipment of a printing of one of our books. Boxes were stacked high, and it would take quite some work to empty them onto our shelves. Late in the afternoon, however, Clay came out of our little office to find Joel, sweating profusely in the Texas summer heat, busily at work. He had already emptied thirty boxes of books, placing them neatly onto the shelves, and had only two more to go.

"Joel, this is amazing! What made you decide to do this?" we asked.

"Well, when I was thinking about the ant and how he carried so much more than we could ever imagine possible, I thought, *I want to be like that ant! I want to be strong and dependable.* Today, something came into my head and told me to empty the boxes of books." (Yes, he really said that when he was nine years old. I think maybe the Holy Spirit came into his head!) We couldn't have planned this lesson for Joel; it came about as part of our regular routine.

How does nature fit into your day?

DECEMBER 31

The people who know their God will display strength and take action.

DANIEL 11:32

BUBBLING UP IN MY HEART FROM an early age was a desire to know the greatness of God. I had a hunger to meet people who had a desire for greatness, excellence, and vision in their lives. I always believed that if someone really knew the God who created this exquisite universe, they would have an exceptional sense of life, beauty, power, love, and purpose.

When I came across today's verse, my deep desire was validated. It seemed to say the power of God in a person would cause them to reflect His reality.

What does it mean to display strength? We face constant challenges in which we could become discouraged and bitter or develop a victim mentality that suggests we are unfairly limited by our difficult circumstances. However, this verse in Daniel suggests that in every circumstance, when one is walking with God, strength will be available.

Taking action means taking initiative to do something, pursuing the harvest field of the lost, working diligently, and engaging resources for much-needed Kingdom work. Even as Christ obeyed the Father in everything, ultimately yielding His very life to redeem us, so His Spirit inside of us should compel us to action. Passivity and laziness are never seen in the character of God.

Consequently, when we are in the presence of God and in His Word daily, we see that He has compassion on the poor, so we have compassion for the poor. He is holy, so we are to be holy. He forgives us, so we are compelled to forgive. He is the servant leader, so we serve those around us.

Do people see life, goodness, love, compassion, excellence of character, and generosity of spirit when they are in your presence? How might you display strength and take action in your own life?

ABOUT THE AUTHOR

✴

Sally Clarkson is the beloved author of multiple bestselling books, including *Girls' Club* with her daughters, Sarah and Joy; *The Lifegiving Home* with her daughter Sarah; *Desperate* with Sarah Mae; *Different* with her son Nathan; and *Own Your Life*. As a mother of four, she has inspired thousands of women through conferences, resources, and books with Whole Heart Ministries (wholeheart.org). She has also advocated relentlessly for the power of motherhood and the influence of home through her Mom Heart conferences (momheart.org), speaking to audiences on several continents.

Discipleship and mentoring women to understand how to love God in a more personal way and how to live a satisfying Christian life are threads through all of her messages. Sally encourages many through her blogs, podcasts, and websites. You can find her on her blog at Sallyclarkson.com. Her popular podcast, *At Home with Sally and Friends*, which has over a million downloads, can be found on iTunes and Stitcher. She regularly teaches at conferences and on webcasts, and she participates in international discipleship ministry in venues all over the world.

SALLY CLARKSON

Books and Resources to Help You Own Your Life

Sally has served Christ in ministry for four decades. She and Clay started Whole Heart Ministries in 1994 to serve Christian parents. Since then, Sally has spoken to thousands of women at her Mom Heart Conferences and written numerous inspirational books about motherhood, faith, and life. She is a regular mom blogger.

ONLINE

SallyClarkson.com—Personal blog for Christian women
MomHeart.com—Ministry blog for Christian mothers
WholeHeart.org—Ministry website, blog, and store
MomHeartConference.com—Ministry conference website
SallyClarkson.com/podcast—*At Home with Sally Clarkson and Friends* podcast

IN PRINT

Own Your Life (Tyndale House)

The Lifegiving Home (Tyndale House)

The Lifegiving Home Experience (Tyndale House)

The Lifegiving Table (Tyndale House)

The Lifegiving Table Experience (Tyndale House)

The Lifegiving Parent (Tyndale House)

The Lifegiving Parent Experience (Tyndale House)

Different (Tyndale House)

A Different Kind of Hero (Tyndale House)

You Are Loved (with Angela Perritt, Love God Greatly)

Seasons of a Mother's Heart (Apologia)

Educating the WholeHearted Child (Apologia)

The Mission of Motherhood (WaterBrook)

The Ministry of Motherhood (WaterBrook)

Dancing with My Father (WaterBrook)

The Mom Walk (Whole Heart Press)

Desperate (with Sarah Mae, Thomas Nelson)

10 Gifts of Wisdom (Home for Good Books)

CONTACT INFORMATION

Whole Heart Ministries | Mom Heart Ministry
PO Box 3445 | Monument, CO 80132
719.488.4466 | 888.488.4466 | 888.FAX.2WHM

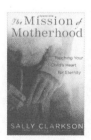    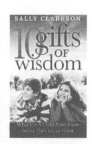

BOOKS BY SALLY CLARKSON

OWN YOUR LIFE

THE LIFEGIVING HOME (with Sarah Clarkson)

THE LIFEGIVING HOME EXPERIENCE (with Joel Clarkson)

THE LIFEGIVING TABLE

THE LIFEGIVING TABLE EXPERIENCE (with Joel & Joy Clarkson)

THE LIFEGIVING PARENT (with Clay Clarkson)

THE LIFEGIVING PARENT EXPERIENCE (with Clay Clarkson)

DIFFERENT (with Nathan Clarkson)

A DIFFERENT KIND OF HERO (with Joel Clarkson)

THE MISSION OF MOTHERHOOD

THE MINISTRY OF MOTHERHOOD

YOU ARE LOVED BIBLE STUDY (with Angela Perritt)

DESPERATE (with Sarah Mae)

GIRLS' CLUB (with Joy & Sarah Clarkson)

GIRLS' CLUB EXPERIENCE (with Joy Clarkson)

MOM HEART MOMENTS

Visit her online at **SALLYCLARKSON.COM**

CP1190